Prentice-Hall

Contemporary Topics in Accounting Series

ALFRED RAPPAPORT, SERIES EDITOR

ACCOUNTING AND HUMAN INFORMATION PROCESSING: THEORY AND APPLICATIONS

ACCOUNTING AND HUMAN INFORMATION PROCESSING: THEORY AND APPLICATIONS

ROBERT LIBBY

University of Michigan

PRENTICE-HALL, INC., ENGLEWOOD CLIFFS, NEW JERSEY 07632

LIBRARY OF CONGRESS CATALOGING IN PUBLICATION DATA

Libby, Robert.
   Accounting and human information processing.

   (Contemporary topics in accounting series)
   Bibliography: p.
   Includes index.
   1. Accounting—Decision making. I Title.
HF5657.L47   657'.072   81-7394
ISBN 0-13-001818-X   AACR2
ISBN 0-13-001800-7 (pbk.)

Editorial production/supervision by Richard C. Laveglia
Manufacturing Buyer: Ray Keating

© 1981 BY PRENTICE-HALL, INC., ENGLEWOOD CLIFFS, N.J. 07632

PRINTED IN THE UNITED STATES OF AMERICA

10 9 8 7 6 5 4 3 2 1

Prentice-Hall International, Inc., *London*
Prentice-Hall of Australia Pty. Limited, *Sydney*
Prentice-Hall of Canada, Ltd., *Toronto*
Prentice-Hall of India Private Limited, *New Delhi*
Prentice-Hall of Japan, Inc., *Tokyo*
Prentice-Hall of Southeast Asia Pte. Ltd., *Singapore*
Whitehall Books Limited, *Wellington, New Zealand*

To Patricia

Contents

Foreword

Accounting, broadly conceived as the measurement and communication of economic information relevant to decision makers, has undergone dramatic changes during the past decade. Recent advances in quantitative methods, the behavioral sciences, and information technology are influencing current thinking in financial as well as managerial accounting. Leasing, pension plans, the use of convertible securities and warrants in mergers and acquisitions, inflation, and corporate diversification are but a few of the challenging problems facing the accountant.

These developments and the very pervasiveness of accounting activity make it difficult for teachers, students, public accountants, and financial executives to gain convenient access to current thinking on key topics in the field. Journal articles, while current, must often of necessity give only cursory treatment or present a single point of view. Many of the important developments in the field have not crystalized to a point where they can be easily incorporated into textbooks. Further, because textbooks must necessarily limit the space devoted to any one topic, key topics often do not get the attention they properly deserve.

The Contemporary Topics series attempts to fill this gap by covering significant contemporary developments in accounting through brief, but self-contained, studies. These independent studies provide the reader with up-to-date coverage of key topics. For the practitioner, the series offers a succinct overview of developments in research and practice in areas of special interest to him. The series enables the teacher to design courses with maximum flexibility and to expose his students to authoritative analysis of controversial problems.

ALFRED RAPPAPORT

Preface

Concern with the quality of decisions made by users of accounting information and by accountants themselves provides the common thread running through most efforts aimed at improving the accounting and auditing processes. This concern has led to progress in the facet of accounting research which is the subject of this book—human information processing and decision making. The purpose of this research is to *describe* actual decision behavior in accounting contexts, to evaluate its quality, and to suggest remedies for any discovered deficiencies.

Behavioral decision making, a new and rapidly growing area of accounting research, is beginning to have a major impact on accounting practice. The basic psychological discipline which underlies the accounting research is more mature and vital. As evidence of this, a recent literature review (Slovic, Fischhoff, and Lichtenstein, 1977) discovered more than 1,000 journal articles on the subject of behavioral decision making which had been published between 1971 and 1975. A significant portion of this research addressed questions of interest to accountants. However, no single source has integrated this voluminous research and described its implications in a form suitable for accounting students and interested practitioners.

This book was written to bridge the gap between the basic theory of human decision making and its applications to accounting. It was motivated by the frustrations experienced as a result of teaching this material solely from original articles. The purpose of the book, therefore, is to synthesize the psychology and accounting literature in a form comprehensible to accounting students and practitioners who have little formal training in the behavioral sciences. In addition, it provides a basis and some directions for further study for those who are so inclined. The book is intended for a variety of reader groups, including accounting practitioners responsible for implementing research findings, Ph.D. students wishing an introduction to this field, and MBA and advanced undergraduate students in courses discussing current topics in accounting or providing an introduction to accounting research. The reader is assumed to have no special behavioral science background and only minimal statistical training. The structure of the book, described next, allows great flexibility in the depth of topic coverage.

The book is structured in four parts:

1. Chapter 1 discusses the motivation for accountants' interest in decision making and develops a general framework for describing decision behavior and for experimental research.

2. The next three chapters discuss each of the three major approaches to the study of decision making: regression models, probabilistic judgment, and predecisional behavior. Each chapter (a) describes the research approach, (b) uses key studies to illustrate the principal research findings and their implications for accounting, and (c) discusses some difficult conceptual and methodological problems faced by researchers using the approach. Each chapter represents an incremental addition to an overall picture of human decision-making abilities.

3. The final chapter discusses methods for improving decision making which take advantage of human decision-making strengths, but help correct the weaknesses that are discussed in the prior three chapters. Applications of these decision aids to accounting problems are presented.

4. Three appendixes present comprehensive reviews of the accounting studies which have been conducted within each of the three research approaches discussed in the book.

An important feature of the book is the flexibility which results from the organization of the first four chapters. In each chapter, the more difficult conceptual and methodological issues are presented in a separate section. These sections were written for more advanced readers interested in conducting this type of research and may be skipped with no loss of continuity. Similarly, assignment of the appendixes is optional and is appropriate when a comprehensive review of the accounting literature is desired.

Acknowledgments

I am indebted to many people for their help at various stages in the preparation of this book. Cornelius Casey, Robin Hogarth, David Larker, Barry Lewis, John Payne, Alfred Rappaport, Larry Tomassini, and Frank Yates all provided many helpful suggestions on the manuscript. A special note of appreciation is due to my colleagues Nicholas Dopuch, Hillel Einhorn, and Edward Joyce, whose insightful ideas, enthusiasm for this research, and encouragement for my work are reflected throughout the book, to Paul Danos whose continuing suggestions helped motivate me to complete the book, and to Barry Lewis for his insightful contributions to the materials in the appendices. Important assistance was provided by many students at the University of Michigan, especially Judy Klein, Garry Marchant, and Nancy Preis. Terry Bradley and Janet Vaughn provided professional secretarial support. Elizabeth Vernon provided expert editorial assistance.

ACCOUNTING AND HUMAN INFORMATION PROCESSING: THEORY AND APPLICATIONS

CHAPTER ONE

Introduction

Decision behavior forms much of the basis for general standards of accounting and auditing practice. Consider, for example, such questions as the following:

1. What changes in the income statement and balance sheet accounts would alter a user's decisions?
2. How are decisions affected by changes in accounting principles?
3. What internal control attributes affect the auditor's reliance on the overall system?
4. When will standardized procedures improve audit decisions?
5. Will traditional auditing methods be cost effective in detecting fraud?
6. Do "Big 8" accounting firms dominate the decisions of accounting policy boards?
7. Which changes in accounting report format will affect performance evaluations by managers?

The first two questions are of major concern to the Financial Accounting Standards Board (FASB) in its attempts to develop materiality standards and to eliminate accounting alternatives. Questions 3 and 4 are being examined by numerous public accounting firms attempting to improve their audit programs. Questions 5 and 6 form the basis for regulatory action being considered by both Congress and the Securities and Exchange Commission. The answer to the last question has a major impact on designers of management information systems.

Answers to these questions have traditionally been supported by an informal consensus of practitioners' experience. It is only in recent years that accounting researchers have endeavored to provide systematic evidence which bears on these basic issues. Researchers have discovered that similar questions have been examined in other disciplines, such as economics, finance, and psychology. Those who attempt to answer questions which require descriptions of individual behavior have turned to a branch of psychology called *behavioral decision theory,* which has its roots in cognitive psychology, economics, and statistics.

Given the importance of decision making in all phases of human endeavor, it is not surprising that a vital literature in psychology has developed.[1] Further, decision making is being studied in the context of a variety of applied disciplines, such as engineering, law, medicine, marketing, and accounting. The goal of much of this work is to describe actual decision behavior, evaluate its quality, and develop and test theories of the underlying psychological processes which produce the behavior. In addition, these descriptions reveal flaws in the behavior and often suggest remedies for these deficiencies.

The purpose of this book is to demonstrate how behavioral decision theory can enrich our understanding of accounting problems. This chapter will develop a general framework for describing judgment and decision making. Later chapters discuss alternative approaches to the analysis of decision behavior and the implications of this research for accounting policy making.

GENERAL FRAMEWORK FOR ANALYZING DECISION MAKING

The purpose of this book is to demonstrate what research in judgment and decision making[2] offers to accountants. To meet this goal, a very basic question must first be addressed: *Why should accountants be interested in individual judgment and decision making?* The general answer is that decision making is an intrinsic part of the current practice of accounting. Decision making is the basis for the demand for accountants' services and

---

[1] Hogarth (1980) and Nisbett and Ross (1980) illustrate the breadth of this literature.

[2] The terms *judgment* and *decision making* are often used interchangeably. When distinguished, judgment usually refers to the process of estimating outcomes and their consequences, while decision making involves an evaluation of these consequences which leads to a choice among the alternatives. Judgment, as well as tastes and preferences, provides the input for decisions. The differences in meaning become more evident as we progress through the book.

is involved in many of their more difficult duties. First, the demand for the accountant's product, *information,* is generated by those who believe that accounting information will aid them in their decision making. Investors, lenders, employees, government, and the management of a firm are affected by the information choices accountants make. For example, when reports are developed for a manager who makes production-planning decisions, the choice of level of data aggregation, number of periods, report format, and accuracy of the information might all affect the decision maker's performance. Since the impact of the accountant's choice will be, in part, a function of how the information is processed by the decision maker, the accountant must learn how users' decisions are made.

Second, accountants themselves are called upon to make countless complex decisions. For example, the accountant must (1) determine the content of reports provided to decision makers, (2) estimate, in the context of giving tax and accounting advice, how different regulations will be interpreted by authorities, (3) decide how to combine the results of various parts of an audit to produce an appropriate audit report, and (4) predict the demand for audit services in order to plan personnel needs. The quality of these decisions, among others, will determine the accountant's success in the marketplace. Whether accountants are concerned with their own or others' decisions, the focus of their concern is on the *improvement* of decisions.

Improving Decisions

What, then, are the available options for improving decisions? Figure 1–1 illustrates three basic options:

1. Changing the information (area A).
2. Educating the decision maker to change the way he or she processes information (area B).
3. Replacing the decision maker with a model (area C).

In addition, some combination of these three options might be employed. In Figure 1–1, these combinations are represented by areas D, E, F, and G.

Accountants have traditionally tended toward the first approach, changing the information. However, the impact of this option is not unaffected by decisions regarding the other choices. The impact of a change in information will be determined, at least in part, by how the information is used. Further, the characteristics of the information will in turn affect the way the information is processed. Stated more simply, the information set and the method chosen to process the information have an interactive effect on the quality of decisions.

Some would argue that there is no need to understand how infor-

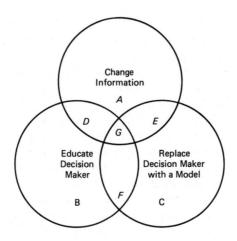

FIGURE 1–1

Decision improvement options

Source: Libby [1976b, Figure 1]

mation is being used, but only the optimal way different sets of information can be processed and the best combination of information and processing methods. However, before one can decide that a change is necessary, a baseline is needed to measure the incremental benefits of the change. This calls for an understanding of how decisions are currently being made and a measure of current decision performance. Perhaps more important is that knowledge of how decisions are being made highlights flaws and inconsistencies in the process, which are clues to specific methods of improving decisions. Our first step toward this ultimate goal of *improving decisions* is to study a general framework for describing how decisions are made.

A Structure for Representing Decision Situations

In most decision-making situations, judgments about the environment must be made in the absence of direct contact with the object or event to be judged. In such circumstances, "most likely" judgments are formed on the basis of information or cues whose relationships to the object or event of interest are imperfect or probabilistic. That is, judgments and decisions are made under conditions of *uncertainty* about the relationships between cues and events. For example, bankers evaluating a loan application must predict whether or not the customer will default on loan payments in the future. They must make this judgment on the basis of such indicators as financial statements, interviews, plant visits, and loan history, which both individually and collectively are imperfectly related to the future default-nondefault.

Let us examine a situation of decision making under uncertainty with which most readers should be familiar—the graduate business school admissions decision. Figure 1–2 presents a general structure which highlights the important features of this situation. When making this decision, the admissions committee (decision maker) attempts to predict an applicant's future success as a student and in the job market. Future success will be represented by $. However, the committee cannot judge this future event directly, as it has yet to take place. As in most situations, the decision maker is separated from the event of interest by space or time.

On what basis, then, can this judgment of future success be made? The applicant usually provides a number of cues, including GMAT scores, grade point average (GPA), quality of the undergraduate school attended, recommendations, participation in extracurricular activities, and answers to subjective questions. None of these individual cues or combinations are perfect indicators of future success. Some of them, however, may be probabilistically related to this event. In Figure 1–2, these imperfect relationships are denoted by broken lines.

One would also expect that in most cases these cues will come in related bundles; that is, some of the cues will contain information redundant with that provided by other cues. For example, one could speculate that the school quality index will be negatively related to GPA and that GMAT scores will be positively related to both GPA and school quality. In Figure 1–2, the relationships between cues are expressed with broken lines.

On the basis of these cues, the committee will make a rating which indicates their most likely estimate of the candidate's success. The cues will be used to varying degrees, and the relative reliance on different cues is likely to change over time as a result of fatigue, special circumstances, learning, and so on. The resulting probabilistic relationship between each cue and the judgment is also represented in Figure 1–2 by broken lines.

The final relationship in Figure 1–2, which will be called judgmental *achievement,* is the focus of our schematic representation of decision making under uncertainty. The achievement measure comprises two factors: (1) measurement of the accuracy of the judgments and (2) determination of the consequences of any error. The accuracy of the judgments can be measured after the student has completed his or her education by comparing estimated and actual performance. The consequences of the error will be a function of the action or choice which results from the judgment and the decision maker's preferences for outcomes.

To review, the model in Figure 1–2, which is an adaptation of Brunswik's (1952) lens model, portrays the decision maker as (1) being separated from the event of interest by time or space, (2) faced with multiple

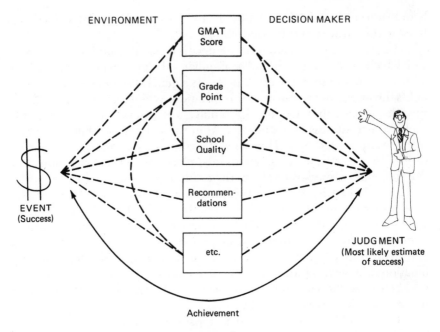

ENVIRONMENT

DECISION MAKER

GMAT
Score

Grade
Point

School
Quality

Recommen-
dations

etc.

EVENT
(Success)

JUDGMENT
(Most likely estimate
of success)

Achievement

FIGURE 1–2

The simple lens model

overlapping cues which are imperfect predictors of the environmental state, and (3) probabilistically combining these cues to form a judgment. In effect, the environment is observed through a "lens" of imperfect cues.

The focus of the model is on judgmental achievement. The model suggests that judgmental achievement will be a function of *both* the environment (the model's left side) and the decision maker (the right side). This dual effect implies that a complete understanding of decision making requires that the decision maker and the environment be studied jointly.

This structure is very general and can be applied to almost any decision-making scheme. Again, consider a simplified commercial lending decision in which the principal task of the loan officer is to predict loan default. Loan default-nondefault is mainly a function of the future cash flows which will be available to the customer to service the debt. The customer provides a number of cues, some of which are probabilistically related to future cash flows. These include indicators of liquidity, leverage, and profitability drawn from financial statements, management evaluations resulting from interviews, plant visits, discussions with other knowledgeable parties, and outside credit ratings. No individual cue or combination of cues is a perfect predictor of future cash flows, and there is overlap in the information (e.g., credit ratings are closely associated with profitability and liquidity measures). In making this judgment, the loan officer combines these cues into a prediction of future cash flows. Even if the banker's judgmental policy is highly stable over time, some inconsistencies are likely to arise, which will result in a probabilistic relationship between the cues and the final judgment. At the end of the term of each loan, the officer's prediction of cash flows can be compared with the actual event, and any resulting losses can be computed to measure achievement. While this example is highly simplified, it illustrates the generality of the framework and its importance for accountants. The model's principal concern with information-processing *achievement* in an uncertain world coincides both with accountants' interest in *improving* the decisions made by users of accounting information and their more recent attention to the quality of their own decisions.

Basic Questions about Decision Making

This simplified lens model portrays the individual interacting with the uncertain environment. The relationships in the model suggest the following research questions,[3] which are fundamental to an understanding of decision making:

1. What information about the event is available to decision makers?
2. How accurate is the information?
3. How is the information combined in forming judgments?
4. How accurate are the judgments?
5. What attributes of the information set, the context, and the decision maker affect the quality of the judgments?
6. How might the quality of judgments be improved?

The first two questions address the nature of the decision environment. Questions 3 and 4 pertain to a particular decision maker's process. Question 5 asks how characteristics of the environment and decision process interact in affecting the decisions. Finally, the last question suggests the goal of applied decision research—improvement in the quality of judgments. The general model presented therefore provides both a method of integrating these questions and a systematic method for structuring decision-related accounting issues. In later chapters, several formal models for integrating the questions posed by the model will be discussed, and the research studies which attempt to answer one or more of these questions will be described.

Each of the preceding questions is composed of subparts, which are presented in Figure 1–3 under the headings of the information environ-

---

[3]See Newell (1968) for a more extensive set of questions.

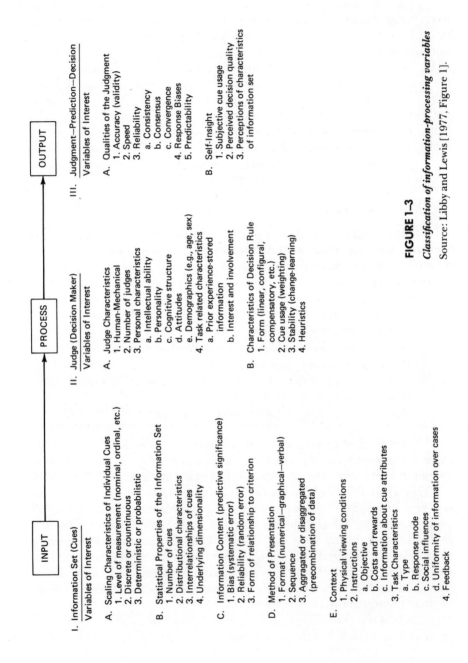

INPUT → PROCESS → OUTPUT

I. Information Set (Cues)
Variables of Interest

A. Scaling Characteristics of Individual Cues
   1. Level of measurement (nominal, ordinal, etc.)
   2. Discrete or countinuous
   3. Deterministic or probabilistic

B. Statistical Properties of the Information Set
   1. Number of cues
   2. Distributional characteristics
   3. Interrelationships of cues
   4. Underlying dimensionality

C. Information Content (predictive significance)
   1. Bias (systematic error)
   2. Reliability (random error)
   3. Form of relationship to criterion

D. Method of Presentation
   1. Format (numerical–graphical–verbal)
   2. Sequence
   3. Aggragated or disaggregated
      (precombination of data)

E. Context
   1. Physical viewing conditions
   2. Instructions
      a. Objective
      b. Costs and rewards
      c. Information about cue attributes
   3. Task Characteristics
      a. Type
      b. Response mode
      c. Social influences
      d. Uniformity of information over cases
   4. Feedback

II. Judge (Decision Maker)
Variables of Interest

A. Judge Characteristics
   1. Human-Mechanical
   2. Number of judges
   3. Personal characteristics
      a. Intellectual ability
      b. Personality
      c. Cognitive structure
      d. Attitudes
      e. Demographics (e.g., age, sex)
   4. Task related characteristics
      a. Prior experience-stored
         information
      b. Interest and involvement

B. Characteristics of Decision Rule
   1. Form (linear, configural,
      compensatory, etc.)
   2. Cue usage (weighting)
   3. Stability (change-learning)
   4. Heuristics

III. Judgment—Prediction—Decision
Variables of Interest

A. Qualities of the Judgment
   1. Accuracy (validity)
   2. Speed
   3. Reliability
      a. Consistency
      b. Consensus
      c. Convergence
   4. Response Biases
   5. Predictability

B. Self-Insight
   1. Subjective cue usage
   2. Perceived decision quality
   3. Perceptions of characteristics
      of information set

FIGURE 1-3

Classification of information-processing variables

Source: Libby and Lewis [1977, Figure 1].

ment, the decision maker, and his or her judgments. Although this listing is not exhaustive, these are many of the subparts or attributes which make up the substance of most accounting research questions. Accountants addressed many questions about decision making before they began applying behavioral decision theory, but they did not look upon these "accounting problems" as being composed of a series of underlying information-processing variables. Viewing the problem of interest in terms of the underlying variables leads the researcher to the appropriate psychological theory and evidence which can help to set expectations about what might be found in the accounting situation. Methodologies which have proved useful in similar situations may also be discovered.

Fortunately, psychologists have studied many of the variables in which we are interested, in situations very similar to those which characterize the practice of accounting. For example, a number of studies of individual accounting behavior have examined the impact on decisions of adding supplementary inflation-adjusted information to traditional financial statement presentations (see Dyckman, 1975, for a review). Not one of these studies made any prediction about the potential effects of this change. This deficiency can probably be attributed to the failure of the researchers to analyze the alterations in the underlying information environment caused by the accounting change. Had they done so, they might have examined the change in potentially important variables, such as the number of cues, their interrelationships, and their predictive ability. Further, the literature suggests that the effects of the change might be mediated by the decision maker's lack of experience with this type of data. These issues have been studied extensively in the multiple-cue probability learning literature, which will be discussed in Chapter 2. The findings of the psychological research could have helped set the early accounting researchers' expectations, which would have guided them in their conceptualization of the problem and in their experimental design. Further, methodologies which are more suitable for addressing these issues than those used in the early studies have since been developed.

Each of the following three chapters discusses a body of literature founded on a different representation of the judgment process, each of which focuses attention on different basic issues. As the chapters progress, the representations become increasingly complex, while the related literatures become less well developed. In each chapter, the principal issues and their implications for accounting will be discussed and illustrated.

Before the specific approaches to the study of judgment and decision making are examined, we will make a small investment in discussing the experimental approach to hypothesis testing to illustrate how it relates to other research approaches. This section is of principal interest to more advanced readers. The discussion will aid in an understanding of the strengths and weaknesses of the specific research studies we will later evaluate. In keeping with the purpose of this book, the discussion will be in summary form. Those requiring a more detailed presentation are referred to standard methodology texts, such as that by Kerlinger (1973).

THEORY VALIDATION

A general framework for theory validation will help to illustrate the research process. This framework is usually called the *predictive validity* model. In its simplest form, a theory specifies relationships between concepts. For example, concept A, intelligence, is assumed to affect concept B, academic achievement. Researchers who might attempt to test this theory are faced with a problem. Neither of these two concepts, intelligence and academic achievement, can be directly measured, because concepts themselves are not observable. The researcher must therefore develop operational or observable definitions of these concepts. For example, scores on an IQ test might be used as the operational definition of intelligence, and school grades might be used as the operational definition of academic achievement. In addition, the researcher must be concerned with other factors, such as social background, that could affect or moderate the relationship.

Accounting researchers who attempt to test theoretical relationships are faced with the same problems. Figure 1–4 illustrates the conceptual network implicit in a study by Ashton (1976). Ashton hypothesized that decision rules (concept B) would be insufficiently adjusted in response to changes in accounting rules (concept A). He studied this question in a product pricing decision context. The independent variable, change in accounting rule, was operationally defined as a change from full to direct cost inventory accounting, or vice versa. The change in decision rule, the dependent variable, was operationally defined as a change in a certain statistical indicator called "cross-temporal model validity.[4] Ashton also controlled for two moderating variables: information about the change in accounting rules and the importance of the change.

Again, because a researcher can never directly test the relationship between two concepts (link 1 in Figure 1–4), the theory must be tested by assessing the relationship between the operational definitions of the independent and dependent variables (link 4 in Figure 1–4). Implicit in this framework are the assumptions that links 2 and 3, which relate the concepts to the operational definitions, are valid, and that other factors that

---

[4]This statistic measured the change in a linear representation of the subject's decision process. The use of linear representations of judgment will be discussed in Chapter 2. Ashton's study is described in detail in Appendix A.

might affect the dependent variable (link 5) either have been controlled for or have no effect.

The evaluation of the validity of a study will then be a function of the appraisal of links 1, 2, 3, and 5. Once it has been determined that a logically consistent theoretical framework is being employed (link 1), the evaluator should look closely at the ways in which variables are operationalized (links 2 and 3) and other factors are controlled for (link 5). If there is a major flaw in the theoretical relationship, or if the operationalization and control are not appropriate, the results of the study are of little value no matter how clever the procedures or how sophisticated the analysis.

EXPERIMENTAL DESIGN

Next, the design of the experiment must be considered.[5] The major purpose of experimental design is to arrange observations of effects and causes or treatments so that we can be sure that observed effects are the result of our treatments, thereby producing what is called *internal validity*. In the example in Figure 1–4, the researcher would attempt to arrange observations of decision rule changes and accounting changes to ensure that any changes in the former were caused by changes in the latter. A second important goal of experimental design is *external validity*, or the ability to generalize results beyond the specific tasks, measurement methods, and actors of a specific study. Both internal and external validity are

FIGURE 1–4

Conceptual network

Source: Libby [1976c, Figure 1]

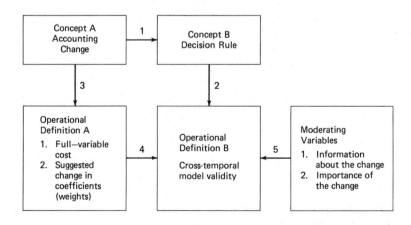

[5]Campbell and Stanley (1963) is the primary reference on this subject.

affected by how the variables in a study are treated. In any research study, the principal variables of interest can be treated in the following ways:

X = independent variable or treatment. The values of independent variables are established prior to execution of the study. They can either be systematically manipulated, as they normally are in experiments, or they can be measured in natural settings, as they normally are in econometric studies.

O = dependent variable or observation. The dependent variable, which is allowed to vary freely in response to the independent variable, is measured. This is the place in the study where new information is gathered.

The remaining variables in the study can be treated by the following:

K = holding constant. The variable is held constant at one value across all values of the independent variables.

M = matching. Matching assures that the distribution of the variable is equal across levels of the independent variables.

R = randomizing. Randomizing ensures that the distribution of the variable is unbiased or is equally probable across levels of the independent variables.

Z = ignoring (intentionally or unintentionally). Variables are ignored intentionally if we have thought about them and have decided they logically should have no effect.

These six modes of treatment of variables can be used to compare two often-used accounting research approaches: econometric studies and experimental studies. Our framework for comparing different experimental designs is based on Campbell and Stanley's (1963) scheme. Three of these designs are presented in Figure 1–5.

Most studies of stock-price reactions to actual accounting changes ("efficient markets" studies) use either designs 1 or 2 (see Dyckman, Downes, and Magee, 1975, for a review). We will first examine design 1, the static group comparison design as presented in Figure 1–6. In this design, the effect of the treatment variable, the accounting change, is determined by comparing certain attributes of security returns between a group of companies exhibiting one level of the independent variable and a group exhibiting a second level of the independent variable. Note that the *measured* independent variable (X) and the observation (O) are *not* the only modes of treatment used in these studies. A reexamination of the predictive validity framework depicted in Figure 1–4 will indicate that, while the independent and dependent variables have been specified, we have yet to consider the other potential moderating factors which might

No. 1: Static group comparison:

$$X \quad O_1$$
$$O_2$$

No. 2: One-group pretest-posttest design:

$$O_1 \quad X \quad O_2$$

No. 3: Posttest only control group design:

$$R \left\{ \begin{array}{l} X \ O_1 \\ \\ O_2 \end{array} \right.$$

FIGURE 1–5

Some experimental and quasi-experimental designs

Adapted from Campbell and Stanley (1963)

affect the dependent variable. How can these remaining variables be treated in a stock-price study? Some may be held constant (K); for example, we can decide to consider only firms with certain characteristics (e.g., New York Stock Exchange firms only). The two groups can also be matched (M) on certain variables (e.g., size or industry). The remaining variables are treated by Z; they are ignored. Often, the decision to consciously ignore certain variables is based upon the results of prior research. Other times, these variables are *assumed* to be randomly distributed across levels of the independent variables. Because it is impractical to hold constant or match many variables, a large number of potentially relevant factors must be ignored in stock-price studies.

Accounting studies using the static group comparison design face two major problems in determining the effect of the treatment. Each problem creates a competing hypothesis which could explain observed differences in behavior. First, even before receiving the treatment, the groups may be systematically different on some variables which were ignored or ineffectively matched. This results in what are called *selection biases.* Second, even if the groups are assumed from the beginning to be equivalent, they may experience *differential mortality;* that is, the dropout

FIGURE 1–6

Design 1: Static group comparison

$$(K, M, Z) \left\{ \begin{array}{l} X \qquad\qquad O \\ \\ \\ O \end{array} \right.$$

MEASURED   OBSERVED
DESIGN PARTITION

rate may be different between the two experimental groups. For example, more of the firms using one accounting method may drop out of a sample as a result of failure or merger.

Many efficient market studies employ a second design, the one-group pretest-posttest design (Figure 1–5, design 2). In this design, the same dependent variable (relating to stock returns) is observed both before and after receipt of the treatment (accounting change) to determine its effect. The variable observed is usually some measure of portfolio returns which is "preobserved" when the portfolio is formulated. This design faces different threats to internal validity, the most important of which, to accountants, is *history*. History becomes a rival hypothesis when other change-producing events occur between the pretest and posttest observations. For example, a change in government regulations may take place contemporaneously with the accounting event of interest. This design would not allow the effect of the accounting change to be disentangled from the effect of the change in government regulation. Other threats to internal validity intrinsic to these designs are discussed by Campbell and Stanley (1963).

In contrast, laboratory and field experiments investigating individual decisions use a different design. In this case, design 3, the posttest only control group design presented in Figure 1–7 is commonly used. Note that this design is very similar to design 1, except that variables which are not held constant or matched are not ignored, but are randomized. Instead of *assuming* that other important variables are randomly distributed, such a distribution is assured by randomly assigning participants to the experimental groups. This design eliminates the remaining threats to internal validity. Experiments based on this design also tend to use more of mode K, holding moderating variables constant, to simplify the experimental task.

Note the major differences between designs 1 and 2, which are employed in stock-price studies, and design 3, which is used in experimental studies. In stock-price studies, by necessity, a number of variables are treated with mode Z; they are ignored. Treating variables in this fashion threatens the *internal validity* of the study. Recent studies of the effects of the new oil and gas accounting standards on drilling companies illustrate

FIGURE 1–7

Design 3: Posttest only control group

```
                       X                  0
        (K, M) R  {
                                          0
            MANIPULATED        OBSERVED
            DESIGN PARTITION
```

these problems. In most stock-price studies, the effects of other potentially relevant events are assumed to be distributed randomly across levels of our independent variable (whether the company used full-cost or successful-efforts accounting before the change). However, mode Z does not assure this distribution. In the oil and gas case, there is some evidence that companies with different economic characteristics choose different accounting methods. This produces potential *selection biases*. Events relevant to drillers' stock prices, such as the issue of a new government regulation or a change in oil prices, may have also occurred contemporaneously with the issue of the new accounting standard. In instances where accounting choices and economic attributes may be related, one cannot expect that the effects of these other events will be randomly distributed. As a result, there will be no method for discriminating between the effects on stock prices of our independent variable, the accounting policy change, and these contemporaneous events. In capital-market studies, however, the treatment variable (X) is *measured* in the real world, the actors and context are also observed in the real world, and diverse populations are usually sampled (little K is used). All these factors minimize threats to external validity.

Alternatively, experimental studies treat many variables by holding them constant and employ a *manipulated* independent variable, which, by its nature, is in part contrived. These practices and questions about the representativeness of contexts and subjects create important threats to *external validity* for experimental studies. However, since variables which are not matched, held constant, or treated as independent variables are controlled for through randomization, most threats to the internal validity of these studies are eliminated.

A likely question to arise at this point is "Must *all* potential sources of invalidity, both internal and external, be eliminated for a study to make a contribution?" The answer is "Definitely not." However, given the different strengths and weaknesses of the two research approaches that have been discussed, it should be clear that they are complementary.[6] This complementarity supports the view of research as an interative process of evidence gathering in which the use of various methodologies with different strengths and weaknesses increases the diagnostic value of the findings.

CONCLUDING COMMENTS

In the following three chapters, different methods for representing judgment are presented. Each chapter is organized as follows. First, the

---

[6]Stock-price studies and individual-decision studies also differ greatly in their goals, as the relationship between individual and aggregate market behavior is quite complex. This example was chosen only to illustrate the different experimental design problems faced by the two types of research.

method is described. Second, sample research studies which illustrate the principal research findings and their accounting implications are examined. And, third, some important methodological and conceptual problems faced in using the method are discussed. Each of these chapters helps to build a general picture of the strengths and weaknesses of human decision making. The final chapter summarizes many of these findings through a discussion of decision-aiding techniques tailored to human cognitive abilities and limitations. Some directions for future research are also presented.

DISCUSSION QUESTIONS

1. Referring to the decision improvement options in Figure 1–1, explain how recommendations to change the information set can be affected by the other two options.
2. Choose a judgment task for which accounting information is used or which accountants often perform and describe it in terms of the simple lens model in Figure 1–2.
3. Choose one of the following articles dealing with the accounting aggregation issue:
   a. Abdel-khalik, A. R. "The Effect of Aggregating Accounting Reports on the Quality of the Lending Decision: An Empirical Investigation," *Journal of Accounting Research* (Supplement 1973), pp. 104–162.
   b. Casey, Jr., C. J. "Variation in Accounting Information Load: The Effect on Loan Officers' Predictions of Bankruptcy," *Accounting Review* (January 1980), pp. 36–49.
   c. Barefield, R. M. "The Effect of Aggregation on Decision Making Success: A Laboratory Study," *Journal of Accounting Research* (Autumn 1972), pp. 229–242.
   Then try to determine the underlying information-processing variables that were manipulated in the experimental treatments (use Figure 1–3).
4. For one of the following articles, (a) draw the conceptual network implicit in the study in the format of Figure 1–4, (b) indicate the mode of treatment of each variable, and (c) indicate the experimental design employed (see Figure 1–5).
   a. Hofstedt, T. R. "Some Behavioral Parameters of Financial Analysis," *Accounting Review* (October 1972), pp. 679–692.
   b. Dickhaut, J. "Alternative Information Structures and Probability Revisions," *Accounting Review* (January 1973), pp. 61–79.
   c. Tomassini, L. A. "Assessing the Impact of Human Resource Accounting: An Experimental Study of Managerial Decision Preferences," *Accounting Review* (October 1977), pp. 904–914.
5. Provide a brief discussion or description of each of the following:
   a. Operational definition
   b. Internal validity

    c. External validity

    d. History

    e. Selection biases

6. Compare the threats to internal and external validity faced in most experimental and efficient markets studies.

7. Discuss and evaluate the following statement: "Experimental studies cannot be generalized to 'real-world' behaviors because all experiments by their nature involve abstraction."

CHAPTER TWO

Representations of Human Judgment: Regression, ANOVA, and Multidimensional Scaling

Brunswik's lens model, as presented in Chapter 1, is a general structure which highlights many important characteristics of decision making under uncertainty. It portrays the individual judging an event which cannot be directly observed through a "lens" of cues whose relationships to both the event and the judge are uncertain. The interaction between the individual and the environment is described by a number of relationships, including those among the cues, those between the cues and the criterion event, those between the cues and the judge's response, and those between the criterion event and the judge's response. While Brunswik (1952) proposed the use of correlation statistics to measure these relationships, it was Hursch, Hammond, and Hursch (1964) and Tucker (1964) who developed the rigorous analytical framework for the model, using regression and correlation statistics.

Research structured around this analytical framework is the focus of this chapter, which is organized in three sections. First, the analytical framework developed around the regression form of the lens model is presented. In the second section, representative research examples are presented as vehicles for discussing the basic methodology, the central research issues, and the accounting-related findings. Detailed reviews of accounting studies which use the model are presented in Appendix A. The final section raises more complex conceptual and methodological issues. This latter section is of interest principally to those who wish to conduct judgment research or to critically evaluate individual studies.

REGRESSION FORM OF THE LENS MODEL

The regression formulation of the lens model is presented in Figure 2–1. This formulation is formally identical to the simple model depicted in Figure 1–2. As before, the three elements of the model are (1) the *task environment* as defined by the *cue set* $(X_1, X_2, \ldots, X_k)$, (2) the *criterion event* on the left side of the model (Y_e), and (3) the *judge's estimate* of the event on the right side of the model (Y_s). The *relationships* among these elements are now represented by a series of correlation coefficients which are summarized in the lens model equation.

The cue set $(X_1, X_2, \ldots, X_k)$ and the matrix of intercorrelations between cues (r_{ij}) define the task environment. The relationships of the cues to the criterion and to the judgment are measured by both univariate and multivariate correlations. On the environmental (left) side of the model, the univariate relationship between each cue (X_i) and the criterion event (Y_e) is indicated by the correlation (r_{ie}) and is usually called the *ecological validity* of the cue. This correlation can be interpreted as measuring the relevance of the *i*th cue to predicting the criterion event, independent of

FIGURE 2–1

Regression formulation of the lens model

Source: Dudycha and Naylor [1966, Figure 1]

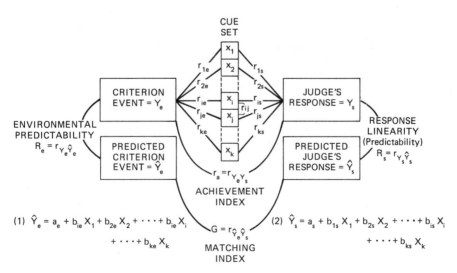

the other cues. To determine the multivariate relationship between *all* of the cues and the criterion event, the following linear regression model is formed:

$$\hat{Y}_e = a_e + b_{1e}X_1 + b_{2e}X_2 + \cdots + b_{ke}X_k, \qquad Y_e = \hat{Y}_e + u_e$$

The multivariate relationship between the cues and the criterion is then assessed by the correlation of the criterion event (Y_e) and the *prediction* of the criterion event from the preceding model ($\hat{Y}_e$). This measure is called *environmental predictability* ($R_e = r_{Y_e \hat{Y}_e}$) and can be interpreted as indicating the relevance of the complete cue set to predicting the event.

A series of analogous correlations is computed to describe the decision maker's judgment process. The decision maker's reliance on individual cues is measured by the univariate correlation between the cue (X_i) and the response (Y_s) and is called the *utilization coefficient* (r_{is}). This correlation may be positive or negative and takes values from zero to one. If a cue is ignored or *not* selected by the judge, it is given a zero weight. Again, the multivariate equivalent relating all the cues to the decision maker's response is assessed by forming the linear regression

$$\hat{Y}_s = a_s + b_{1s}X_1 + b_{2s}X_2 + \cdots + b_{ks}X_k, \qquad Y_s = \hat{Y}_s + u_s$$

and correlating the actual judgment (Y_s) with the model's *prediction* of the judgment ($\hat{Y}_s$). This measure is called *response linearity* ($R_s = r_{Y_s \hat{Y}_s}$) and under certain assumptions indicates the predictability or consistency of the judgment. The similarity of the decision maker's weightings of cues to the environmental relationships is assessed by comparing the two linear regression models. This is accomplished by correlating the predictions of the two equations to form the *matching index* ($G = r_{\hat{Y}_e \hat{Y}_s}$). In certain circumstances,[1] this index can be treated as an overall measure of the accuracy of cue weighting or utilization, because the effects of human inconsistency and environmental unpredictability are eliminated in the regressions.

The judge's performance is summarized in the *achievement index* ($r_a = r_{Y_e Y_s}$), which indicates the correspondence between the subject's response and the environmental event. This index provides a direct ex post measure of judgment accuracy, which is the focal point of this research.

Table 2–1 summarizes the lens model statistics. The following lens model equation explains achievement (r_a) in terms of the other components of the model:

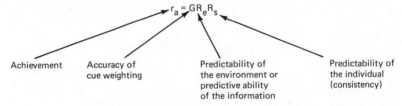

| Achievement | Accuracy of cue weighting | Predictability of the environment or predictive ability of the information | Predictability of the individual (consistency) |

[1] If the linear models of the environment and decision maker capture all the reliable variance in each system, this interpretation is appropriate.

The equation[2] indicates that achievement will be a function of three factors: (1) the weighting of the cues relative to their weighting in the environment, (2) the predictability of the environment (i.e., the predictive ability of the information), and (3) the predictability of the individual (i.e., his or her consistency). It further indicates that these three terms are combined multiplicatively.

TABLE 2–1

Lens Model Statistics

Symbol	Name	Definition
r_{ie}	Ecological validity	$r_{X_i Y_e}$
R_e	Environmental predictability	$R_{Y_e \hat{Y}_e}$
r_{is}	Utilization coefficient	$r_{X_i Y_s}$
R_s	Response linearity (predictability)	$R_{Y_s \hat{Y}_s}$
G	Matching index	$r_{\hat{Y}_e \hat{Y}_s}$
r_a	Achievement	$r_{Y_e Y_s}$

Observed values of R_s are likely to be less than 1, because decision makers usually are not perfectly consistent. R_e in most cases will also be less than 1, because the environment normally is not perfectly predictable. Finally, the failure of most decision makers to employ the ex post optimal weighting strategy[3] would make the first term (G, the matching index) less than 1. Combining these three potential sources of error in a multiplicative fashion would lead one to expect that, in general, judgmental achievement will not be particularly high, which is consistent with empirical observation. This equation is a useful analytical tool because it both sets our expectations of the level of judgmental achievement *and* explains the causes of observed nonoptimal behavior.[4]

The regression formulation of the lens model and the closely associated technique, *analysis of variance,* have been employed extensively in the investigation of decision making. Some examples from accounting and other contexts will illustrate the central research issues and how they are addressed.

---

[2]This is a reduced form of the equation, which is based on the assumption that there is no significant relationship between the residuals (u) of the two regression equations. This is nearly true in most situations.

[3]The strategy implicit in the environmental model.

[4]While the equation is a useful tool for setting expectations and analyzing results, it must be used with some caution when evaluating empirical data. When certain of the assumptions of regression are violated, as is usually the case, both the equation and its interpretation become much more complex.

RESEARCH EVIDENCE

Many researchers in diverse disciplines such as psychology, law, marketing, and accounting have found the regression form of the lens model to be a useful representation of human judgment policies. In the typical study, decision makers evaluate a large number of cases on a simple rating scale. The cases contain a small predetermined set of cues whose values vary from case to case; these cues are presented in the context of unchanging background information. This structure is necessary to allow accurate assessment of the parameters of the equation. As will be discussed later in this chapter, however, this structure limits the dimensions of decision behavior that may be analyzed. It is important to note that the algebraic models resulting from these studies simply indicate the functional relationship between the cues and judgment. These, like *all* models, are abstractions and do not purport to represent "real" mental processes.

Much of this research is classified into one of three categories. Studies in the first category, *clinical versus statistical prediction,* address the accuracy of human judgment and the relative accuracy of humans and simple statistical models. In accounting, these issues have been addressed most often in business failure, stock price, and earnings prediction contexts. The second group, *multiple cue probability learning* research, examines the effects of characteristics of the information environment and of feedback on learning decision rules. Accounting research in this area has most often been applied to management control problems. Research in the third category, *policy capturing,* investigates the relative importance of different cues in the judgment process and consensus among decision makers. Internal control evaluation and materiality judgments have received greatest attention in this portion of the accounting literature. Examples which illustrate the methodology and principal conclusions of each type of study, as well as their accounting implications, are presented in this section.

Clinical versus statistical prediction

Much of early decision research focused on the *accuracy* of unaided human judgment (see Goldberg, 1968). Frequently, the research was aimed at resolving the controversy over the relative accuracy of human (clinical) judgment and simple statistical classification models. Issues of consistency over time and consensus among judges were also addressed because they relate directly to accuracy.[5] Often, the contributions to ac-

---

[5]If there is only one correct answer, inconsistency over time limits individual accuracy, while lack of consensus among judges sets a limit on the average accuracy of a group of judges. For example, if 10 business firms are classified as successful or failed businesses on two separate occasions, and these classifications are in agreement for 8 of 10 firms, a maximum of 18 of the 20 predictions could be correct. The same holds true if two judges evaluate the same 10 firms and agree in only 8 of 10 cases.

curacy were analyzed through the lens model equation. More recent research has provided explanations for many of the early results.

In studies of judgmental accuracy, the experimental cases are usually abstracted from real cases where the criterion event has already been observed. This allows more realistic inferences to be drawn concerning judgmental achievement. Two examples, one from a nonaccounting context and one from an accounting context, will illustrate how the key issues are addressed.

DIAGNOSING PSYCHOSIS

Early research into these questions focused upon diagnoses made by clinical psychologists. One of the most comprehensive studies of clinical psychologists' judgments is Goldberg's (1965) analysis of data gathered by Meehl (1959). In the study, 29 clinical psychologists (including 13 Ph.D.-level clinicians and 16 advanced graduate students at the University of Minnesota) evaluated 861 Minnesota Multiphasic Personality Inventory (MMPI) profiles taken from patients at seven hospitals and clinics around the country. Each patient profile consisted of 11 scores representing the degree of similarity in the manner in which certain questions were answered by the respondents and by other patients suffering from a well-defined form of mental illness. Each profile had previously been classified as psychotic (coded 1) or neurotic (coded 0) on the basis of more extensive information. The clinical psychologists rated each profile, using an 11-step forced normal distribution which ranged from least likely to be judged psychotic in the later diagnosis to most likely. Judgmental achievement (r_a, the achievement index in Figure 2–1) was measured by computing the correlation between the clinicians' judgments (Y_s) and the actual final diagnoses (Y_e). The results were disappointing. Achievement (r_a) ranged from .14 to only .39, with a median of .28. There was also little agreement among the clinicians.

In most studies of this type, judgmental achievement is compared with (1) the accuracy of the environmental regression model (the environmental event regressed on the cues) in predicting the outcome of a new set of cases, $R_{e(cv)}$,[6] and (2) the accuracy of the regression model of the subject (based upon regressing the subject's responses on the cues) in predicting the environmental event ($r_{\hat{Y}_s Y_e}$). Because of the surface simplicity of regression models, it was thought at one time that the environmental regression model would set a minimum standard against which to judge the accuracy of the more complex human judge. It quickly became evident, however, that the minimum standard actually exceeded the maximum human performance (Dawes and Corrigan, 1974, p. 97). Goldberg (1965) reported that the validity of the environmental regression model, $R_{e(cv)}$, was .46, compared to the median individual achievement (r_a) of .28.

---

[6]This index is called *cross-validated* environmental predictability.

The earlier discussion of the lens model equation suggests the likely cause of this result. First, unlike the human, the model is perfectly consistent over time. Second, when the assumptions of linear regression are met, the model uses the optimal cue weighting pattern, while the human is likely to misweight cues. Both potential sources of error put the human at a disadvantage in this situation.

When the linear regression models of the judges' responses were constructed, they provided accurate predictions of the judges' behavior. The linear predictability of the judges (R_s) ranged from .58 to .86, with an average of .78. After further analyzing of the same data, Goldberg (1970) reported a more startling result. He measured the accuracy of the subject regression model or *model of man* in predicting the environmental event $(r_{\hat{Y}_s Y_e})$. Goldberg reported that 86% of the models of the clinicians were significantly more accurate than the clinicians from whom the models were derived $(r_{\hat{Y}_s Y_e} > r_{Y_s Y_e})$. The average validity of the models of man was .31, compared to average human performance of .28.

The superior performance of the models of the clinicians over the clinicians themselves (called *bootstrapping*) at first seems surprising and paradoxical. Dawes (1971, p. 182) explained that this phenomenon is due to the fact that

> a mathematical model by its very nature is an abstraction of the process it models; hence, if the decision maker's behavior involves following valid principles but following them poorly, these valid principles will be abstracted by the model—as long as the deviations from these principles are not systematically related to the variables the decision maker is considering.

In this argument, decision behavior is conceived of as consisting of two components: (1) decision rules containing some validity and (2) random errors caused by fatigue, headaches, boredom, quality of recent cases considered, and the like. By approximating the combination rules of the decision maker and eliminating random error in the decisions, the models of the decision maker are able to outperform the decision makers themselves (Goldberg, 1970). This is the same line of reasoning followed earlier by Bowman (1963) in his "management coefficients theory." More simply stated, for bootstrapping to occur, the loss in accuracy caused by the subject's inconsistency over time must be greater than the increase in accuracy gained by using the information in a way not captured by the linear model.

To summarize, both environmental and bootstrapping models are likely to outperform humans, since they both eliminate error caused by human inconsistency. Further, the environmental model removes error resulting from misweighting of cues. Only if the linear models fit the task poorly, or if the clinicians can assess information unavailable to the models, can people outperform models.

When evaluating a loan applicant, the banker's primary task is to judge the prospect's ability to make the required payments. The major role of financial information in detecting poor credit risks or failure-prone firms is well established. Libby (1975a, b) studied these accounting-based judgments using the lens model framework. In particular, he examined the accuracy, consistency (over time), and consensus of loan officers' predictions of business failure made on the basis of accounting ratios and the ability of a linear model to predict these judgments. In the study, 43 experienced loan officers made business-failure predictions for 70 real firms drawn from Moody's Industrials (including 10 repeats) on the basis of five-ratio financial profiles. (Two sample ratio profiles are presented in Figure 2–2.) Half of these firms had previously failed within 3 years of the financial statement date. To remain consistent with the accounting literature, the lens model statistics were measured by the percentage of correct predictions (hit rates), rather than by the correlation coefficients used by Goldberg.

The bankers' predictions were quite accurate. Their achievement (r_a) ranged from 45% to 83% correct and averaged 74% correct. Environmental predictability (R_e), which sets an upper limit for achievement, was 85% as determined by a linear discriminant analysis model.[7] Nine judges performed within 4% of the environmental predictability. As in studies of other types of decision makers, linear models were able, on average, to predict 88% of the judges' responses (R_s). The officers were also quite consistent over even a 1-week time period (mean = 89%), and they agreed with one another an average of 80% of the time. While the loan officers' performance was marginally more accurate (when compared to environmental predictability) than Goldberg's psychologists, the results were quite similar and lend support for the generalizability of the psychological results.

ACCURACY OF LINEAR MODELS

Dawes and Corrigan (1974) have suggested a compelling reason for the efficacy of linear models in predicting both judgments and events even when numerous assumptions are violated. They suggest that in most judgment situations the relationships between the cues and the criterion event are *conditionally monotonic* or can be rescaled to be so. This condition requires that higher values of a particular cue imply a higher value on the criterion, regardless of the value of the other cues. In our graduate admissions study, for example, this condition would require that, on aver-

---

[7]The linear discriminant analysis model is a classification technique, which in this case reduced to a simple linear regression.

FIRM: 31

Given the following information:

$\dfrac{\text{NET INCOME}}{\text{TOTAL ASSETS}}$	-0.353
$\dfrac{\text{CURRENT ASSETS}}{\text{TOTAL ASSETS}}$	0.593
$\dfrac{\text{CASH}}{\text{TOTAL ASSETS}}$	0.008
$\dfrac{\text{CURRENT ASSETS}}{\text{CURRENT LIABILITIES}}$	0.880
$\dfrac{\text{SALES}}{\text{CURRENT ASSETS}}$	2.906

I. My best estimate is that within the next three years this firm will: *(Circle one)*

FAIL............................-
NOT Fail........................+

II. My level of confidence in my prediction can best be described as: *(Circle one)*

NOT Very Confident..........1
Confident.....................3
VERY Confident..............5

IBM digit # *(Please (ignore)*

11

12

FIRM: 32

Given the following information:

$\dfrac{\text{NET INCOME}}{\text{TOTAL ASSETS}}$	0.116
$\dfrac{\text{CURRENT ASSETS}}{\text{TOTAL ASSETS}}$	0.165
$\dfrac{\text{CASH}}{\text{TOTAL ASSETS}}$	0.011
$\dfrac{\text{CURRENT ASSETS}}{\text{CURRENT LIABILITIES}}$	2.049
$\dfrac{\text{SALES}}{\text{CURRENT ASSETS}}$	0.481

I. My best estimate is that within the next three years this firm will: *(Circle one)*

FAIL............................-
NOT Fail........................+

II. My level of confidence in my prediction can best be described as: *(Circle one)*

NOT Very Confident..........1
Confident.....................3
VERY Confident..............5

IBM digit # *(Please (ignore)*

13

14

FIGURE 2-2 Sample case

Source: Libby [1975a, Figure 3]

age, students with higher GMAT scores be more "successful," regardless of their undergraduate cumulative grade points. In such cases, it has been shown that the outputs of nonlinear functions are highly correlated with the output of a linear model. Two additional conditions contribute to this result. First, in the preceding situations, error in the independent variables makes the output of nonlinear functions more linear. Second, the relative weights derived from a regression analysis are unaffected by error in the dependent variable. This further illustrates the wisdom of Brunswik's assertion that the study of psychology requires the simultaneous investigation of the individual *and* the environment. The nature of the environment (conditional monotonicity and error) explains the accuracy of the models.

Dawes and Corrigan also present an even more interesting result. Using the data from Goldberg's psychological diagnosis study and four others, they constructed linear models with *equal* weights and compared their ability to predict the criterion with both human predictions and the predictions of models of man. Only the signs of the predictor variables were chosen a priori. Across all five studies, the equal weighting model produced the highest achievement, suggesting that linear models are also robust to deviations from optimal weights.[8] Furthermore, this finding implies that the most crucial element in decision making may be the selection of variables and not the determination of their weights. The results are also important in that they suggest a number of decision-aiding techniques.

SUMMARY

Sawyer (1966), Slovic and Lichtenstein (1971), and Dawes and Corrigan (1974) provide complete reviews of the extensive "Clinical versus Statistical Prediction" literature. Even though these research studies involve a wide variety of situations differing greatly in (1) the type and training of the decision maker, (2) the type of cue (e.g., numerical versus nonnumerical), (3) the reality of the experimental task, and (4) the type and reliability of the criterion, the results paint a consistent picture. In many important decision-making situations, the environmental predictability (R_e) of available information is low. However, even in situations where environmental predictability is relatively high, poor judgmental achievement (r_a) is the norm.[9]

Both human inconsistency (low R_s) and misweighting of cues (low G) contribute to the poor achievement. Combining quantitative information

---

[8]This issue is discussed in detail in Einhorn and Hogarth (1975), Newman (1977), Wainer (1976, 1978), Keren and Newman (1978), McClelland (1979), and others.

[9]Among the accounting studies, there are some notable exceptions to this finding, such as Libby's (1975) business-failure experiment and others discussed in Appendix A.

in repetitive tasks does not appear to be a function that people perform well. Thus, in these situations, replacing people with statistical models (e.g., environmental regression models, models of man, and equal weighting models) shows promise for increasing predictive accuracy. Even in situations where the human judge has access to information unavailable to the models, human performance usually falls short of model accuracy (see, e.g., Dawes, 1971). Where the statistical models cannot be used because of certain attributes of the task, a variety of other techniques has been designed to eliminate inconsistency and misweighting. Different variations of these techniques are currently being used in practice by accountants, particularly in the areas of financial analysis and auditing. A number of these decision-aiding methods and their accounting applications will be discussed in Chapter 5.

Multiple cue probability learning

Multiple cue probability learning (MCPL) research is aimed at determining what environmental conditions promote or deter learning in tasks such as business-failure prediction and others described in the previous section, which require that judges predict a criterion event from a set of probabilistically related cues. The environmental attributes receiving the greatest attention are (1) task predictability (R_e), (2) the functional form of cue-criterion relationships (e.g., positive linear, negative linear, quadratic, U shaped), (3) the number of cues, (4) cue validity distributions, and (5) cue intercorrelations. Decision aids which involve educating the decision maker (option 2 in Figure 1–1) through feedback are also discussed in this literature. As many of these task variables are controlled by the accountant, the MCPL literature should provide fertile ground for those interested in information systems design and managerial accounting.

The lens model equation presented earlier usually provides the framework for analyzing results. In the analysis, environmental or task predictability (R_e) is an independent variable, and achievement (r_a), as a function of matching (G), and linear consistency (R_s) are the dependent variables. As you will recall from the description of the lens model equation, G measures the similarity between the decision maker's weightings of cues and the environmental relationships as modeled by their respective regression equations $(G = r_{\hat{Y}_e \hat{Y}_s})$ and is interpreted here as indicating *task knowledge*. R_s under certain circumstances[10] measures response consistency and is interpreted in this literature as indicating how consistently the judge can apply her or his task knowledge. In the MCPL literature, this index is called *cognitive control* $(R_s = r_{Y_s \hat{Y}_s})$. This interpretation of the lens model equation is as follows:

[10]This holds when the linear model captures all reliable judgmental variance.

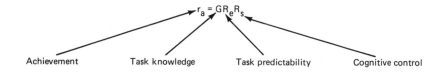

$$r_a = GR_eR_s$$

Achievement Task knowledge Task predictability Cognitive control

LEARNING AN ABSTRACT TASK

In the typical MCPL experiment, artificial task environments are created to allow manipulation of the independent variables of interest. The experimental cases are usually simulated on the basis of prespecified intercue and cue-criterion relationships. Subjects are then "taught" by various types of feedback to perform the task. For the most part, these tasks are highly abstract, with no empirical referents given for either the cues or the criterion event. For example, Hammond, Summers, and Deane (1973) presented subjects with three unlabeled vertical 10-point scales (the cues) and asked them to predict a fourth unlabeled scale value for each case. The purpose of the study was to measure the effectiveness of three types of feedback: (1) *outcome feedback,* where subjects are given the correct answer after each case, (2) *task-properties feedback,* where the correlation between each cue and the criterion event (r_{ie}) is indicated, and (3) a combination of the two. The number of cues (three), the functional relationship between cues and criterion (inverted-U shape), the ecological validity of the individual cues (r_{ie} = .8, .4, and .2), the cue intercorrelations (zero), and the environmental predictability (R_e = .88) were held constant in the experiment. Achievement (r_a), knowledge (G), and cognitive control (R_s) were measured. The authors hypothesized that outcome feedback would be detrimental to learning for the following reason: In tasks where the relationships between cues and criterion are probabilistic, the erroneous information (noise) in the outcome feedback would result in response inconsistency or lack of cognitive control (R_s), which in turn would decrease achievement (r_a). The results were consistent with the hypothesis. Achievement scores indicated little learning in the outcome feedback group, while the task-properties feedback group quickly learned the task. More importantly, the latter group also outperformed the subjects receiving both types of feedback. Analysis of knowledge (G) and cognitive control (R_s) suggested that the result was due to the detrimental effects of outcome feedback on cognitive control.

A MORE REALISTIC ENVIRONMENT

The role of different types of feedback in learning is of obvious importance to accountants concerned with performance evaluation and management control. Subjects' difficulty in dealing with outcome feedback should create concern because most control systems are based on this form of feedback. However, as noted previously, most of the literature in this area has studied the learning of generic tasks. Thus, a question arises as to whether learning from outcome feedback is facilitated by other variables in more realistic environments. This issue was addressed by Muchinsky and Dudycha (1974), who compared student subjects' performance in abstract and comparable "meaningful" environments. They compared learning of a two-cue prediction task under two conditions. The first was the typical abstract task where cues and event were labeled "cue 1," "cue 2," and "criterion." The second was a consumer-credit scoring task where cues and event were labeled "average monthly debt," "average number of creditors," and "credit score." Muchinsky and Dudycha also varied the sign of the cue validities and the sign of the cue redundancies. The experiment was carried out twice under differing levels of environmental predictability (R_e = .52 and .92). In both experiments, achievement was dramatically higher in the meaningful environments. Furthermore, previously discovered additional difficulties in learning negative relationships were eliminated in the meaningful environment. The studies in abstract settings appear to have understated human learning ability.

LEARNING AND MANAGEMENT CONTROL

The importance of a meaningful task environment to the learning of environmental relationships was brought home even more strongly in an accounting study. Harrell (1977) analyzed Air Force officers' ability to learn environmental relationships from the same two types of feedback studied by Hammond, Summers, and Deane (1973) in the abstract task example: (1) task-properties feedback and (2) outcome feedback. Both are traditionally a part of management control systems. Task properties indicating the relative importance of different cues are frequently presented in the form of company policies, though usually in nonquantitative form. Outcome feedback is often presented when one's superior indicates the judgment he or she would have made in the same situation. The experimental situation closely resembled the way in which actual Air Force training wings are evaluated. Not only were the wing commanders able to learn from *both* types of feedback, but they were able to determine when the two types were in agreement or disagreement and to adjust their policies accordingly.[11] This study is discussed in more detail in Appendix A.

These highly different findings seem to result from the lack of real-world referents for the cues and the criterion event in the abstract tasks used in earlier studies.[12] The research discussed in Chapters 3 and 4 sug-

[11]Note that Harrell interprets the results differently.

[12]Greater subject motivation and training and the high level of environmental predictability (R_e = 1) also may contribute to the result.

gests that cue patterns are learned in the form of prototypes or simple causal theories. The lack of such a framework in the abstract tasks substantially complicates learning. As most management-control systems employ both types of feedback (task properties *and* outcome feedback), these recent results are more reassuring.

SUMMARY

Slovic and Lichtenstein (1971), Brehmer (1976), Castellan (1977), and Slovic, Fischhoff, and Lichtenstein (1977) provide partial reviews of the MCPL literature. In addition to the conclusions already discussed, these studies suggest that: (1) linear consistency (R_s) increases as task predictability (R_e) increases; (2) positive linear functions are relatively easy to learn, while negative linear and nonlinear functions are more difficult; (3) the addition of less valid cues to a set containing more valid cues decreases performance; (4) subjects take insufficient note of cue redundancies, which results in the overweighting of redundant information; and (5) less important cues are often overweighted and more important cues are underweighted. A number of accounting researchers are beginning to investigate this area, and their work is discussed in more detail in Appendix A.

Policy-capturing studies: ANOVA and multidimensional scaling

The main concerns of policy capturing research are between-judge *consensus,* the relative importance of individual cues in the judgment process, the functional form (linear, quadratic, etc.) of the judgment rule, and the judges' own *self-insight* or awareness of their judgmental processes. Judgmental consensus has become an increasingly important issue to professional decision makers. Where the lack of objective criterion data makes the direct measurement of achievement impossible, the consensus judgment of experts often serves as a substitute criterion. Since most accounting situations can be so characterized, consensus judgments provide the backbone for much of accounting practice. In fact, a major objective of professional training in degree programs and continuing professional education is to promote consensus in professional judgment, and most standard setting in the accounting profession involves the codification of a consensus of expert opinions rather than scientific findings or objective measurements. These standards themselves are designed to promote consensus in practice. Within firms, detailed procedure manuals and review processes are also designed to ensure consensus. Finally, when the accountant's judgment is questioned in litigation or regulatory proceedings, his or her defense requires the demonstration that "generally accepted" or consensus procedures were followed.

Knowledge of the relative importance of individual cues in the judgment process and the functional form of the judgment rule can aid in training novice decision makers and provide an explanation of between-judge disagreement. Explicit specification of judgmental policies can also serve as a starting point for the evaluation of these policies. These issues are usually addressed by building algebraic models of the relationships between cues and judgments. This process is often called *policy capturing*. Accountants' interest in policy capturing goes back to Horrigan's (1966) econometric study of bond raters' judgmental rules.[13] More recent research has used an experimental approach and has focused on audit and disclosure judgments.

The studies described under the heading "Clinical versus Statistical Prediction" used actual cases drawn from the environment so that realistic inferences concerning judgmental accuracy could be drawn. However, as the lens model suggests, the cues in real settings are likely to be interrelated. This problem, called multicollinearity, clouds the inferences concerning the relative importance of different cues that may be drawn from the cue utilization coefficients. This has led many researchers to turn to a method similar to regression, which is called *analysis of variance* (ANOVA). In addition, many multiattribute judgments are made based on cues which are ill-defined and unquantified. This requires a technique which identifies the cues on which judgments are based and then scales each object on each cue. Judgment researchers have used *multidimensional scaling* for this purpose. Both approaches are described next.

ANOVA STUDIES

When experimental cases are constructed following analysis of variance designs, multicollinearity is eliminated and interactive effects[14] of cues can be measured. In such cases, each cue is first partitioned into a few discrete levels, and hypothetical cases are developed by forming all unique combinations of cue values (a completely crossed *factorial* design) or by a special sampling of these combinations (a fractional replication design). The percentage of variance accounted for by the individual cues (the main effects) and the interactions of the cues (see footnote 14) can then be measured by use of the ω^2 statistic (Hays, 1963, p. 324). The individual ω^2 statistics are interpreted as (squared) utilization coefficients (r_{is}^2), and their sum is interpreted in a manner similar to linear predictability (R_s^2). A complete description of the technique is available in Hoffman, Slovic, and Rorer (1968).

The ANOVA method has been applied to a variety of situations. One of the most interesting studies examined decisions made by radiologists. Hoffman, Slovic, and Rorer (1968) studied radiologists' judgments

---

[13]Horrigan analyzed archival data relating to actual bond ratings.

[14]Interactions occur when the effect of one cue differs depending on the levels of other cues. This phenomenon is discussed more thoroughly in the next section.

of the malignancy of gastric ulcers. Major issues of interest included the relative weights placed on different diagnostic signs, the consistency of judgments over time, and between-judge consensus. Six practicing radiologists and three radiologists-in-training from a major medical school judged a set of 96 cases on a seven-point benign-malignant scale. Each case contained five cues which could take one of two levels and one cue with three possible levels. These 96 cases were constructed on the basis of a completely crossed 3×2^5 factorial design. The diagnostic signs were presented on stimulus cards (not actual radiographs) where, except for the three-level cue, the existence or nonexistence of the sign was indicated by a "yes" or "no," respectively. Each participant evaluated the set of 96 cases twice.

Consistency of the judges over time was high, ranging from $r = .6$ to .92. However, pairwise agreement between judges, or consensus, was low, ranging from $r = -.11$ to .83. Computation of the ω^2 statistics indicated that, on the average, 90% of reliable judgment variance was accounted for by the linear additive components (main effects), and the largest interaction of cues accounted for less than 2% of the variance. Each judge appeared to place major emphasis on relatively few cues (from one to three). As suggested by the low between-subject agreement, the weights placed on the individual signs varied greatly from subject to subject. These results are consistent with the studies in the Clinical versus Statistical Judgment category, where judges demonstrated little agreement among themselves but were linearly predictable and reliable over time.[15]

Ashton (1974a) used Hoffman, Slovic, and Rorer's (1968) methodology to study cue utilization, consistency, and consensus of auditors' internal control judgments and their self-insight into their judgment processes. This study is of particular interest because it attacked the conventional wisdom that it was impossible to subject the auditor's professional judgment to vigorous scientific inquiry. More recently, auditors have begun to reevaluate this stand because of (1) pressures from the courts and regulators to explain procedures, (2) the need to reduce inefficiencies in audit resource allocations resulting from inconsistent procedures, and (3) interest in developing more effective teaching techniques. In Ashton's study, each of 63 practicing auditors judged the strength of the internal control in a payroll subsystem on the basis of six dichotomous internal control factors. Thirty-two cases were formed by a one-half replication of a 2^6 factorial design. (A sample case is presented in Figure 2–3.) The cases were administered a second time 6 to 13 weeks later. Like the radiologists in the Hoffman, Slovic, and Rorer study, the auditors were very consistent over time ($r = .81$). Also, 80% of the variance in their

---

[15] The fact that the radiologists did not agree on a diagnosis is very disconcerting, because two different diagnoses obviously cannot both be correct. The implications for the patient are quite alarming.

judgments was accounted for by the linear additive components. However, unlike the case of the radiologists, there was considerable consensus among the auditors' evaluations. This suggests that auditors have developed a generally accepted definition of "good" internal control. The auditors also exhibited greater than usual self-insight into their cue-weighting patterns. The ω^2 statistics suggested that factors related to separation of duties were of greatest importance to the auditors' judgments. In the next section, a related method which is useful when the factors affecting judgment are less well understood is discussed.

MULTIDIMENSIONAL SCALING

As we have discussed, regression modeling requires the quantification of cues. However, many multiattribute judgments are made on the basis of cues which may be not only unquantified, but also ill-defined. Multidimensional scaling (MDS) is a method by which expressed relationships between objects can be represented within a geometric distance model. The model identifies both the cues or dimensions on which objects differ and the perceived value of each object on each cue. The technique has helped researchers better understand a variety of global judgments, ranging from color perceptions to product preferences. The major advantage of this approach is that it does not require prespecification of relevant cues, which makes it a useful tool for exploratory research. The technique also allows the subjects to evaluate the objects on the basis of their own perceptual frameworks and, thus, independent of much of the experimenter's bias.

Some more recent algorithms (e.g., INDSCAL) provide a measure of perceptual differences between individuals, which are represented in the model by differential weighting (or stretching) of a common set of

FIGURE 2–3
Sample case

Source: Ashton [1974a, Table 1]

Case No. ____	Yes	No
1. Are the tasks of both timekeeping and payment of employees adequately separated from the task of payroll preparation?	X	
2. Are the tasks of both payroll preparation and payment of employees adequately separated from the task of payroll bank account reconciliation?		X
3. Are the names on the payroll checked periodically against the active employee file of the personnel department?		X
4. Are formal procedures established for changing names on the payroll, pay rates, and deductions?	X	
5. Is the payroll audited periodically by internal auditors?	X	
6. Was the internal control over payroll found to be satisfactory during the previous audit?	X	

extremely weak	very weak	substantial weakness	some weakness	not quite adequate	adequate to strong
1	2	3	4	5	6

dimensions. The square roots of these weights indicate the relative importance of each dimension to the individual subject and can be interpreted in a manner similar to utilization coefficients (r_{is}). A subject who weights a dimension more heavily perceives the distances between the objects on that dimension to be greater than does a subject who places a lesser weight on that dimension. The analysis also measures the "fit" between the representation in the derived dimensions and the subjects' original similarity ratings for each individual, which is similar to linear predictability (R_s). Detailed descriptions of the method are available in Carroll and Chang (1970) and Green and Rao (1972). One hypothetical and one actual research example, both drawn from Libby (1979a), will illustrate the technique.

If a group of car buyers were to rate the similarity of all pairs of 10 different automobiles, and these individuals determined similarity on the basis of two aspects of the automobile, price and "sportiness," MDS could uncover these two dimensions or cues from the 45 relationships presented in the individuals' judgments of similarity. The placement of each object on each dimension could be represented on a two-dimensional map similar to Figure 2–4. This map is often referred to as the *object space*. The placement on the two dimensions of one's own product relative to other products might suggest an approach to market segmentation or an advertising strategy aimed at changing the perceived location of one's product on one or more of the dimensions. If one were interested in targeting a campaign to certain types of buyers, the weights placed by different car buyers on the different dimensions would help cluster the potential customers.

FIGURE 2–4
Hypothetical perceptual map or object space of automobiles

Source: Libby [1979a, Figure 4]

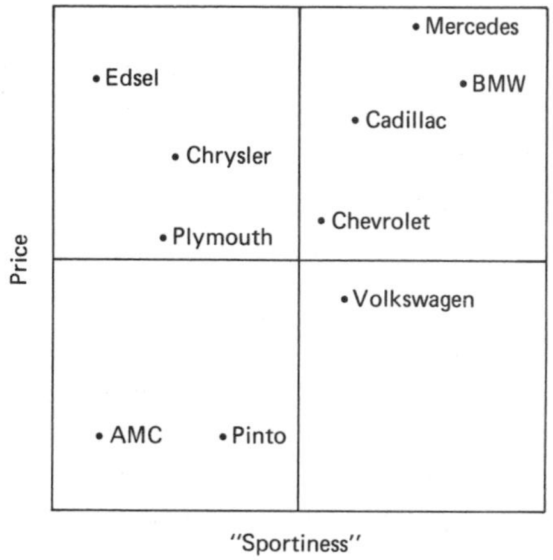

"Sportiness"

In an accounting application, Libby (1979a) determined and compared the way in which 30 "Big 8" audit partners and 28 "money center" commercial lenders perceived messages intended to be communicated by different audit reports. Allegations of differences in perceptions had served as a rationale for suggested changes in the audit reporting framework. The research question was conceptualized as a question of differential weighting of the cues intended by the reports. As the cues were not well specified, MDS was employed. Each subject evaluated the similarity of the messages intended by all pairs of 10 different audit reports (unqualified and qualified by different types of uncertainty and scope qualifications and disclaimers) and rated the reports on 13 adjective rating scales. An MDS algorithm called INDSCAL was used to build representations of the participants' perceptual structures, and the auditors and bankers were compared using three methods: (1) comparison of separate group models, (2) comparison of average cue weights in a composite (all-subject) model, and (3) comparison of responses to the adjective rating scales. A two-dimensional (or two-cue) model was built. Contrary to the beliefs of a number of policy makers, all measures indicated highly similar perceptions between the two groups of subjects. The two dimensions were tentatively identified as "need for additional information" and "amount of audit judgment required." Differences between the qualified and disclaimer opinions were twice as great as differences between the unqualified and qualified reports. The source of the scope limitation (client versus circumstance imposed) appeared to be important, while the source of the uncertainty (asset realization versus litigation) appeared to be of little consequence.

SUMMARY

Professional judgments about a wide variety of tasks have been studied using ANOVA and MDS. The studies described here illustrate many of the typical findings. Like the decision makers in the earlier-mentioned studies of "Clinical versus Statistical Judgment," these judges are consistent over time and their processes are well approximated by linear additive models. They also exhibit varying degrees of consensus and self-insight into their cue weightings. Observed differences in cue weighting pinpoint the cause of disagreements. Furthermore, the judges seem to emphasize a few key variables in forming these judgments, even when a great deal of additional information is available.

Generalizations from the research to date

Recent review articles (e.g., Slovic, Fischhoff, and Lichtenstein, 1977, p. 12) note the high volume of research that has been conducted using the regression model and associated analytical methods. A wide variety of laboratory and real-world judges has served as subjects, including admissions committees, fish hatchery employees, bankers, teachers, doctors, judges, consumers, and many others. The approach has also been particularly useful to accountants. Conclusions which can be drawn about decision behavior in general and accounting issues in particular will next be reviewed.

GENERAL CONCLUSIONS

A surprisingly consistent picture of the human decision maker can be drawn from this research. Linear models can account for most of the reliable variance in human judgment. However, the accuracy of the linear representation is due in part to the mathematical characteristics of the models and tasks, as well as to characteristics of actual combination rules. People's judgment rules are probably not always linear, but involve a combination of functional rules, which we will discuss in more detail later in this chapter. People also appear to rely on a relatively small subset of available data. Achievement has with some exceptions been quite poor, while consistency over time has been relatively high, and results on between-judge consensus have been mixed. Both inconsistency and inaccurate cue weighting contribute to the less-than-optimal measures of achievement.

Many attributes of the information set and context have major effects on a judge's ability to learn the relationships between cues and events, and the learning literature continues to progress toward the stage of theoretical development where accurate task-specific predictions can be made. Some of the relationships that have been discovered are contrary to conventional wisdom. For example, adding cues that increase environmental predictability often increases confidence in judgment, but has no effect on achievement.

The improvement of human decisions continues to receive much attention from researchers. Studies of the characteristics of human judgment have led to the development of many aids designed to alleviate the negative effects of specific attributes of judgments. Some of these are discussed in detail in the final chapter.

ACCOUNTING ISSUES

The regression approach to modeling has been used in more than 30 studies to analyze judgments in accounting contexts. Important areas such as materiality judgments, lending decisions, and the determination of litigation risk have been investigated. Many of the general conclusions about decision behavior that we have just summarized have been confirmed, but with some important exceptions. Some of the key findings of these studies are very briefly discussed next. Readers with an interest in the details of the research are referred to Appendix A, which reviews the individual studies.

The usefulness of accounting ratio information has been addressed in four studies concerning the accuracy of loan officers' bankruptcy predictions. Performance has been high relative both to environmental predictability and to the performance of other decision makers on different tasks. Also, high levels of consistency and consensus among bankers were reported. A recent study suggests that the selection of cues, as opposed to their relative weighting, is the key to accuracy in the task.

With respect to multiple cue probability learning, three issues have been addressed. First, three studies suggested that novice decision makers did not sufficiently adjust their decision rules in response to a change in the algorithm used to compute the accounting numbers. This behavior has been called *functional fixity*. Second, in three different accounting tasks, decision makers appeared able to learn quite easily from both outcome feedback and task-properties feedback. These studies further support the importance of meaningful environments to the learning process and suggest that earlier research has understated human abilities. Third, decision makers were better able to analyze financial data when it was presented in the form of multidimensional graphics rather than standard ratios. Other possibilities for improving accounting report format have received surprisingly little attention in the accounting literature. These possibilities are discussed in more detail in Chapter 5.

Policy-capturing studies have addressed a number of important accounting issues. Of particular interest are those dealing with internal control evaluations and their relationship to audit program planning. These studies have indicated a high degree of consensus in internal control evaluations. However, this level of consensus does not appear to carry over to audit planning decisions, which suggests that highly different decision rules are brought to bear on the latter situation. These findings have led to changes in certain audit practices aimed at eliminating the source of inconsistency. Some of these techniques are discussed in Chapter 5. As expected, separation of duties appeared to dominate internal control judgments.

The determinants of materiality judgments have also received considerable attention. The impact on net income played the greatest role in these judgments. However, the disclosure criterion cutoff changed for different disclosure items. Other studies have indicated the relative unimportance of "subject to" qualified audit reports in the commercial lending decision and little evidence of block voting or "Big 8" dominance of accounting policy making. Clearly, the FASB has taken unpopular outlying positions in many cases. The accounting studies which led to these conclusions and others are reviewed in detail in Appendix A.

While use of the regression framework has produced many important findings in accounting and other disciplines, its use is not without limitations. In the next section, a number of conceptual and methodological problems inherent in the framework are discussed.

CONCEPTUAL AND METHODOLOGICAL PROBLEMS

When employing the regression approach to the study of judgment, the researcher must make a number of difficult choices related to task construction, process modeling, and performance measurement. The strengths and weaknesses of the available alternatives and how the purpose of the study can guide these choices will be discussed in this section. While this discussion does not represent a comprehensive review of methods, it illustrates how the construction of an experiment can affect the results and conclusions of a study.

Task construction

While a number of notable studies using regression-related modeling techniques have analyzed archival data resulting from actual decisions,[16] most studies are laboratory or field experiments. In these experiments, to allow the researcher to estimate the parameters of the regression formulation of the lens model, each subject normally evaluates a large number of cases, which are represented by the same cue set. The experimental cases can be constructed in three ways. First, experimental cases can be abstracted from a representative group of actual cases, as was done in the clinical versus statistical judgment studies (e.g., Libby, 1975a, b). A second possibility is to build fabricated cases representative of realistic relationships. For example, Boatsman and Robertson (1974) estimated the joint distribution of certain financial statement variables and used this distribution as the basis for building their experimental cases. The third alternative is to use fabricated cases which are *not* representative of realistic relationships, as Ashton (1974a) and others have done in many of the policy-capturing and multiple cue probability learning studies. The first two alternatives, in which an attempt is made to maintain the realistic statistical properties of the cues and events, are called *representative designs*. The latter alternative, which often is based upon an orthogonal ANOVA model, is called a *systematic design*.

The relative benefits of the two approaches are usually described in terms of a trade-off between the ability to measure either cue usage or performance. As most cues are correlated in the environment, the interpretation of cue-usage coefficients derived from a representative design

[16]See, e.g., Horrigan's (1966) study of bond raters, Dawes (1971) study of a graduate admissions committee, and Brown's (1981) study of respondents to FASB discussion memoranda. These types of studies are extremely important and should receive more attention.

is often difficult. The use of fabricated cases based on orthogonal designs eliminates this problem. In studies where cue utilization was the focal point of interest, such as the Hoffman, Slovic, and Rorer (1968) study of radiologists and Ashton's (1974a) and Joyce's (1976) studies of auditors' internal control judgments, such a design was necessary. This design is also often chosen as a result of difficulties in assessing realistic cue relationships.

DETERMINING CUE USAGE

While the interpretability of weights is a virtue of the ANOVA approach, a number of significant interpretation problems remain. First, in ANOVA the main effect of a cue on judgment is measured by the difference between the mean responses to the cases having each of the two levels of the cue. Relative cue importance is normally compared by means of a ratio of the magnitude of the two effects. If a continuous variable is dichotomized, this measure of importance will be affected by the specific values which are chosen for each variable. To illustrate the implications of this problem, consider an accounting example in which the relative effects on the subjective probability of failure of the current ratio and the return on total assets are examined. As can be seen in Figure 2–5, when a dichotomous scale is used for the current ratio, the slope of the function

FIGURE 2–5

Effect of dichotomizing continuous cues

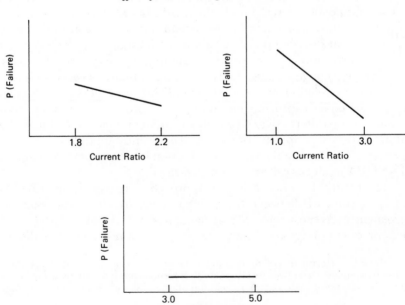

representing its effect on judgment may depend on which segment of the underlying continuous function is extracted. In Figure 2–5, three different pairs of values were chosen at random. Each pair would produce highly differing indications of cue importance. The Hofstedt and Hughes (1977) study of the determinants of materiality judgments suffers from this problem because the choice of cue values determined the results.

In Ashton's (1974a) and Joyce's (1976) studies, the real-world equivalents to the cues presented in the cases take on dichotomous values, eliminating this problem. Other authors attempt to eliminate the problem by using a high-low dichotomy. However, this presents an additional problem, as the terms may have different meanings for different cues and for different subjects. If differential perceptions of the meaning of "high" and "low" exist, these differences will artificially decrease between-judge agreement or consensus.

REPRESENTATIVE DESIGN

Since cases developed from orthogonal designs are fabricated, performance measurement is impossible unless the criterion event is also fabricated. In Goldberg's (1965, 1970) study of psychologists and Libby's (1975b) study of bank loan officers, a representative design was utilized because they were designed primarily to measure performance. However, there are two other, often overlooked, reasons to consider representative design. Basic to Brunswik's theory of probabilistic functionalism is the tenet that behavior is a *joint product* of the observing system *and* the environmental system. More simply, when the basic structure of a task is changed so that it is not representative of the environment, the behavior of the subjects may also change, and the results may no longer be closely related to the real-world problem of interest. A convincing explanation and illustration of the representative design problem is presented in Hammond and Stewart (1974).

The way in which altering the environmental system may affect the conclusions of a study will be illustrated with a hypothetical accounting experiment. Suppose that a researcher wanted to measure the consensus among accountants in the application of Accounting Principles Board (APB) Opinion 18 rules for choosing between the cost and equity methods of accounting for investments. The basic research issue is between-judge consensus: whether different accountants make the same judgment in the same situation. Accountants have expressed great concern over the consistency of application of accounting rules, and to some extent this concern has affected our judgments in accounting policy making, leading to more detailed rules.

In APB 18 the criterion for application of the equity method is the investor's ability to exercise "significant influence" over the financial and operating policies of the investee. The ability to exercise that influence is presumed, in the absence of other evidence to the contrary, when the investor owns 20% or more of the voting stock. Significant influence (or the lack thereof) can also be evidenced by (1) representation on the board of directors, (2) participation in decision making, (3) intercompany transactions, (4) exchange of personnel, or (5) technological dependency. These cues may be taken as sufficient evidence of significant influence in the absence of the 20% ownership, or they may indicate lack of significant influence in the presence of 20% or greater ownership. Note that in the real world these cues are highly correlated.

Suppose the following experiment was conducted. Experimental cases containing the six cues indicative of significant influence have been constructed in a nonrepresentative fashion using the following factorial design. The stock ownership cue takes on three levels (6%, 19%, and 40%) and the other five cues are dichotomous (high or low). All possible combinations of the six cues have been formed, resulting in a fully replicated 3×2^5 factorial design. Each member of a group of auditors has evaluated the 96 cases. For purposes of the discussion, assume that their responses to the cases were identical to what they would be if they were confronted with the *same* cases in the real world, and that they are perfectly consistent over time. This assumption eliminates other external validity problems and removes the random element from the process. If little consensus among auditors is found in this experiment, would one expect similar results in real-world applications of APB 18? Given the identity assumption, the initial reaction might be "yes." However, let us examine the question more closely. Remember first that the interrelationships among the cues have been altered. Given that the subjects are consistent over time and the cues are uncorrelated, any lack of consensus in the experimental judgments must have resulted from different weighting of cues, and, likewise, differential weighting must result in lack of consensus. However, in the real world, different weighting of cues (called *disagreement in principle*) does *not* necessarily imply lack of between-judge consensus (*disagreement in fact*). Thus, if two judges differentially weight two cues which happen to have a high positive correlation, very little between-judge inconsistency should result. As positive multicollinearity increases, the effect of the differential weighting decreases.

The orthogonal design ensured that different decisions *must* result from differential weightings. In the real-world situation, multicollinearity exists to a high degree and, as a result, the extent of the disagreement would decrease. The way in which this experiment was designed actually magnified the inconsistency; the experimental setting was so different from the real world that the results of the study were not directly relevant to the research question of interest.

Next, remember that the distribution of cases has also been altered. Fully one-third of the cases were on the borderline of the 20% ownership rule (19%). If most disagreements occur in borderline cases where, for example, the investor owns between 18% and 22% of the stock, and if such cases are overrepresented in our sample, this will tend to further magnify the level of disagreement. Note that Libby's (1975a, b) use of 50% failed firms in his bankruptcy prediction study also significantly altered the distribution and thus may suffer from the same problem. The reader should recognize that changing either the cue interrelationships or the case distributions affects the *external validity* of the results.

What would happen if policy decisions were based on this experiment? To decrease the experimentally observed inconsistency, more detailed rules might be prescribed. In reality, however, the inconsistency may not be as great as the experiment would lead us to believe, and more rules may not be necessary.

This example was *not* designed to discourage use of orthogonal designs, but to emphasize the importance of letting the purpose of the study guide the choice of design. Clearly, in this hypothetical case, the policy issue of interest should have led to the use of a more representative design.

CASE CONSTRUCTION

Once the researcher has decided on the type of design to be employed, the construction of the individual cases must be addressed. First, one must decide what data to include in each case and how many cases should be presented to each participant. Many real-world tasks of interest are characterized by the availability of large amounts of data. An attempt to mimic this data availability in an experiment requires that, to build stable models, the number of cases presented be increased as the number of cues in each case increases. The conflicting motivation to make the subjects' task manageable must also be dealt with.

This conflict usually requires that, in practice, the real-world task be abstracted to some degree. Often, a useful form of abstraction is to focus on the relevant component of the decision of interest. This was done both by Ashton (1974a) and Libby (1975a, b). The normative theory of decision making in the task and advice from expert decision makers will provide the most important guidance in this phase of task construction. As illustrated by the sample cases presented in Figures 2–2 and 2–3, Ashton and Libby employed a high level of abstraction. However, this degree of abstraction is *not* required by the methodology. Libby (1979b) reports an example in which more realistic data representations, including nearly complete financial statements, were used.

The conflict between manageability and realism can further be resolved by presenting cases in the context of extensive background data which is held constant across all cases. Increasing concern for this aspect of case design is evidenced in the internal control studies discussed in Appendix A. The three exemplar experimental tasks were developed by

Ashton (1974a), Joyce (1976), and Mock and Turner (1979). Each represented a major step forward in increasing the fidelity of the background data; in fact, this art has developed to the point where the Mock and Turner (1979) paradigm closely replicates a portion of the standard audit procedures of Peat, Marwick, Mitchell and Company. The impact of the researcher's choice of both the fidelity of the background data and the level at which these cues are held constant has received little scientific attention.

Process modeling

Most studies conducted within the regression framework have as one of their goals the production of a mathematical representation of the environmental and decision sides of the lens. In the representation, the judge is portrayed as considering all available information in a single global judgment. However, this method does not measure the *actual* mental process which produces this judgment—nor does any other modeling method. *All* modeling approaches provide only surface representations of relationships between inputs and outputs. Even different psychophysical measurements of the same behavior sometimes imply different processes. Yet the implications of different types of models in terms of the mental process they suggest can be important. A number of compensatory and noncompensatory models are discussed next.

COMPENSATORY MODELS

Most regression studies represent the process as a linear additive regression model of the form

$$Y = a + b_1X_1 + b_2X_2 + \cdots + b_kX_k + u$$

Linear regression models are a type of *compensatory* model. In a compensatory model, a high score on one cue offsets a low score on another. The degree of offset will be determined by the relative weights (b_i) placed on the cues (X_i). This process of trading off attributes is integral to most day-to-day decisions. When choosing an automobile, we would all like to find a car which is luxurious *and* inexpensive or fast *and* fuel-efficient. However, we usually must trade some luxury for cost savings and some speed for fuel economy. Indeed, most would agree that determining the proper trade-offs in a compensatory model is the most difficult activity in decision making. In light of this, it is ironic that linear models are frequently referred to as "simple" because of their statistical features. (Einhorn, Kleinmuntz, and Kleinmuntz, 1979, discuss this issue in detail.)

The analysis of variance (ANOVA) method provides a simple way to add *interactions* of cues in a linear model. When two cues interact in their effects on judgment, the level of one cue affects the impact of the second. Figure 2–6 presents, in graphical form, two examples of two-cue interactions. In example (a), the relative enjoyment experienced from consuming a bottle of white or red wine (cue 1) depends upon the type of main course which is consumed, fish or beef (cue 2). In this type of interaction, where the sign of the slope of the line changes, conditional monotonicity is violated. You will recall from the earlier discussion that this violation decreases the power of linear models. In example (b), smoking and the use of birth-control pills both increase the probability of developing cancer. However, the increase in probability caused by the drug is much greater if the woman also smokes cigarettes. Note that while taking the pill *and* smoking each *independently* increase cancer risk, the combined effects of the two are greater than the sum of the two individual effects. This is called a *positive interaction*, where the effect of one trait is increased by the existence of a second trait. Note also that the lines on the graph do not have to intersect to produce an interaction. It is sufficient that they be nonparallel.

FIGURE 2–6

Examples of interactions

Source: Examples (a) and (b) were suggested by Hillel Einhorn and Edward J. Joyce, respectively.

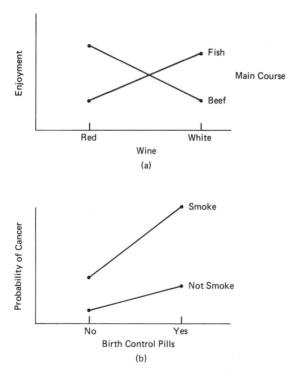

In noncompensatory models, a high score on one variable cannot compensate for a low score on another. The two types of noncompensatory models that have received the greatest attention are the *conjunctive* and *disjunctive* models (see Einhorn, 1970). *Conjunctive* or multiple-cutoff models require that some minimum level of performance be exceeded on *all* variables ($X_i \geq X_c$ for all i). The resulting choice is actually based on the level of the worst attribute. For example, football players are usually in excellent physical condition, but seldom are inducted into the Army. This results because the Army uses a conjunctive model for assessing physical condition. Each potential inductee must meet *all* minimum standards on a variety of physical attributes. A football player whose knee is held together with pins doesn't pass the Army physical regardless of his other physical attributes. Research has suggested that such models are often used for prescreening of alternatives.

Disjunctive models require outstanding performance on at least one variable ($X_i \geq X_n$ for any i, where X_n is very high). This is equivalent to judging alternatives on the basis of their best attribute. For example, promotion guidelines at some universities require that the individual must be *either* an outstanding teacher *or* an outstanding researcher. Individuals who are good teachers *and* researchers, but are outstanding on neither attribute, would not be promoted under such a rule. Research suggests that many decisions are made using some *combination* of rules, such as conjunctive for prescreening and disjunctive or compensatory for final choices (see, e.g., Payne, 1976). Conjunctive models are used for prescreening because they can eliminate most of the alternatives while producing few obvious anomalies and can be employed at low cost. The most difficult and thus the most expensive part of decision making involves, in the compensatory model, the evaluation of trade-offs and, in the disjunctive model, arriving at a definition of "very high" for each variable. Johnson (1979) discusses the effort required by different decision rules.

Understanding the nature of decision rules can provide relevant insights for accounting policy making. For example, if the FASB attempted to develop explicit materiality guidelines based on the way in which these decisions are currently being made, it would face a two-part task. First, the relevant cues would need to be determined. They might decide, for instance, that the important cues are the size of the disclosure item as a percentage of (1) net income, (2) the specific asset or liability, and (3) total assets. However, before the rules are complete, they must also specify the nature of the cue combination rule. If items are disclosed on the basis of reaching any one or more cutoffs on the preceding three cues, a disjunctive model is being used. If high values on the net income cue may be offset by low values on the total asset or specific asset cue, use of a compensatory model is implied. These different rules will result in different disclosure decisions in many situations. The analysis of the functional form of the process model is addressed in more detail in Chapter 4.

Performance measurement

The final issue we will discuss is the measurement of decision achievement. Frequently, this presents an insurmountable problem. Assessing achievement requires measures of both the judgment and the criterion event. In many accounting decisions, the criterion event is not even well specified, let alone easily observed and measured. As a result, many accounting studies using regression and ANOVA look only at the judgment side of the lens. Even when an observable criterion is specified, other often overlooked problems face the researcher (Einhorn and Hogarth, 1978). First, the success or failure of rejected candidates is often difficult to observe. For example, in our graduate admissions study, the success or failure of a student who is admitted to the program could be simply measured in terms of his or her starting salary. However, it is virtually impossible to track the failure or success of a student who is rejected. Similarly, bankers rarely become aware of the success or failure of loan applicants who have been rejected. This performance measurement problem is exaggerated further if the criterion event is not independent of the judgment. This second difficulty occurs in both the graduate-admissions and business-failure-prediction examples, where the act of selection itself affects future success. For example, assume that success is measured by starting salary, and completion of the masters program on average results in a $3,000 salary premium over the salaries of comparable students not completing the program. Even if students are accepted at random, it is likely that in the short run the $3,000 edge will cause accepted students to appear more successful than their rejected colleagues. It will be impossible to completely separate the effect of the MBA program from the accuracy of the admissions decision. Similarly, the act of granting a loan may itself increase the recipient business's chance of success.

From the prior discussion in Chapter 1, the reader should recognize this as a problem of *internal validity*. Elimination of this problem would require not only following up rejected individuals, but *accepting* a sample of those who are judged as *rejections*. Of course, most organizations are unwilling to make this investment in the evaluation of their selection procedures.

Like measures of cue utilization, performance measures will also be affected by the construction of the task and, in particular, the distribution of cases. For example, if marginal cases which are particularly difficult to predict are overrepresented in the sample, performance is likely to be adversely affected. Similar problems occur if only selected candidates make up the case sample. For example, if a sample of loan candidates containing only those applicants who were successful is evaluated, type I errors will probably be understated.

Finally, measurement of performance requires the researcher to specify a loss function for errors. This process is complex in that the relationship between judgment and choice must be specified and the cost of choosing one action when another is more appropriate must be measured. In many studies, this has been done only implicitly. The most frequently used measure has been the correlation coefficient (r_a). The use of a correlational measure implies (1) no penalty for misspecification of the mean, (2) no penalty for misspecification of the variance, and (3) a squared loss function for other errors. Many psychologists have deemphasized this problem by blurring the distinction between a judgment or probability estimate and a decision or action choice. However, consideration of this distinction may lead one to conclude that much behavior that appears to be nonoptimal might be optimal if payoffs were appropriately specified. Einhorn and Schact (1977) discuss the conditions which determine the effects of inaccurate judgments on decision quality.

CONCLUDING COMMENTS

As Einhorn (1976) has indicated, the methods and experiments that we have discussed for the most part place the decision maker in a passive role in which he or she responds on a predetermined scale to cases containing a small, predetermined information set. While less structured tasks *have* been modeled with the techniques we have discussed (e.g., the bond-rating models), the resulting models are still highly abstract and indicate little about the sequence of steps taken in most complex decision situations. This level of analysis highlights important attributes of judgment, but it fails to capture some of the richness of real situations. The next area of research we will discuss considers additional elements, including prior knowledge, a sequential revision process, and judgments of probability distributions on future events. It also formally addresses the difference between a judgment and a decision.

DISCUSSION QUESTIONS

1. Provide a brief discussion or description of each of the following:
   a. Criterion event
   b. Ecological validity
   c. Environmental predictability
   d. Utilization coefficient
   e. Response linearity
   f. Achievement index
   g. Matching index
   h. Conditional monotonicity
   i. Conjunctive model
   j. Disjunctive model
   k. Interaction
2. How is the information environment defined within the lens model?
3. Distinguish between "environmental regression models" and "models of man" and explain why both are likely to be more accurate than human judges in situations where the models can be constructed. List some characteristics of common business decisions which would limit the usefulness of the models.

4. Dawes and Corrigan (1974) suggest that, in most situations, cues and criteria are "conditionally monotonic." Describe one accounting-related situation where this condition holds and one where it does not hold.

5. Discuss the roles of "task-properties feedback" and "outcome feedback" in a business decision-making situation.

6. Explain why learning may be easier in a meaningful task environment than in an abstract task environment.

7. Explain the benefits of examining the impact of a change in the information set in terms of the components of the simplified lens-model equation (G, R_e, R_s), as opposed to only the global measure of achievement (r_a).

8. Explain how evidence concerning cue weighting, consistency, consensus, and self-insight into auditor's internal control judgments might be of interest to the executive officers of a major CPA firm (see e.g., Ashton, 1974a).

9. Explain the meaning of "cue usage" as measured by the "utilization coefficient." When cue usage is different from perceived cue usage, subjects are usually judged to have poor self-insight. What are the potential implications of poor self-insight for the teaching of decision rules?

10. What are the advantages and disadvantages of systematic and representative designs?

11. How might the hypothetical experiment discussed in the chapter related to application of APB 18 be redesigned to eliminate the specific weaknesses suggested?

12. Discuss the costs associated with constructing more complex case materials in policy-capturing research.

13. Goldberg's study of the diagnosis of psychotics and Libby's study of business-failure prediction are presented as similar studies. What is the major difference between the events predicted in each study? What is the significance of this difference in terms of drawing valid conclusions? (*Hint:* Consider the statement, "Goldberg's study really examines judgmental consensus.")

14. Obtaining an acceptable sample of "rejected candidates" is often necessary to provide the data base for evaluation of a decision model. Why do you believe that most organizations are unwilling to make this investment in evaluation?

15. In light of the discussion of performance measurement, indicate the weaknesses in the interpretation of the accuracy results in Libby's (1975b) business-failure-prediction study. (*Hint:* Consider base rates, the costs of error, and the self-fulfilling prophecy" problem, among others.)

16. Choose one study using regression and one study using ANOVA from Appendix A. Critically evaluate each study in terms of the conceptual and methodological problems discussed in the last section of Chapter 2.

17. Make a list of 10 important accounting-related decisions. Classify them into two categories depending on whether an external criterion measure is typically available. Consider what differences exist in the research questions one might ask with regard to each.

CHAPTER THREE

Representations of
Human Judgment:
Exploring Predecisional
Behavior

Judgments such as medical diagnoses or internal control evaluations are normally made to provide a basis for choices between alternatives, such as medical treatments or substantive testing levels. Similarly, predictions of future events such as employment success or business failure provide a basis for school admission or loan-granting decisions. Economists and statisticians (e.g., von Neumann and Morgenstern, 1947; Savage, 1954) have constructed a theory of rational choice for these types of situations. This theory, often called *statistical decision theory*, presents a normative or prescriptive model, but it also furnished psychologists (e.g., Edwards, 1954) with a rigorous framework and a point of departure for building a *descriptive* model of decision making under uncertainty. Bayes's theorem and the concept of subjective or personal probabilities have received the greatest attention in descriptive research. The resulting literature is often categorized under the title *probabilistic judgment.*

This chapter is organized in three parts. The first part describes the probabilistic judgment model and compares it to the regression version of the lens model discussed in Chapter 2. In the second section, associated research methodologies, the principal research issues and findings, and their implications for accounting are discussed. (Appendix B reviews the related accounting literature in detail.) The third section presents a discussion of the more difficult conceptual and methodological issues of interest to more advanced readers.

LENS MODEL AS A PROBABILISTIC JUDGMENT MODEL

The decision-theory model decomposes the decision process into two components: (1) *probability judgment,* which is closely related to the regression version of the lens model, and (2) *risky choice*, where probability judgments are combined with utilities for outcomes to determine action choices. The graduate-admissions example developed in Chapter 1 will first be used to examine the probability judgment model and to compare it with the regression version of the lens model. The completed probability judgment version of the lens model is presented in Figure 3–1.

As was discussed earlier, the regression model represents the decision process at a very high level of abstraction. The decision maker is

FIGURE 3–1

Probabilistic formulation of the lens model

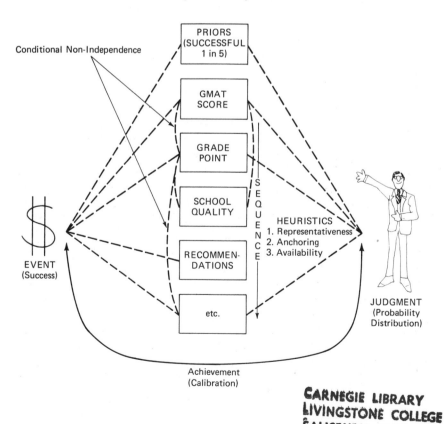

portrayed as combining a number of imperfect cues into a categorical judgment which indicates his or her *best estimate* of the true state of the future event (success). No *temporal sequence* is specified in the process state. By contrast, the probability judgment model describes the decision maker as estimating a probability *distribution* over each possible state or event (level of success) in a *sequential process* where initial expectations, often called *prior probabilities,* are revised on the basis of each new piece of information (GPA, GMAT score, etc.). In the graduate-admissions task, these initial expectations are likely to be based on the success rates of earlier years' applicants. The normative side of the regression version of the model contains the *least-squares optimal* cue combination rule. However, the human judgmental process is usually represented by a linear model containing both *systematic bias* (misweighting) and *random error* (unreliability). In the probabilistic judgment model, *Bayes's theorem* is the normative method for revising probability estimates on the basis of new information. Most recent research suggests that the revision process used by the decision maker is fundamentally different from the normative model. This research indicates that decision makers employ a number of simple decision *heuristics* which allow them to solve complex problems usng their *limited cognitive abilities.* The simple decision rules that people employ are efficient and, in many cases, accurate. In some situations, however, they can lead to significant biases.

In both models, achievement is judged by comparing the human judgment with the actual outcome or with the normative solution. In place of the correlation coefficients used in the regression model, judgments are compared with subsequent events through measures of *calibration.* A judge is considered to be well calibrated if "over the long run, for all propositions assigned a given probability, the proportion true equals the probability assigned. Thus, across all the occasions that the assessor assigns the probability .7, 70% should be true" (Lichtenstein and Fischhoff, 1980, p. 149). Comparisons with the Bayesian solution are normally made with scoring rules. The comparison of the two models is summarized in Table 3–1. The probabilistic judgment model described thus far is very similar to the regression model. Both contain a normative aspect and a descriptive aspect and focus on task achievement in an uncertain environment. While the measure of judgmental achievement completes the regression formulation, the complete decision-theory model provides considerable additional detail.

As was suggested at the end of Chapter 2, determining the practical effect of an error in judging a most likely outcome or a probability distribution requires specification of (1) the relationship between the judgment and choice and (2) the costs of choosing the wrong alternative. These issues are addressed in the second stage of the decision-theory model where alternative *actions* must be specified (admit or reject the applicant)

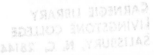

TABLE 3–1

Comparison of Regression
and Probabilistic Judgment Models

| Components | Representation | |
	Regression	Probability Judgment
Judgment response	"Best" estimate	Probability distribution
Process representation	Represented by linear model with error; no sequence specified	Sequential revision of priors based on simplifying heuristics
Optimal model	Environmental linear regression model	Bayes's theorem
Achievement	Correlation with actual outcomes or comparison with environmental model	Calibration based on actual outcomes or comparison with Bayesian response

and values or *utilities* must be assigned to all combinations of choices and environmental states or events (e.g., accepting an applicant who becomes president of Chase Manhattan Bank, rejecting the same applicant). Decision theory represents these combinations as utility or loss functions, payoff matrixes, scoring rules, or as rules for weighting certain attributes of the probability distribution over outcomes (e.g., the mean and variance of the distribution). The final action selection or *choice* is made by combining the probabilities and utilities and choosing the alternative with the highest expected utility. The lens model only implicitly considers the details of the second stage of the decision-theory model where they are encompassed in the measure of achievement.

A simplified cost-variance investigation decision will further illustrate this framework. Bierman and Dyckman (1976, Chapter 22) and Kaplan (forthcoming, Chapter 10) analyze this decision problem in detail. We will assume the simplest case where the system observed by the manager may be in either of two states (in control or out of control) and the manager may perform either of two actions (investigate or not investigate). Furthermore, assume that the cost-variance report is *not* a perfect indicator of the environmental state, but that the actual investigation *does* reveal the true environmental state with certainty, and all out-of-control processes which are investigated are corrected.[1]

In this task the decision makers are modeled as if they perform the two tasks encompassed in the decision-theory model. First, *probabilities* are assigned to each possible environmental state (in or out of control). In this stage, the decision maker may call on both his or her prior experience

[1]These are extreme assumptions. The real-world situation is much more complex. See the just cited references for illustrations.

concerning the state of the process and the data in the cost-variance report to assess these probabilities. Bayes's theorem is the appropriate method for combining prior experience and new information. However, the psychology literature suggests that human decision makers estimate these probabilities by using a basically different process, which involves a series of heuristics or simplified judgment rules. In the second stage of the model, the decision maker measures the *utility* or cost of each of the four state-choice combinations (in or out of control and investigate or not investigate). These costs could include the direct costs of investigation (both monetary and motivational), the cost of correcting the process, and the monetary and motivational costs of allowing the process to operate in the out-of-control state. These monetary and nonmonetary costs are converted to a common utility scale and then combined with the probabilities to determine the expected utility of each action choice. The alternative with the highest expected utility is chosen. This second operation is often referred to as *risky choice*. The experimental literature suggests that the actual process used in this second stage again involves use of simplifying heuristics. In summary, although the normative model posits a complex two-step process, the experimental literature suggests that decision makers use simplifying heuristics in response to their information-processing limitations. As indicated earlier, probability judgment has received the principal attention in the descriptive literature. This literature will be discussed in detail in the remainder of the chapter. Libby and Fishburn (1977) discuss the risky-choice literature.

RESEARCH EVIDENCE

Probability judgment has been the subject of extensive research in the basic disciplines of psychology, statistics, and economics, and in applied fields such as medicine, natural resource management, and business. We will discuss a sampling of the issues most relevant to accounting and business that have been addressed in the more recent descriptive literature, much of which has been reviewed by Hogarth (1975). A detailed discussion of normative decision theory is beyond the scope of this book; interested readers are referred to the classic works by Savage (1954) and Raiffa (1968) and more recent decision-theory texts (e.g., Winkler, 1972).

Intuitive judgment versus the Bayesian model

Bayes's theorem is the appropriate method for updating one's beliefs in light of new evidence. In the case of a simple binomial event, the simple ratio or odds form of Bayes's theorem states that

$$\frac{P(H_1 \,|D)}{P(H_2 \,|D)} = \frac{P(D\,|H_1)}{P(D\,|H_2)} \quad \frac{P(H_1)}{P(H_2)}$$

$$\uparrow \qquad\qquad \uparrow \qquad\qquad \uparrow$$

| Posterior odds | Likelihood ratio | Prior odds |

where H_1 and H_2 are the alternative hypotheses and D is a datum.

The prior odds measure initial expectations about the rate of occurrence of each hypothesis before the receipt of new data. These odds are also referred to as the expected *base rate* of outcomes. The likelihood ratio determines the amount by which these prior expectations should be revised in light of the new data and is considered a measure of the informativeness or "diagnostic value" of the new data. These revised probabilities are reflected in the posterior odds. However, this method of updating prior beliefs on the basis of new data is often counterintuitive. Consider the following example. Suppose that you are in charge of security for a large department store. A recent audit has indicated that losses due to employee theft have risen to 10% of sales. In response to your superior's concern, you institute a mandatory lie detector screening program for the employees. Prior research indicates that 2% of all employees steal. In addition, field studies have indicated that the probability that the employee will produce a "deceptive" response on the lie detector if he or she did in fact lie (a true positive) is .9. The probability of producing the "deceptive" response if the employee did not lie (a false positive) is .12. If an employee produced a "deceptive" response to the question, "Did you steal from the store?" what is the probability that the employee did in fact steal from the store? Most people would suggest that it is quite high, around .8. However, use of Bayes's theorem indicates that the true probability is much lower:

$$\frac{P(S\,|D)}{P(\overline{S}\,|D)} = \frac{P(D|\,S)}{P(D|\,\overline{S})} \cdot \frac{P(S)}{P(\overline{S})}$$

$$= \frac{.9}{.12} \cdot \frac{.02}{.98}$$

$$= \frac{.153}{1}$$

where S = steal
$\overline{S}$ = not steal
D = "deceptive" response to the question, "Did you steal?"

Thus, there is little more than a 13% chance that this employee actually stole from the store.[2] For your information, the diagnostic value of

[2]Note that .153/1 odds is equal to a 13% probability (= .153/1.153).

actual lie detector tests is much lower (approximately 2/1 as opposed to 7.5/1 in this example). However, improving the diagnostic value of the lie detector test to 44/1 would only increase the probability that the employee stole to .5. It appears that, in this case, most people either intuitively extract more information from the data than is really there or that they ignore the prior probabilities. In real-world situations where there are multiple data sources and conditional independence of data is violated, these inferences are much more complex. In such situations, the diagnostic value (informativeness) of a datum will vary depending on what information preceded its arrival.

These problems become even more pronounced when the judgment requires a multiple stage or cascaded inference (see Schum and Du-Charme, 1971). Consider this example.[3] You plan to introduce a new product two months from now, after additional engineering work is completed. If your major competitor plans to introduce a similar product before that time, you will employ an engineering shortcut which will allow introduction in one month. Your only source of information about activities at your competitor's research facility is an industrial spy.

Let

H_1 = event (competitor introduces new product)
D = increased activity at competitor's proving ground
$D*$ = spy reports increased activity at competitor's proving ground

Assume (1) the probability that the competitor will introduce the new product given increased activity $[p(H_1|D)]$ is .75 and (2) the probability that there is increased activity at the competitor's proving ground given that the spy reports such activity $[p(D|D*)]$ is 1.

What is the probability that the competitor will bring out the new product, given that the spy reports increased activity at the competitor's proving ground $[p(H_1|D*)]$? Most people would believe it to be .75. In reality, however, the probability could be anywhere from 0 to 1. The information given is not sufficient to answer the question. The following two Venn diagrams illustrate this point. In Figure 3–2(a), $p(H_1|D)$ = .75 and $p(D|D*)$ = 1, but $p(H_1|D*)$ is 1. A positive response from the spy is actually a stronger indicator of the competitor's plans than is actual knowledge of high activity. Alternatively, the same two conditions hold in Figure 3–2(b), but there $p(H_1|D*)$ = 0. The solution depends on where we place the $D*$ circle inside the D circle. Intuitively, one assumes that $p(D|D*)$ = 1 implies that D and $D*$ are the same, which leads to the conclusion that $p(D*|D)$ = 1. This is a logical fallacy, since conditional probabilities are different from joint probabilities [$p(A|B) \neq p(A \cap B)$], while $p(B|A)$ + $p(\overline{B}|A)$ = 1, $p(A|B)$ + $p(A|\overline{B})$ $\neq$ 1. However, even after this explanation is presented, the answer .75 still has great intuitive appeal.

[3]Einhorn (1980) suggested this example in another context.

Early research in probabilistic judgment focused mainly on comparisons of intuitive probability judgments and the normative model. The typical experimental paradigm was the "bookbag and poker chip" experiment. In this type of experiment, subjects are usually presented with two bookbags which have different proportions of red and white chips. The task is to estimate the probability that the predominantly red (white) bag is being sampled from. Subjects are first required to accept that there is a .5 prior probability for each bag. They are then presented with sample drawings (with replacement), after each of which the subject is asked to estimate the posterior probability. These subjective probabilities are then compared with the normatively determined posteriors to measure achievement. Other variations are also used. In similar experiments, subjects are presented with prior probabilities and new data and are then asked to estimate both the likelihood ratios and the posterior probabilities. The stated priors and assessed likelihood ratios are combined using Bayes's theorem and are then compared with the assessed posteriors. The difference between the two measures the quality of the integration process. Both variations address the question of whether probabilities are revised in accordance with the normative model. This research is reviewed in Slovic and Lichtenstein (1971).

FIGURE 3–2

Cascaded inference examples

(a)   p (H$_1$|D*) = 1

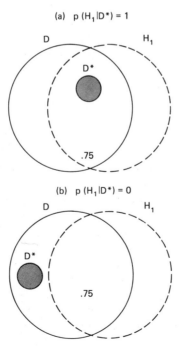

(b)   p (H$_1$|D*) = 0

The earliest studies (see Edwards, 1968) suggested that subjects revised their prior probabilities to a lesser extent than Bayes's theorem would suggest. This behavior was termed *conservatism*. Later results were more inconsistent. In some situations subjects made correct revisions, in others the revisions were conservative, and in still others they were radical (extreme). Subjects also appeared to be attending to factors that, according to the normative model, they should not (e.g., sample proportions) and disregarding factors that the normative model suggested should be considered (e.g., sample size). While Bayes's theorem is the appropriate mechanism for revising opinions under conditions of uncertainty, this research suggested that its usefulness as a foundation for a descriptive theory of decision making under uncertainty was quite limited.

In recent years, psychologists have focused attention on the possibility that humans employ a revision process which is fundamentally different from that implicit in Bayes's theorem. Tversky and Kahneman (1974) suggested that decision makers assess probabilities by means of heuristic procedures. Accounting research on probability judgment has focused on the heuristics used in accounting contexts and on the practical issue of how to elicit subjective probabilities.

Heuristics and biases

Most recent theoretical and empirical analyses of human inference processes are based on the seminal work of Amos Tversky and Daniel Kahneman, which is summarized in their 1974 paper. They suggest that observed biases in judgments of probability are caused by the use of heuristic procedures or rules of thumb. Judges use these heuristics because they reduce complex inference tasks to more manageable proportions. Tversky and Kahneman describe three of these heuristics, which they believe account for many of the findings in probability judgment research: representativeness, availability, and anchoring and adjustment. Swieringa and others (1976) introduced this research into the accounting literature.

REPRESENTATIVENESS

When the representativeness heuristic (Kahneman and Tversky, 1972) is used, the probability that B came from A is evaluated by how much B resembles A. This approach, where class membership of an object is judged by its similarity to the stereotypical class member, leads to several systematic biases in probability estimation, including (1) insensitivity to prior probabilities, (2) disregard for the impact of sample size on the variance of the sampling distribution, (3) misperceptions of the likelihood of different sequences resulting from a random process, and (4) insensitivity to the predictability of data, which results in unwarranted confidence in judgment and misconceptions of regression toward the mean (e.g., that extreme values of predictor variables are likely to produce less extreme outcomes). These biases will be discussed in some detail.

You will recall from our discussion of Bayes's theorem that the posterior odds are a function of *both* the prior odds or base rate and the likelihood ratio for the new data. If judgments are based only on the similarity of the case-specific data to some stereotype (their representativeness), these prior odds will be neglected. This bias was illustrated in our lie detector example, where we overestimated the probability that the employee was a thief because the low base rate of theft was ignored. Might accountants or auditors ever fall prey to the same bias in similar situations? A recent example illustrates that the answer is likely to be yes. Auditors are currently reevaluating their role in the detection of management fraud. A number of authors have suggested developing a client-screening program to alert auditors and directors to the warning signs of fraud (e.g., Sorenson and Sorenson, 1980, and AICPA, 1979). These systems usually first involve identifying the attributes of stereotypical fraud-prone companies (e.g., poor internal control, deteriorating earnings, association of management with known criminals). The likelihood of fraud in prospective client companies is then judged by their similarity to the stereotype (their representativeness). These "red-flag" approaches do not formally consider the base rate [4] of management fraud, which appears to be quite low.

Would auditors fail to consider the prior probability of management fraud when using these techniques? Joyce and Biddle (1981b) presented the following question to a group of senior and in-charge auditors:

> A team of accountants and psychologists has developed a procedure to test for the existence of management involvement in fraudulent activities. The procedure consists of developing a personality profile of key managers and relating this profile to a master profile compiled from interviews conducted by clinical psychologists with a substantial number of individuals who have admitted to perpetrating material frauds. If the manager's profile is sufficiently similar to the master profile, the test signals "fraud." If there isn't sufficient similarity, the test signals "no fraud." In the last 18 months, the procedure has been tested rather extensively in the field by a national public accounting firm and they have found the following:
>
> — If a key manager has been involved in a material fraud, the test procedure indicates "fraud" 8 times out of 10.
> — If a key manager has *not* been involved in a material fraud, the test will nonetheless indicate "fraud" 4 times out of 100.
> — The evidence indicates that about 1 key manager in 100 has been involved in material fraud.

[4]Sorenson and Sorenson (1980) discuss base rates but do not indicate the magnitude of the problem faced in predicting low base rate events.

Based on these results, what is your assessment of the probability that a key manager who receives a "fraud" test signal is actually involved in fraudulent activities? (Circle the number below which is closest to your probability estimate.)

0   .1   .2   .3   .4   .5   .6   .7   .8   .9   1.0

The problem specifies the three pieces of information necessary for solving this problem: (1) the positive hit rate of 80%, which means that the test signals "fraud" 8 times in 10 when a fraud has been committed, (2) the false positive rate of 4%, which indicates that 4 times in 100 an innocent manager will be judged guilty by the test, and (3) the base rate incidence of fraud in the population of all managers, which is 1 in 100 cases. The correct answer to this problem according to Bayes's theorem is .168. The mean probability estimate given by the auditors was .521. While base rates appear to have been considered in this judgment,[5] this consideration was not sufficient.

Underweighting of prior probabilities in this experimental situation is particularly distressing, because this problem is an almost perfect analog to the "rare disease" prediction problem used to introduce prior probabilities in many introductory statistics texts (e.g., Hamburg, 1977, p. 78; Winkler, 1972, p. 43). Further study indicated that subjects also misunderstood the significance of the false positive rate. They failed to recognize that the validity of the test is a function of both the positive hit rate *and* the false positive rate. Failure to properly weigh this latter measure could result in many innocent managers being implicated by the test. The failure of even experts in the fraud-detection area to give adequate consideration to false positives is illustrated in a recent *Journal of Accountancy* article by Romney, Albrecht, and Cherrington (1980), who developed a fraud-risk questionnaire based solely on the positive hit rate.

If population membership is judged solely on the basis of the similarity of sample characteristics to the population characteristics (representativeness), judges will also neglect the fact that small samples tend to be *less* representative of underlying populations than large samples. *Insensitivity to sample size* has been observed in a number of experimental situations. Kahneman and Tversky (1972) asked a group of undergraduate students the following question:

A certain town is served by two hospitals. In the larger hospital about 45 babies are born each day, and in the smaller hospital about 15 babies are born each day. As you know, about 50 percent of all babies are boys. However, the exact percentage varies from day to day. Sometimes it may be higher than 50 percent, sometimes lower.

For a period of 1 year, each hospital recorded the days on which more than 60 percent of the babies born were boys. Which hospital do you think recorded more such days?

[5]Complete neglect would result in an answer of .952.

> The larger hospital (21)
> The smaller hospital (21)
> About the same (that is, within 5 percent of each other) (53)
>   (The values in parentheses are the number of undergraduate students who chose each answer.)

The majority of the subjects thought the events were equally likely, presumably because they were equally representative of the population. The fact that the smaller sample mean will tend to be less like the population mean because of its higher variance was not considered.

Since most audit tests are conducted on a sampling basis, this type of behavior could have serious consequences for the evaluation of test results. However, since this basic tenet of statistics—the relationship of sample size to sample variance—is usually taught to young auditors at least twice (in statistics and auditing courses), you might expect that this bias would be of little import in auditing. As a preliminary test for this bias in auditing, Gibbins (1977) asked 37 experienced auditors a question similar to Kahneman and Tversky's:

> A local industrial company has two departments. In the larger department about 45 sales invoices are completed each day; in the smaller department about 15 sales invoices are completed each day. About 50 percent of all sales invoices completed in each department specify discounts from the company's list prices. However, the exact percentage varies from day to day. Sometimes it may be higher than 50 percent, sometimes lower.
>   For a period of 1 year, and for each department, a member of the auditor's staff kept track of the number of days on which more than 60 percent of the sales invoices specified discounts. Which department do you think showed the greater number of such days?
>   a. Larger department (3)
>   b. Smaller department (19)
>   c. Same (15)

The number of auditors choosing each response is indicated in parentheses. While their performance was superior to that of Kahneman and Tversky's undergraduates, fully 41% of the subjects appeared to exhibit the same intuitive behavior as the students.

If the predicted outcome of a probabilistic process is that which is maximally *representative* of the inputs to the process, extreme inputs should produce equally extreme predictions of outputs. However, if the process is stationary (has not changed), the output observation is more likely to be less extreme because of *regression toward the mean*. Most people find this concept particularly counterintuitive. This feeling is pervasive even among the highly educated and explains many "surprises" in everyday life. For example, most of my colleagues are consistently surprised when MBA students with high GMAT scores do not live up to their "potential" on other tests. Even if the high scorer is of superior intellect, if one test is not a perfect predictor of the next, then, *on average*, high scorers will decline and low scorers will improve.

This phenomenon occurs in any stationary system with an error or stochastic element. For example, sons of extremely tall fathers are more likely than not to be shorter than their fathers (even though their genetic systems are different from those of the average individual). Because genetic systems are probabilistic, the tall father is more likely to have resulted from a higher than average drawing from the system, and the next drawing (the son) *on average* should be lower.

Failure to understand this concept is highly detrimental to learning. A particularly interesting case was observed by Tversky and Kahneman (1974):

> In a discussion of flight training, experienced instructors noted that praise for an exceptionally smooth landing is typically followed by a poorer landing on the next try, while harsh criticism after a rough landing is usually followed by an improvement on the next try. The instructors concluded that verbal rewards are detrimental to learning, while verbal punishments are beneficial, contrary to accepted psychological doctrine. This conclusion is unwarranted because of the presence of regression toward the mean. As in other cases of repeated examination, an improvement will usually follow a poor performance and a deterioration will usually follow an outstanding performance, even if the instructor does not respond to the trainee's achievement on the first attempt. Because the instructors had praised their trainees after good landings and admonished them after poor ones, they reached the erroneous and potentially harmful conclusion that punishment is more effective than reward. Thus, the failure to understand the effect of regression leads one to overestimate the effectiveness of punishment and to underestimate the effectiveness of reward.

Again, one might expect that statistically sophisticated individuals such as financial analysts and accountants would not be subject to this bias. However, it was not until the early 1970s that researchers (Vasichek, 1973; Blume, 1975) formally recognized that sample *betas* (which measure the systematic risk of a security) are biased estimates of the true underlying beta because of statistical regression toward the mean. Blume (1975, pp. 788, 789) explains this phenomenon with a simplified example attributed to Harry Markowitz. In the example, he assumes the following:

> 1. The true security beta can take on three values: .8, 1, and 1.2.
>
> 2. Sample beta ($\hat{\beta}$) is measured with the following error distribution: 60% probability that the estimate contains no measurement error, 20% probability that it understates the true value by .2, and 20% probability that it overstates the probability by .2.

Table 3–2 presents the probability of $\hat{\beta}$ given each value of β. When analysts are faced with an estimated $\hat{\beta}$, they must assess the expected value of β given $\hat{\beta}$ [$E(\beta|\hat{\beta})$]. The bottom row of the table contains the expected value of β given each value of $\hat{\beta}$. Note that the expected value is equal to $\hat{\beta}$ only when $\hat{\beta}$ equals the grand mean of β. In cases where $\hat{\beta}$ is above or below this value, the expected value of β is less extreme (closer to the mean) than the sample estimate. As Foster (1978) notes, a number of techniques to adjust $\hat{\beta}$ for regression have been developed at universities and investment firms.

TABLE 3–2

Probability of $\hat{\beta}$ Given β

		.6	.8	1.0	1.2	1.4
	.8	.2	.6	.2		
β	1.0		.2	.6	.2	
	1.2			.2	.6	.2
$E(\beta|\hat{\beta})$		*	.85	1.00	1.15	*

*Given the restrictions on the values of β and the error assumptions in this example, these values are determined with certainty to be .8 and 1.2, respectively.
Source: Blume [1975, Table 2]

This phenomenon should partially account for Lev's (1969) observation that firm financial ratios tend to regress toward industry-wide averages. Remember that the process that determines the firm's current ratio at a particular point in time is a stochastic process. As in our tall fathers and shorter sons example, the observation following an extremely high or low observation is likely to be less extreme. Yet many traditional financial statement analysts tend to attribute all of this change to a conscious effort on the part of management to adjust their ratios to industry-wide averages. Hogarth (1980) notes that "management by exception" is also subject to this bias. As only extremely high or low performance instigates a management intervention, even a totally ineffective intervention is more likely than not to be followed by a less extreme observation. This would tend to convince most managers of the effectiveness of their method of intervening.

Why do many investors still believe that future stock prices can be predicted from patterns of past prices by means of such techniques as point and figure charts? The representativeness heuristic again provides a possible explanation. As Kahneman and Tversky (1972) suggested, people expect that even short sequences from a *random process* will be maximally *representative* of the underlying characteristics of the process. As a result, they found that people believe that a sequence of random coin flips resulting in H-T-H-T-T-H is more likely than the sequence H-H-H-T-T-T, when in reality they are equally likely. This belief often causes people to see patterns when there are none. With respect to "peaks" in stock prices, for example, the same bias would lead the point and figure chartist to conclude that a price increase following a "double peak" was the result of a systematic process, when in fact it resulted from the random walk of stock prices. The availability heuristic, which we will discuss next, will tend to reinforce this belief because instances where events co-occur are more easily remembered than instances where they do not. This leads to what Chapman and Chapman (1969) call *illusory correlation*.

AVAILABILITY

When the decision maker uses the judgmental heuristic called availability (Tversky and Kahneman, 1973), the frequency or probability of occurrence of an event is judged by the ease with which similar events are brought to mind. Resulting biases due to retrievability of instances and biases due to imaginability have important potential consequences for business judgment. When we judge the probability of events we have previously experienced, sensational and vivid events are more easily remembered. Overestimation of the probability of these events and underestimation of less spectacular events often result.

Lichtenstein and others (1978) present an extremely interesting illustration of this bias. A group of college students and members of the League of Women Voters participated in an experiment in which they compared the frequency of occurrence of pairs of lethal events. Table 3–3 contains some sample pairs from the experiment. Please take a moment to choose the more common cause of death from each pair.

Although the majority of subjects chose cause A for all pairs, the less memorable cause in column B is actually the more frequent occurrence. In fact, although lightning kills *52 times* as many people as botulism, the majority of the subjects judged botulism the more likely cause.[6] Among other explanations, the authors demonstrate an association between the

TABLE 3-3

Sample Pairs of Causes of Death

Pair	Cause A	Cause B
1	Poisoning	Tuberculosis
2	Leukemia	Emphysema
3	Homicide	Suicide
4	Botulism	Lightning
5	All accidents	Stroke

[6]This study was conducted shortly after the Bon Vivant Soup botulism case.

amount of newspaper publicity given to a cause and its perceived likelihood of occurrence. The results suggest that the media misinform the public by both overreporting spectacular events and underreporting more mundane events.

Watts and Zimmerman (1979) unknowingly call attention to the importance of availability in determining regulatory action. They point out that proponents of increasing government regulation of business consider the benefits of eliminating the relatively small number of *observed* abuses but do not consider the large number of cases where the current system has worked. They attribute this bias to a tendency among lawyers and politicians to concentrate on extremes rather than means. More likely, our legislators are responding to their constituents' use of the availability heuristic in judging the frequency of fraudulent activities. If the Lichtenstein and others (1978) study were replicated with fraudulent corporate acts in place of causes of death, the results would quite likely be similar. The frequency of major embezzlement, bankruptcy, and other spectacular events would be overestimated, and these overestimates would be highly correlated with press reporting.[7] If this is true, then the legislators are probably reacting to their constituents' wishes, and not to some innate or learned tendency.

Availability will also cause biases owing to the imaginability of events. These biases are of particular importance to internal control system designers and evaluators. The development of a fail-safe control system requires that we specify what could go wrong with the system. When the system to be controlled is complex and new technology is employed, as in data-base information systems and nuclear reactors, prior experience may not be sufficient to make this judgment. Understanding of the design of the system and the ability to *imagine* possible system failures must fill the gap in experience. Such judgments may be beyond our cognitive abilities. The Brown's Ferry nuclear reactor fire, which almost caused the world's largest reactor to melt down, is a classic example. No one had imagined that a technician would search for an air leak with a candle when such behavior was directly prohibited in the procedures manuals. Difficulties in predicting the imaginative ways that humans can devise to defeat a system have led to many such failures. In the final chapter, we will discuss an aid called a fault-tree, which has been designed to help deal with these problems.

ANCHORING AND ADJUSTMENT

The final heuristic discussed by Tversky and Kahneman (1974) is anchoring and adjustment. Individuals often evaluate a sequence of new information by choosing an initial estimate or anchor against which future adjustments may be made as additional information is received.

---

[7]This hypothesis has not been tested.

Much of the early research in probability judgment (see Slovic and Lichtenstein, 1971) suggested that these adjustments typically are insufficient. Many readers will recognize that an anchoring and adjustment rule is standard procedure in audit planning. Often, prior years' workpapers are adjusted in the process of devising the current year's audit program. The possibility that this reliance on prior years' procedures results in insufficient adjustment in light of changing circumstances has been of concern to auditors for some time. Budgeting behavior may follow similar patterns.

Joyce and Biddle (1981a) investigated this issue in one of their experiments. They examined the effect of changes in internal control systems on the extensiveness of substantive (detailed) tests. Half of the participating auditors received the following instructions:

> You are conducting a routine year-end audit of a large closely held tire wholesaler. Your firm has conducted its annual audit for the last three years. During that time no significant errors were discovered by the audit tests and unqualified opinions were issued. The management and employees of the client seem both competent and trustworthy. You are about to plan your substantive tests of the sales and collection cycle.

> You review the client's system of internal control to identify the types of errors that could occur in the system and whether specific controls exist which would prevent or detect such errors. The first error you consider is "sales recorded for goods not shipped." Your review of the relevant controls for this error reveals the following:
> (1) There is adequate control over back orders and partial shipments.
> (2) There is adequate control of access to the shipping area.
> (3) Prenumbered shipping documents are not used.
> (4) Sales invoices are matched to shipping documents.
> (5) The accounts receivable billing clerk also performs clerical duties for the shipping department.
> (6) Regular shipping reports are prepared and reviewed monthly.
> (7) Overdue accounts receivable are investigated.
> (8) Unmatched sales invoices are independently reviewed and followed up.
> Your compliance tests and observations of the system confirm the system is operating as just described.
> 1. Based on this information, indicate below the extensiveness of the substantive (detailed) tests you would perform in this engagement to test for the specific error "sales recorded for goods not shipped." (Circle one number.)

Minimum Audit Tests								Most Extensive Audit Tests	
1	2	3	4	5	6	7	8	9	10

> 2. Suppose that instead of the preceding system description, you had received one that was identical except for the following (assume your compliance tests and observations of the system confirmed this description as well):

(3) Prenumbered shipping documents are used.

(5) Shipping is segregated from the billing function.

Based on this different information, indicate below the extensiveness of the substantive (detailed) tests you would perform in this engagement to test for the specific error "sales recorded for goods not shipped." (Circle one number.)

Minimum Audit Tests									Most Extensive Audit Tests
1	2	3	4	5	6	7	8	9	10

The other half of the participants received the same instructions except that the order was changed: they received the stronger internal control system first, made an extensiveness rating, and then received the weaker system and made a second extensiveness rating. The anchoring and adjustment heuristic would suggest that subjects would anchor on their initial judgment and then adjust from that point, with the following results: (1) when the weaker system followed the stronger system, the subjects would perform less extensive testing than when the weaker system was presented first; (2) when the stronger system followed the weaker system, the subjects would perform more extensive testing than when the stronger system was presented first. (Note that a higher extensiveness rating denotes a less adequate system.) While the second prediction was valid (when the stronger system followed the weaker, more extensive tests were performed than when it was presented first), not only was the first prediction incorrect, but the opposite behavior was in evidence. The extensiveness rating for the weaker system following the stronger system was significantly higher than the rating for the initially weaker system. These results are summarized in Table 3–4. The auditors appear to be applying a rule which is basically different from anchoring and which is consistent with a conservative approach to such judgments. A change from a stronger to a weaker system appears to be viewed as a "red flag," which results in more extensive than normal substantive tests. On the other

TABLE 3-4

Internal Control Anchoring Example

		Internal Control		
		Stronger	Weaker	
Order Condition	A (stronger to weaker)	2.79 ⟶ 6.29		4.54
	B (weaker to stronger)	3.24 ⟵ 5.47		4.36
		3.02	5.88	

Source: Joyce and Biddle [1981a, Figure 10].

hand, a system improvement may be regarded with some skepticism until the results of substantive tests support its effectiveness.

Generalizations from the research to date

Virtually all business decisions are made under conditions of uncertainty. Each of these decisions requires that, explicitly or implicitly, probability assessments be made. For example, plant-expansion decisions are based on probabilistic assessments of future demand, raw materials, and labor costs. Many of the other examples have illustrated how the decision to issue an audit report is preceded by a series of probability assessments made from sample evidence. The literature just discussed suggests that accountants and other business decision makers approach these judgments with many of the same simplifying heuristics as their less sophisticated counterparts. Furthermore, the results indicate that in some cases accountants have developed their own unique rules of thumb (e.g., the anchoring example). These heuristics make complex tasks cognitively tractable, but may result in biased probability assessments. Both academics and practitioners are expressing increasing concern that these biases may adversely affect decision quality. This concern is best exhibited in the Peat, Marwick, Mitchell and Company manager training program, where audit managers are routinely sensitized to these potential biases. More detailed prescriptions for change in the way these assessments are made awaits further research which better explains the circumstances in which we use different heuristics and when their use adversely affects decision performance. These issues will be addressed briefly in the final section of this chapter.

CONCEPTUAL AND METHODOLOGICAL PROBLEMS

The preceding discussion suggests a number of conceptual and operational problems facing the reader who wishes either to implement the results of the research or to conduct research in this area. Most of the operational problems inherent in the probabilistic judgment framework are similar to those in regression modeling. For example, cue interrelationships cloud the interpretation of weights in regression modeling. In probability judgment, weights are derived from the implied diagnostic value of the data. In cases of conditional nonindependence, this interpretation is also clouded. Given these similarities, this section will focus primarily on more recent research aimed at filling the conceptual gaps in our understanding of probabilistic judgment and risky choice.

When are data perceived to be diagnostic?

The need to refine Tversky and Kahneman's initial theoretical statements was recognized as additional research (e.g., Olson, 1976; Swieringa and others, 1976) indicated that the judgmental impacts of both base rates and new data were sensitive to seemingly minor alterations of task characteristics. Two other theoretical problems were also noted. First, a single heuristic can explain more than one behavior pattern. For example, judgments of the group membership of an object on the basis of its similarity to the typical group member (its representativeness) will depend on which attributes of the object are being attended to. Attention to different subsets of attributes could easily lead to radically different judgments. Second, in some situations combinations of heuristics can explain virtually all possible behavior. For example, both conservative and radical probability revisions can be accounted for by anchoring and representativeness, respectively. The potentially tautological nature of the theory motivated a number of researchers to address the conditions under which different judgmental heuristics will be used and to relate them to specific cognitive strategies employed in light of specific cognitive limitations. These modifications in the theory are currently in a state of flux, but they represent positive developments for the future.

Three papers present closely related ideas. Tversky and Kahneman (1980) suggest that judgments under uncertainty are made in terms of causes and effects. While individuals can reason both causally (from causes to effects) and diagnostically (from effects to causes), the authors present evidence indicating that causal information has a greater impact than equally informative diagnostic data. Further, data which are not obviously part of the chain of cause and effect (incidental data) appear to be almost completely dominated by either causal or diagnostic data. Bar-Hillel (1980) suggests that the impact of information is a function of its perceived relevance, one potential indicator of which is causality. Einhorn and Hogarth (1981) present a similar idea in which informativeness of data is a function of the initial representation of the problem or sample space. They point out that *no* probability is unconditional, and that the relevance of data is a function of the conditioning arguments implicitly used to define the judgment problem or sample space.

The importance of causal reasoning is further illustrated by Shaklee and Fischhoff (1979), who conceptualize the inference process as a search for a sufficient causal explanation. In this model, the impact of data will be a function of the point in the decision sequence at which it is received. Data suggesting possible causal relationships will receive high weightings early in the process. After a sufficient causal explanation has been developed, additional evidence pointing to alternative causes will be underweighted and supporting evidence will be overweighted.

Recognition of the importance of task determinants of judgmental behavior belatedly confirms Brunswik's (1952, 1956) basic precepts, which we discussed in prior chapters. It has also increased concern over the representativeness of many experimental paradigms used to study probability judgment. For example, while most experimental tasks employ conditionally independent data, conditional independence is violated in many actual situations where learning takes place. The application of judgment rules learned in a conditionally dependent environment to the unrealistic experimental task may make nearly optimal behavior appear conservative (e.g., Winkler and Murphy, 1973). Concerns with problem definition and the dynamics of judgmental behavior point out the complementary nature of probability judgment research and the theory and methodology developed in the problem-solving area (Newell and Simon, 1972), which we will discuss in Chapter 4.

Functional Heuristics

Assessing the operational significance of biases in probability judgments requires that we specify the choice stage of the decision-theory model. As discussed previously, the circumstances in which different heuristics work well or work poorly are not well specified. It is quite possible that the heuristic assessment may approximate the optimal solution in many situations, and that in others the decision payoffs are insensitive to the resulting biases or are counterbalanced by the heuristics used in the choice process. An extreme view held by many economists and sociobiologists (with which the author is also sympathetic) is that "heuristics exist because they serve useful functions and their benefits outweigh their costs" (Einhorn and Hogarth, 1981). This state of nature is thought by economists to result from the workings of the marketplace, where nonoptimal decision makers are eliminated by competition. Sociobiologists believe that this state results from evolution. Consider a physician who estimates the incidence of disease using the availability heuristic. Sensational cases which have particularly harmful effects on the patient will be more easily remembered. Overestimation of the probability of these catastrophic illnesses is likely to result. If the cost of incorrectly diagnosing a catastrophic illness is death, and the cost of treating a mild illness as if it were a catastrophic one is discomfort due to the side effects of drugs, the physician who is led by the availability heuristic to make the second type of error may be preferable. In this example, the utilities for choice outcomes affect the doctor's assessment of the probability of disease occurrence, and the resulting bias is functional. Einhorn and Hogarth (1981) suggest the even more disturbing possibility that what appears to be nonoptimal behavior may result from using inappropriate assumptions to estimate the optimal solution. It is likely that use of many heuristics is functional, but that some result from our inability to learn appropriate decision rules in a probabilistic environment (see Einhorn and Hogarth, 1978).

Note on assessment

As suggested earlier, the researcher attempting to conduct research within the probability judgment framework is faced with most of the same operational problems related to task construction and representative design, process modeling, and performance measurement that we discussed in Chapter 2. The most important additional problem concerns the effect of imposing a probabilistic framework on the experimental setting. In most situations, people are not experienced in specifying the required probabilities. In both regression and probabilistic judgment studies, subjects often are not what Winkler has called "substantive experts"; they are not familiar with the substantive area. However, in most probabilistic judgment studies, even the "substantive experts" are usually not "normative experts"; they do not know how to express judgments in terms of probabilities. The only extensively studied group that has demonstrated both types of expertise is weather forecasters. They are highly trained in both meteorology and the use of probabilities. It is interesting to note that this is the only group whose members have been found to be accurate probability assessors.

This problem is best illustrated when one assesses likelihoods $[P(D|H)]$. Normal human experience would not provide even an intuitive explanation of this term. The author and colleagues have also found that this concept is extremely difficult to convey to students, who many times intuitively equate it with posterior probabilities. The importance of the problem is confirmed by the studies which indicate large discrepancies between probabilities assessed with alternative elicitations. These accounting-related studies are discussed in Appendix B. This lack of "normative expertise" confounds the effects of assessment error in the revision process.

CONCLUDING COMMENTS

Probabilistic judgment research is progressing toward a better understanding of the interaction between human cognitive limitations and environmental characteristics, which determines the way in which information is processed. However, the research still emphasizes the study of more structured decision tasks. The problem-solving literature, which is discussed in the next chapter, addresses many of these same issues in the context of less structured tasks which require the decision maker to formulate the problem, generate hypotheses, and search for information.

DISCUSSION QUESTIONS

1. Describe an accounting-related decision problem in terms of the simple decision-theory model. Discuss both the probabilistic judgment and the risky-choice portions of the task.
2. Explain the role of utility or loss functions in decision theory and contrast this with their role in the regression version of the lens model.

3. Provide a brief discussion or description of each of the following:
   a. Base rate
   b. Diagnostic value of data
   c. False positive
   d. Conservative probability revision
   e. Radical probability revision
   f. Insensitivity to sample size
   g. Regression toward the mean

4. Tversky and Kahneman formulated three heuristics which they claim people use in lieu of Bayes's theorem in many situations.
   a. Identify and define these three heuristics.
   b. State why they are in violation of normative statistical principles.
   c. Give an example of the use of each in some real or hypothetical accounting decision problems.

5. Neglecting both base rates and false-positive rates affects perceptions of one's ability to predict rare events such as business failures and management frauds. Explain how this neglect may lead to misperceptions. Also, discuss how policy makers should consider these factors, along with the costs of type I and type II errors, in developing regulations related to auditors' responsibilities for evaluating the "going concern" assumption and for detecting fraud.

6. Until the advent of credit scoring models (see Chapter 5 for a discussion), much of consumer-credit analysis was performed using intuitively devised rules of thumb, many of which were inaccurate. Explain the following scenario in terms of (1) ignoring sample size, (2) neglecting base rates, and (3) neglecting false positives.

   A newly hired credit analyst employs a lenient policy and grants all credit applications during the first week. One month later the analyst reviews the bad debts resulting from these decisions and finds that four of the customers have failed to pay their bills. After quickly perusing these four customers' applications, it is discovered that 75% of those not paying their bills have light-colored hair. Determined to improve this bad debt record, the analyst adopts a new rule: "Do not lend to people with light-colored hair."

7. Virtually every auditing text discusses the differential validity of audit evidence drawn from different sources (e.g., independent third parties, company management). What should be the relationship between data reliability and the impact of evidence? If auditors used the representativeness heuristic to evaluate audit evidence from different sources, what bias might result?

8. In this chapter, availability biases which result in overestimation of the frequency of striking events are suggested as one cause of certain regulatory actions. Cite some examples of accounting regulation where this scenario appears to be valid. Also, indicate how the utilities one assigns to different outcomes might provide an alternative explanation of this behavior.

9. Reliance on prior years' workpapers in audit program planning appears to be related to the anchoring and adjustment heuristic. What types of errors might result from employing this strategy? What do

Joyce and Biddle's (1981a) results (which are discussed in this chapter) suggest to be the actual strategy used by auditors?

10. Describe an accounting example for which a single heuristic (e.g., representativeness) can explain a variety of behaviors. Then describe an accounting example for which a combination of heuristics would explain all possible behaviors.

11. Tversky and Kahneman (1980) suggest that the impact of evidence depends on whether it is perceived to be causal, diagnostic, or incidental. Explain this statement. Describe accounting situations where information might be perceived as falling into each of the three categories. Then describe a situation where a single piece of evidence plays both a diagnostic and causal role. (*Hint:* Consider the role of the results of compliance tests in evaluating internal control and in predicting errors in accounts.)

CHAPTER FOUR

Representations of Human Judgment: Probabilistic Judgment

Ashton's (1974a) internal control evaluation experiment is typical of the type of decision task facing subjects in most of the research discussed in Chapters 2 and 3. Each participant was required to rate a series of internal control cases on a simple one-dimensional "quality" scale. The information presented included fixed background information and a small set of cues whose values varied from case to case. Einhorn (1976, p. 200) describes four common characteristics of this type of decision task:

(1) the task was well defined, that is, the subject knew what he/she had to do; (2) the subject was given information of some sort; (3) the information given was perfectly reliable; (4) the range of hypotheses that were considered about the data was considerably restricted by having a particular dependent variable.

These highly structured situations lead subjects to play a passive role. In contrast, consider the situation faced by the auditor in attempting to fulfill his or her responsibilities for the detection of questionable corporate acts. The specific actions to be detected are ill-defined, initial warning signs can be explained by a broad range of possibilities, and a large number of avenues for seeking information by which to evaluate these possibilities are open. Einhorn (1976) suggests that many real decision tasks are more similar to this situation, where

> (1) the task is ill-defined; (2) information must be searched for—it is not given; (3) data are rarely perfectly reliable; (4) hypothesis formation, as well as hypothesis confirmation/disconfirmation, occurs within a broad range of possibilities.

Concern for the dynamics of problem definition, hypothesis formation, and information search in these less structured contexts has led decision researchers to develop theories and methodologies for examining these stages of *predecisional behavior*. Research in earlier chapters was primarily concerned with the impact on decision accuracy of misaggregation of data and judgmental inconsistency. In this chapter, the importance of and reason for errors in these predecisional stages will also be discussed.

The theory of problem solving developed by Newell and Simon (1972) and their associates and the measurement techniques which they have developed or refined provide the foundation for much of this research. The basic principles of this theory are found in Simon's (1955) classic article "A Behavioral Model of Rational Choice." He suggests that humans are organisms of limited knowledge and computational capacity. In response to these limitations, simplifications (or heuristics) are deliberately introduced into the choice mechanism.[1] This is often referred to as the principle of *bounded rationality*.

Newell and Simon's more recent research has been concerned with more basic cognitive processes and with how people solve complex problems, given their limited information-processing abilities. They suggest that humans possess a short-term memory with very limited capacity (four to seven "chunks") and a virtually unlimited long-term memory. The structure of these memories and the characteristics of tasks combine to determine the way in which different types of problems are represented in memory. The *cognitive representation* of the task, in turn, determines the way in which the problems are solved. Einhorn and Hogarth (1981) point out that a number of researchers are currently attributing major importance to the effect of problem representation on decision behavior. These researchers include those involved in investigating such topics as causal models (discussed in Chapter 3), similarity judgments (Tversky and Sattath, 1979), and preference reversals in risk taking (Grether and Plott, 1979). Detailed analysis of task demands plays a principal role in research on problem solving, as it does in Brunswik's model.

---

[1]Many of these simplifications involve substitution of noncompensatory screening rules, such as the conjunctive model discussed in Chapter 2, for more complex compensatory rules.

A major portion of this research has as its goal the creation of a computer program which can account for the verbalizations produced by a subject during the process of problem solving. Programs have been developed which describe a variety of problems, ranging from chess moves to textbook problems in thermodynamics (Bhaskar and Simon, 1977) and accounting (Bhaskar and Dillard, 1979). Some of the programs provide only general classifications for analyzing the verbalizations, while others provide detailed sequential predictions of behavior and descriptions of underlying processes. Recent research in problem solving and other areas of information processing is reviewed in Simon (1979).

This basic research has provided the groundwork for recent attempts to investigate predecisional behavior in situations of decision making under uncertainty. Major theoretical and practical contributions are being made by applied researchers in medicine, business, and other areas. While this research is based on Simon's model and methodology, it generally follows a different orientation. As is the case with accounting, the primary objective of most applied decision researchers' interest in describing decision processes is to provide a basis for *improving* judgment. This goal has led them to integrate into their research the prescriptive orientation and many of the theoretical insights from the literature discussed in the prior two chapters.

The discussion in the remainder of this chapter is organized in three parts. First, the most popular approaches for studying predecisional behavior and some common uses are briefly discussed. In the second section, a number of studies illustrating a sampling of the central research issues and methodological approaches are considered. The final section of the chapter is addressed to the more advanced reader and examines some of the extremely difficult conceptual and methodological problems facing researchers using this approach. Accounting research involving the study of predecisional behavior is reviewed in detail in Appendix C.

MEASUREMENT METHODS

Payne, Braunstein, and Carroll (1978) provide a detailed discussion of data-collection techniques associated with the study of predecisional behavior. These methods provide data on the intermediate stages of the decision process, as well as information input and decision output. It is thought that more frequent, time-ordered measurements may provide the basis for a more detailed sequential description of the process. We will briefly discuss three such methods as described in Payne, Braunstein, and Carroll (1978): verbal protocols, eye movements, and explicit information search. These techniques have become particularly popular in marketing (see, e.g., Bettman, 1979; Bettman and Jacoby, 1976; Russo, 1978; Wright, 1974). At the end of this chapter, the strengths and weaknesses of these methods will be evaluated, and the methods will be compared with the input-output approaches discussed earlier.

The use of *verbal protocols* at first appears to be the simplest way of gathering predecisional data. Subjects are normally told to "think aloud" into a tape recorder during the performance of the experimental task. To avoid predisposing the subject to exhibit certain behaviors, more detailed instructions are usually not given. The taped protocol is then transcribed, and an attempt is made to break the protocols into short phrases containing what the coder believes to be a simple assertion. These phrases provide the unit of analysis for further processing and interpretation. They can either be directly coded as a computer program or classified into predetermined formal categories for hypothesis testing. The categories are usually chosen to represent operations (e.g., information search) or knowledge states (e.g., current assets = \$2.5 million) relevant to the researcher's hypotheses. The codings can then be displayed and used in a number of ways. Tree graphs and transition matrixes are particularly useful for testing hypotheses concerning the sequential nature of the process. Various frequency measures are used when cue importance is of interest.

Payne, Braunstein, and Carroll (1978) suggest four major uses of protocol analysis. First, verbal protocols can be used to discover regularities in behavior in *exploratory studies*. In decision situations such as the acceptance of audit engagements, where little systematic literature is available to guide the researcher, the data often provide a basis for forming hypotheses to be tested in further research. Second, as a *supplementary data source* to decision output or information-search measures, the protocols can provide supporting evidence or explanation for behavior. For example, if the algebraic models from Chapter 2 cannot discriminate between reliance on two highly correlated measures of firm liquidity, the protocols may resolve the issue. Third, codings of the protocols can be used to *test hypotheses* such as Payne's (1976) predictions concerning the effect of the number of decision alternatives on the choice of decision rules. Finally, *formal computer models* of sequential behavior can be built and tested by their ability to predict the sequence of operations and knowledge states suggested by the protocols. By making decision rules explicit, these computer models can be used in education and in the evaluation of decision-making policies.

The remaining two data-collection methods provide measures concerning sequential *information search* and use. In business-decision research, Russo's (1978) innovative use of eye movements in marketing research has received the greatest attention. Sequences of eye fixations or the duration of each fixation usually provides the basic data and are interpreted as indicating different processing strategies and relative cue usage, respectively. Eye movements can be measured using a special eye movement recording apparatus or by analyzing videotapes.

Simpler techniques for measuring information search have already found their way into the accounting literature (e.g., Pankoff and Virgil, 1970). These techniques require the decision maker to acquire each piece of information separately, to allow accurate recording. A number of different methods for providing access to information and the recording of choices have been developed. One of the least expensive approaches is the information board. Each piece of information is contained on a card which is placed in a labeled envelope and displayed in matrix form on a board. In this technique, each acquisition must be recorded by the experimenter. More sophisticated techniques using the computer can automatically record each selection, the time interval between selections, and final decisions. The resulting data can be used to assess cue usage by measuring the frequency of cue selection and the time interval between cues. Moreover, the sequence of selections can be used to test different models of the decision process. In the next section, several research studies which have successfully used these techniques to address issues of interest to accountants are discussed.

RESEARCH EVIDENCE

To demonstrate the wide variety of issues and research methods encompassed in this literature and its implications for accounting, research dealing primarily with three different aspects of the decision process will be examined: (1) the structure of "expert" memory, (2) the role of hypotheses in directing information search, and (3) the selection of alternative decision rules. These studies will also illustrate the synergistic relationship between this research and the regression and decision-theory research we have already discussed.

The memory of experts

The importance of professional judgment in areas such as auditing and financial analysis has led a number of researchers to study the characteristics that differentiate experts from novices. Einhorn's (1974) argument for between-judge consensus as a necessary condition for expertise (e.g., Joyce, 1976) and the differences in cue-weighting rules between novices and experts (e.g., Slovic, Fleissner, and Bauman, 1972) have received particular attention in business research. Cognitive psychologists have examined differences in the basic thought processes of novices and experts. Chase and Simon's (1973) replication of DeGroot's (1965) classic study of the memory structure of chess novices and masters presents particularly interesting results. DeGroot found no major differences in a number of the characteristics of the novices' and masters' thought processes, including the number of different moves considered and the search strategies employed. However, while chess masters were found to have the *same* general short-term memory capacity as less experienced players, they were able to remember the location of a *larger number* of chess pieces after glancing at real chess boards. In situations related to their expertise, the masters appeared to be able to effectively expand their memory capacity.

In the experiment, three chess players (a master, a class A player, and a beginner) observed a series of 28 chess boards for a period of 5 seconds each, after which they were asked to reconstruct the board from memory. Twenty of the boards were constructed from actual games presented in chess books and magazines and eight were constructed at random. For the 20 realistic games, the ability to remember the placement of the pieces was closely associated with the experience of the player. To rule out the possibility that this findng resulted from a greater overall memory capacity on the part of the master, the same comparison was also made for the eight random boards. In this case, no difference based on experience was found. These results suggest that the superior performance of the master on the realistic boards was due to the ability to recognize meaningful relationships between pieces that had been seen previously. This allowed the master to store patterns of pieces in short-term memory. The less experienced players were unable to call on this stored experience, which resulted in their storing smaller sequences of pieces in memory. However, in the case of the random boards, the master's experience was irrelevant and in fact may have interfered in the task because the patterns looked unreasonable. Videotape recordings were also used to measure the length of pauses between the placement of pieces as the subjects reconstructed the boards in this and a second experiment. The pause measurements were aimed at determining the size of each "chunk" or pattern of information stored in memory. The results again suggested that the expert encoded a larger number of interrelated pieces in each chunk.

The results of this study suggest that the development of expertise may in part involve storage in memory of a series of meaningful cue patterns which are prototypical of certain class memberships. Recognition of a familiar pattern brings a prototype into short-term memory. In this fashion, a small set of cue values brings to mind a larger set of cues associated with the prototype (see Einhorn, 1976). For instance, financial analysts can often decipher the industry designation of a firm from the relationships between a short series of financial ratios which bring to mind the prototype industry member. This method of memory organization is consistent with use of the representativeness heuristic, which we discussed in Chapter 3. In many cases these prototypes may also take the form of causal theories, as was also suggested in Chapter 3.

Organization of memory on the basis of plausible causal patterns could also explain the poor performance of subjects in the abstract multiple cue probability learning studies discussed in Chapter 2. The abstract situations provide no basis for constructing such patterns. Where realistic cues are used, but natural patterns of interrelationships are disturbed, as in systematic ANOVA designs, one would expect that this basic vehicle for learning and storing multiple relationships would be obstructed. This again points out the importance of Brunswik's concern with the representative design of experiments in which realistic cue interrelationships are maintained.

A model of long-term memory centered around prototypes and associated cues plays the major role in recent theories of expert problem-solving strategies. In these theories, the prototypes take the form of hypotheses which structure further information search and evaluation. This concept was first introduced into the accounting literature by Einhorn (1976).[2] Most of these studies either describe expert problem solving in detail or compare the strategies of experts and novices. Recently, medical researchers have been conducting a number of interesting studies of diagnostic behavior which appear to be closely associated with the research interests of accountants. A sampling of these studies and recent research in accounting contexts is presented in the next section.

Role of the hypothesis in information search

In their comprehensive study of medical problem solving, Elstein, Shulman, and Sprafka (1978) explored the information-processing strategies of expert and nonexpert physicians in the hope of discovering the reasons for the former group's superior performance. Their long-term goal was to develop methods of training physicians to use the processes of the experts. In their 5-year program of study, the authors employed a variety of data-gathering techniques and experimental materials. While the study relied heavily on the research approach developed by Simon, the literature on the lens model and probability judgment (discussed in Chapters 2 and 3 of this book) played an important role in interpreting results and developing further experiments. This latter point illustrates that integration of the literature is one of the major contributions being made by applied decision researchers.[3]

---

[2]The reader will be interested in observing how closely the research results match Einhorn's predictions.

[3]Because the disciplinary interest of applied researchers (medicine, accounting, marketing, etc.) drives their research efforts, they have fewer incentives to dogmatically support one particular view or research approach taken by psychologists.

In a variety of simulated diagnostic situations, Elstein, Shulman, and Sprafka relied principally on verbal protocols and measures of information search to construct and test their model of diagnostic reasoning. Although their research is too voluminous to discuss completely in this chapter, their most complex experiment illustrates the basic research approaches and findings which are relevant to many business and accounting situations. Twenty-four experienced physicians, including seventeen who were judged by their peers to be among the best diagnosticians, participated in the experiments.

In this experiment, the authors performed a *high-fidelity simulation;* that is, the experimental tasks were developed to mimic as closely as possible the actual clinical situation. The authors suggest that this approach not only affects the external validity of the results but greatly improves both practitioners' willingness to participate and their acceptance of results. (Public accountants appear to exhibit the same trait). In this case, the physicians attempted to diagnose a medical complaint presented by a patient in an initial encounter. Actors from the department of theater were trained to simulate the initial complaint and medical and personal history of patients suffering from three types of problems: (1) hematological (related to the blood), (2) gastroenterological (related to the digestive system), and (3) neurological (related to the nervous system). Each doctor was asked to think aloud during the examination or during breaks. Data were gathered by videotaping the entire doctor-patient encounter. A *stimulated recall* method was also employed in which the physician reviewed the videotape and attempted to recall what he or she was thinking about at each point in the session. After the actor-patient provided the chief complaint and was interviewed concerning the medical history and a review of systems, the actor left the room and an assistant who served as a "data bank" entered. The data bank contained all possible clinical test results (blood pressure, blood count, etc.) but no interpretations of their significance. The physician was instructed to solicit any test data he or she felt was necessary to make a diagnosis. Most participants found the simulation highly realistic.

The protocols were coded on the basis of a long list of scoring variables, including measures of the amount of information searched, the timing and number of hypotheses generated, the number of cues acquired, the number of critical cues acquired (as determined by an expert panel), accuracy of cue interpretation, accuracy of problem formulation (hypothesis generation), and accuracy of final diagnosis. The detailed results, presented in Elstein, Shulman, and Sprafka (1978, Chapter 4), are summarized here. First, the general model derived from the study will be presented, and then the relationships between process attributes and accuracy will be discussed.

The authors describe diagnostic problem solving as primarily involving the generation and testing of hypotheses. This process is conducted within short-term and long-term memory as defined in the last section: short-term memory is limited to four to seven chunks, while long-term memory contains a virtually unlimited storage for rough associations between diseases and patterns of symptoms drawn from prior experience.

At the beginning of the process, a small set of hypotheses (potential diagnoses), which are *representative* of the initial data, are retrieved from long-term memory. The authors suggest that disease frequency, and to a lesser extent seriousness, also play some role in hypothesis selection (*availability*). (Note that early hypothesis generation is contrary to procedures actually taught in medical school.) These hypotheses are constructed in terms of prototypical symptom patterns and serve two purposes. First, consistent with Chase and Simon's (1973) results, they allow a greater number of symptoms to be stored in short-term memory by means of chunking patterns of symptoms included in hypotheses. Einhorn and Hogarth (1981) point out that the importance of recognizing natural co-occurrences of environmental cues is also basic to Brunswik's theory, which emphasizes cue redundancy. Second, the prototypical series of symptoms associated with each hypothesis guides the search for additional findings *consistent* with the hypotheses. As additional data are gathered, they are evaluated in a simplified fashion as either *confirming*, *disconfirming*, or *noncontributory* to each hypothesis. Strong disconfirming findings may cause the physician to return to the hypothesis-generation stage. The authors indicate, however, that, when the physician chooses among the competing hypotheses, disconfirming evidence may be underweighted or ignored, particularly toward the end of the process. The tendency to distort negative information toward the end of a process appears to be a common finding (see, e.g., Wallsten, 1978, and Shaklee and Fischhoff, 1980). This behavior suggests an anchoring strategy. Note that all three of Kahneman and Tversky's heuristics appear to play a role at different stages of the process. This implies not only that context may affect heuristic use, but that, within contexts, different heuristics may be used in different decision stages. A consistent pattern of moving from more general to more specific hypotheses was observed in only one of the experimental cases.

As indicated earlier, the authors had hoped to use a comparison of the expert and nonexpert physicians[4] to make prescriptions concerning medical education and practice. But, the analysis failed to uncover significant differences between the two groups—even in diagnostic accuracy. However, a number of characteristics of the decision process were found to be associated with diagnostic accuracy. Accurate diagnosis was weakly

---

[4]All the physicians were experienced. As indicated earlier, the "expert" group was so judged by their peers.

associated with thoroughness of information search and accurate cue interpretation, but the two were uncorrelated. More significantly, errors in *initial hypothesis generation* appeared to account for the *majority* of errors. The ignoring of contradictory evidence contributed to this tendency, because such evidence provided signs which should have resulted in the development of additional hypotheses. For example, in the neurology case, *every* participant who generated the correct hypothesis sometime during the process made the correct final diagnosis. The other subjects ignored contradictory evidence and refused to reformulate the problem to include the correct hypothesis. The authors concluded that the generation of hypotheses is the most important element in clinical diagnosis. They suggest that standard medical workups may serve to increase the number of hypotheses considered and aid in avoiding premature closure. Other aids aimed at this problem are discussed in the final chapter.

Although Pauker and others (1976) take a different approach toward understanding the diagnostic strategy of physicians, their conclusions are quite similar. Their approach is usually associated with the subfield of computer science called *artificial intelligence*. On the basis of introspections and direct observations of behavior, the authors constructed a detailed goal-directed computer program which closely simulated the *detailed* behavior of a group of physicians taking the present illness of a patient with edema (swelling). The program is extremely complex and includes the basic components of human problem-solving systems which we have just discussed. The basic elements of the program are (1) a supervisory program which oversees the operation of various subprocesses, (2) a short-term memory where the patient-specific data interact with general medical knowledge, and (3) a long-term associative memory. The organization of long-term memory is of particular interest: once again it is organized in terms of frames of related facts which are centered around diseases and closely related findings or prototypes. These frames are linked in a complex network through relations such as "may be caused by" and "may be complicated by." The program operates through a process involving mainly hypothesis generation and testing. This article is highly recommended to readers interested in computer modeling of cognitive processes. It illustrates the insights into cognitive processes that can be gained by building these models and the very real possibility that computer models which "think like humans" may be able to replace the decision maker even in these less structured situations.

Many accounting situations have characteristics similar to the medical problems just discussed. Consider the auditor who is faced with results from a statistical analytical review which suggest a basic change in an underlying process which generates the accounting numbers. If the change is judged material, it will be incumbent on the auditor to determine its cause. On the basis of this original "complaint," the auditor must develop a strategy for gathering information which will lead to an appropriate diagnosis. It is likely that the auditor will employ a hypothesis generation and testing approach similar to that of the Elstein, Shulman, and Sprafka (1978) physicians. Two preliminary investigations of this issue in accounting contexts are discussed next.

Bouwman (1980) presents an examination of a financial analysis task which is closely related to these medical examples. He compares expert versus novice financial analysts in an attempt to determine the differences in behavior that the educational process attempts to overcome. Fifteen Dutch accounting students and three professional accountants (CPAs) evaluated four different cases to determine any underlying problem areas. Each case was described by five pages of financial information from the three preceding years. Three of the four cases contained one major problem. Subjects were asked to think aloud while making their evaluations.

The author chose a "typical" student and accountant as the basis of comparison. The protocols were converted into problem behavior graphs which present knowledge states as nodes and operators as arrows between nodes. The student appeared to follow a simple undirected sequential strategy by which information was evaluated in the order presented until a single problem was uncovered. Information was frequently examined on the basis of very simple trends (e.g., sales are up). The information was used to form a series of simple relations which were internally consistent but may have been inconsistent with one another. Instead of developing detailed causal explanations, the student searched for a significant fact which explained the others. When an observed fact was identified as a "problem," little additional information was gathered.

On the other hand, the expert seemed to follow a standard checklist of questions and often examined data in terms of complex trends. He or she appeared to develop a general overall picture of the firm and to classify it under a general category, such as "expanding company," on the basis of initial information acquired. When the stereotype was violated, an in-depth examination to uncover significant causes would be initiated. The problems seemed to be recognized by their similarity to a set of common problems or hypotheses associated with patterns of cues in long-term memory. Both subjects evaluated the quantitative data in qualitative form (confirming, disconfirming, etc.; also see Clarkson and Meltzer, 1960). While the expert accountant appears to be quite similar to the Elstein, Shulman, and Sprafka (1978) physicians, the author notes that the expert also searched for contradictory evidence, whereas the novice did not. Again, it appears that experienced decision makers rely on hypotheses, prototypes, and standard lists of questions (similar to a standard medical workup) to organize and direct information search. Unfortunately, unlike the study of physicians, no attempt was made to associate process characteristics with measures of performance.

Shields (1979) and Biggs and Mock (1980) report similar results in their studies of managers' evaluations of performance reports and auditors' scope decisions. In Shields's (1979) study, each of 12 managers was asked to diagnose the cause of behavior as indicated in each of four performance reports. Each report contained 3 or 9 responsibility units and 6 or 13 performance parameters per unit. The performance parameters were presented on information boards such as those described earlier. Information search and verbal protocol data were gathered. The verbal protocols were coded into 15 categories, and category counts for different portions of the process and statement transition matrixes (which indicate the sequence of operations) were developed. Shields concluded that general goal statements directed the information search in the early stages, after which hypotheses which assumed this role were evoked. The average number of hypotheses evoked was similar to the results of Elstein, Shulman, and Sprafka (1978). However, contrary to their results, the hypotheses appeared to be generated later in the process after a greater portion of the information search was completed.

Biggs and Mock (1980) compared the audit scope decisions relating to accounts receivable confirmation of two inexperienced and two experienced audit seniors. Each auditor was required to think aloud while evaluating a complex audit situation and making sample-size decisions. The cases material was designed to closely mimic the complexity and makeup of the real-world situation. The protocols were converted into flowcharts and summary descriptions called "episode abstracts." Their major finding also is consistent with Bouwman's (1980) results. They found that the novices and experienced participants used distinctly different problem-solving strategies. Like Bouwman's experienced analysts, the experienced audit seniors built an overall picture of the company before making the four sample-size decisions required by the case. The less experienced seniors handled the problem in an ad hoc serial fashion, searching for information relevant to each sample-size decision and solving that part before moving on to the next decision. It appears that the inexperienced personnel were unable to organize the wide-ranging information in terms of predetermined prototypes and were forced to chunk the information in small portions. This was accomplished by cutting the problem into subparts. The experienced seniors' approach to the problem relied on stored information from prior experience, which was brought to bear on developing this overall picture. This latter approach allows greater consideration of the interrelations of the information and the different sample-size decisions.

All four of these studies present a consistent picture of expert problem-solving strategy. The organization of long-term memory and the use of hypotheses and prototypes as chunking devices and as guides for information search are the key concepts underlying most of the results. Newell and Simon (1972) suggest that the few basic constants in human problem-solving systems will interact with the characteristics of the environment in determining behavior. This latter issue is discussed in the next section.

Selection of alternative decision rules

As was suggested at the beginning of the chapter, the major aim of Newell and Simon's theory is to explain how complex problems are solved, given the limitations of human information-processing abilities. The research we have just discussed describes how the characteristics of long- and short-term memory lead a decision maker to use hypotheses as a simple method to guide information search. Simon (1955) suggests that final choices in complex situations will also be made based on simplified rules. In Chapter 2 we discussed a number of alternative mathematical representations of the judgment process and began to discuss their relative difficulty. Simon suggests that in complex situations the "mental arithmetic" required by compensatory models (e.g., the linear additive model) is beyond the cognitive abilities of most individuals. While the mental operations actually employed may differ from those in the model, the model operations themselves are quite complex. Each choice alternative is rated on each relevant attribute, and each attribute is multiplied by its appropriate weight and summed to estimate the overall value of the alternative. This value must then be stored while the next alternative is so evaluated. According to Simon, decision makers respond to the situation by deliberately simplifying the choice mechanism, mainly by employing noncompensatory models.

Payne (1976) developed and tested Simon's basic hypothesis that people respond to complexity by employing simple noncompensatory selection models. This paper is noteworthy for a number of reasons. First, Simon's conceptual hypothesis was used to develop operational hypotheses which could be objectively tested with *multiple* measurement techniques. The use of multiple measurement methods goes a long way toward minimizing many of the objectivity problems associated with this research. Second, Payne relies on the literature developed in all three research traditions discussed in this book. And, third, unlike most of the studies which we have discussed in this section, variables of interest are *manipulated* to test hypotheses. Much of the research in this area involves exposing all subjects to the same treatment, which means that there is no control group for comparison. Testing hypotheses about differences between treatment groups eliminates most threats to internal validity.

Payne (1976) hypothesized that *both* compensatory and noncompensatory models would be used by the same decision maker depending on the demands of the task. Two dimensions of task complexity were varied: the number of choice alternatives and the number of cues available to describe each alternative. As the task became more complex on either or both dimensions, it was expected that subjects would be more likely to employ a noncompensatory rule. Furthermore, in complex tasks, the participants were expected to switch to compensatory rules toward the end of the process when only a few choice alternatives remained.

The use of two compensatory and two noncompensatory decision rules was hypothesized. In Payne's (1976) second (more complex) experiment, 12 subjects selected one-bedroom furnished apartments on the basis of cues presented on information boards.[5] Each subject participated in all 12 experimental conditions, which were formed by all combinations of four levels of number of alternatives (2, 4, 8, and 12) and three levels of number of cues (4, 8, and 12). Each piece of information selected from the boards was recorded and the subjects were asked to think aloud. The information-search statistics were the primary data source. The verbal protocols provided supporting data. Payne determined that the four decision rules implied different levels of two characteristics of information search. First, compensatory models require that the subjects search the same number of cues for each alternative. The noncompensatory models would require that alternatives eliminated early in the process be searched for fewer cues, which would result in varying amounts of search across alternatives. Second, one each of the compensatory and noncompensatory models required either search for different cues within the same alternative or search for the same cue across different alternatives.[6]

The results suggested that, as the number of choice alternatives increased, there was a strong shift from searching the same number of cues to searching variable numbers of cues per alternative. This result supports Simon's basic hypothesis that noncompensatory models will be employed as this dimension of complexity increases. The effect of number of cues was not significant. The choice of search patterns within versus across alternatives appeared to be associated with individual differences and not with complexity.

Biggs (1979) presents an initial analysis of the choice of decision rule made by financial analysts in a complex task. From among five companies, each analyst chose the company with the best earnings prospects on the basis of extensive financial data (10 years' income statements and balance sheets and 2 years' statements of changes). The analysts were asked to think aloud while making their evaluations. The protocols were classified in operator categories which indicated use of four types of compensatory and noncompensatory rules. Biggs's results were less conclusive than

[5]Note that Payne's task differs from the diagnosis tasks just discussed. In the diagnosis tasks, the data were not perfect indicators of environmental states; in Payne's preference task, by contrast, it can be assumed that the data accurately represented the alternative apartments.

[6]See the original article for a complete description of the four models and the measurement techniques.

Payne's (1976). He found evidence of use of all four rules among the analysts. However, he also found that the compensatory models were significantly less efficient than the noncompensatory models in terms of time requirements. Both types of models also resulted in the same choice in most cases.

Payne's (1976) results are closely related to and extend the conclusions of the research we have discussed earlier in this chapter. You will recall that hypothesis-driven information search was a key characteristic of expert judgment. However, little was said about the exact fashion in which the initial small set of hypotheses were reduced to a final choice. If each of Payne's apartments is viewed as similar to a hypothesis, his results suggest that in situations with many alternative initial hypotheses the majority are eliminated by use of simple noncompensatory rules, and the remainder are evaluated by use of the more complex and exact compensatory rule. Biggs's (1979) results suggest that this approach increases the efficiency of the choice process and may often result in the same final choices, depending on the structure of the pool of alternatives. In situations where few initial hypotheses are presented, compensatory rules will be employed. This conclusion indicates that the Elstein, Shulman, and Sprafka (1978) physicians may have zeroed in quickly on a small number of hypotheses by using the simpler noncompensatory strategies and then switched to the compensatory strategy for the final choice. These general findings and the potential errors resulting from early elimination of hypotheses and other characteristics are discussed in the summary to this section.

Generalizations from the research to date

A reasonably consistent *general* picture of *expert* decision strategies emerges from this literature. After being faced with an initial diagnostic problem, experts appear to initiate information-search activity based on standard lists of questions. For example, physicians make extensive use of standard workup procedures, including history taking and laboratory tests; financial analysts compute standard indicators of the basic attributes of a company; and auditors use standard procedures for internal control evaluation and analytical review during the initial stages of an audit. Through their training and experience, these experts have developed a large, complex associative memory which relates evidence to prototypes of problem solutions. Prototypes may take the form of models of causality between events and evidence.

A small number (usually less than seven) of hypothesized solutions which are most representative of the data gathered during the standard workup are retrieved from memory. Failure to retrieve the correct solution at this stage appears to be a major cause of decision error. These failures are likely to result from availability biases related to inexperience with certain solutions that are also difficult to imagine. This type of avail-ability bias should be particularly troublesome in novel auditing situa-tions. For example, in the initial year of an audit engagement, the auditor will not have been able to develop an overall picture of the operating and accounting systems of the client which would serve as a framework for interpreting information. Auditors' recognition of this problem is evident in the emphasis in most audit manuals on "learning the system" during the first year of an audit. This same problem should become even more acute as the detection of questionable corporate acts becomes a greater part of the auditor's responsibility. It is unlikely that even the most expe-rienced auditors will have observed a sufficient number of cases to enable them to develop and store the complex associations between evidence and illegal activities necessary for their recognition. Recent attempts to de-velop fraud-detection decision aids, which are aimed at aiding the hy-pothesis generation process, have produced standard lists of red flags to guide initial fraud reviews and matrixes indicating co-occurrences of "symptoms and diseases" based on past frauds.[7] Both of these approaches are discussed in Elliott and Willingham (1980).

These initial hypotheses serve two functions. First, they organize data in terms of patterns which allow the judge to consider more data within the limited capacity of short-term memory. Second, they guide the search for additional information. Associated with each hypothesis or prototype are additional cues beyond those gathered in the initial workup which are normally indicative of the hypothesized solution. The hy-potheses drive further information search aimed primarily at supporting the *more* likely hypotheses and eliminating the *less* likely. Physicians will order additional diagnostic tests on the basis of these hypotheses and aud-itors will order certain additional substantive tests beyond the initial pro-cedures.

Studies which indicate that the difference between the expert and the novice may be the expert's well-developed memory for systems of hypotheses and associated evidence also have implications for business education. Formal education attempts to help the student to learn these interrelationships through the teaching of causal theories and exposure to representative cases. But the research suggests that concrete experi-ence over a period of years may be a necessary condition for developing this ability. It would appear that the teaching of theories and frameworks provides the novice with an organizing tool by means of which he or she can take full advantage of this experience. Confirmation of these possibil-ities awaits additional studies which relate process differences to perform-ance differences.

---

[7]Any approach to detection of management fraud will be susceptible to the rare events prediction problem discussed in Chapter 3.

The interpretation of data generated in the information-search phase of the process also appears to be highly simplified. Classifying observations into confirming, disconfirming, and neutral categories may ease application of certain decision rules and minimize the difficulty of data storage. For example, elimination of initial hypotheses based on a conjunctive rule would be simplified by rejecting all alternatives which receive a disconfirming score on a cue. A compensatory model involving the summing of confirming and disconfirming evidence as pluses and minuses could then be employed to choose between the final contestants. This latter approach has been called the cognitive balance sheet.

The role of confirming versus disconfirming evidence in this process is not completely clear. It is possible that disconfirming evidence plays its greatest role in paring down the list of initial hypotheses to the few serious competitors. This behavior would be consistent with Payne's (1976) finding of variable information search per alternative. The final solution may then be chosen on the basis of attempts to find confirming evidence, possibly through use of a cognitive balance sheet method. If the search is organized to disconfirm the less popular hypotheses and confirm the initial favorites, maximally diagnostic information will often not be selected and spurious diagnoses are likely to result. This scenario is highly speculative. However, the auditor may be particularly sensitive to this problem. Normally, the client is the first additional source of information approached by the auditor in response to a discovered irregularity . If the client's explanation for the irregularity directs the search for further information, and that search discloses confirming evidence, the auditor may prematurely conclude that the client's explanation is correct. The same behavior may be evident in other tasks, such as variance analysis. The tendency to ignore alternative explanations of the same evidence was also noted in other literature. In the next section, several conceptual and methodological problems presented by this research approach are discussed, and its strengths and weaknesses are compared to those of the approaches discussed in Chapters 2 and 3.

CONCEPTUAL AND METHODOLOGICAL PROBLEMS

The apparent differences between process-tracing models and the linear-regression and decision-theory models discussed in prior chapters result primarily from the difference in emphasis and methodology of the psychological traditions on which the research is based. We share the view held by Payne, Braunstein, and Carroll (1978) and Einhorn, Kleinmuntz, and Kleinmuntz (1979) that all three approaches provide complementary analyses that contribute to the goal of applied decision research: the *improvement* of decisions. The research examples discussed in this chapter were chosen specifically to illustrate the synergistic relationship between the research approaches. In this section, the differences in emphasis and methodology and how they are being narrowed by attempts to combine many of their complementary strengths are discussed. Specific methodological problems inherent in the process-tracing approaches are also reviewed.

Difference in emphasis

When the regression version of the lens model was compared with the decision-theory model, their basic similarity in orientation was noted. The lens model equation focuses attention on achievement and its components, and the decision-theory model focuses on the effects of heuristics on the accuracy of judgment. In both cases, achievement was determined by comparing human judgment with a normative solution, and the process description served to explain observed deficiencies (e.g., the effect of the use of a heuristic). Even in cases where results were purely descriptive, the desired end result of the research program was usually prescriptive. In contrast, the main focus of problem-solving research has been to describe the dynamic processes and supporting knowledge base used in human problem solving.[8] In most studies no attempt was made to relate the characteristics of the resulting computer program to any preferred solution technique. For this reason, the models were not designed to highlight causes of nonoptimal behavior.

It is the author's belief that the close fit between the accountant's interest in the improvement of decisions and the prescriptive orientation driving regression and decision-theory research accounts for the almost immediate popularity of these two approaches among accounting researchers following Slovic's (1969) first financial application. The close similarity of accounting tasks to those studied by psychologists and familiarity with the methodological tools were also contributing factors. The lack of a performance orientation also accounts for the lesser interest in problem-solving research, even though a financial application (Clarkson, 1962) had been published in three different forms fully 7 years before Slovic's paper. Methodological problems with the latter approach contributed to the lack of interest. This observation is supported by the fact that accountants' recent interest in the problem-solving literature has followed innovative integrations of the prescriptive orientation of the lens model and decision-theory research into the problem-solving models (e.g., Payne, 1976; Elstein, Shulman, and Sprafka, 1978). This recent interest has also been supported by advances in computer technology.

[8]This is not true in all cases. In fact, some of the problem-solving models in this literature were built to provide a basis for improving the way computers were programmed (see Simon, 1979).

At the same time that the decision-theory and lens model literature was changing the orientation of and providing a theoretical base for parts of the problem-solving literature, this latter literature was starting to fill an important role in decision research. In the mid-1970s, a number of authors (e.g., Slovic, Fischhoff, and Lichtenstein, 1977) began to express concern over the lack of a theoretical framework to suggest when and why different heuristics would be used and the inability of input-output measurement techniques to provide the necessary evidence. Another group of researchers (e.g., Elstein, Shulman, and Sprafka, 1978) were attempting to study more complex decision situations than appeared amenable to study with the techniques associated with the lens model and decision theory. Neither could deal effectively with the study of information search or provide sufficient detail for discrimination among some competing models. Both groups of researchers turned to cognitive psychology and problem solving for solutions. Many of the studies that have been discussed (e.g., Payne, 1976; Elstein, Shulman, and Sprafka, 1978) are the result of this dissatisfaction.

Difference in methodology

Most of the principal contributors to lens model and decision-theory research in the 1970s were trained in the traditions of mathematical and experimental psychology. These traditions explain the emphasis on developing quantitative models with well-defined variables and relationships and on testing these models in a deductive, experimental fashion. When testing alternative models, the traditional experimentalist would design a study to discriminate between competing models. He or she would deduce the conditions under which the competing models would produce different behavior. In the experiment, the different conditions would be operationalized and manipulated as the independent variables and the affected behavior measured as the dependent variable. In this fashion, the different models serve as the research hypotheses. The experiments reviewed in Chapter 3 on heuristics and biases are examples of this approach.

In contrast, many of the principal contributors to problem-solving research were trained as engineers and computer scientists. In fact, there is nearly total overlap of the subfield of computer science called artificial intelligence and the field of problem-solving research. A primarily inductive tradition dominates much of this research. In these experiments, problems "representative" of a certain situation are developed, data are gathered, and in conjunction with prior evidence an attempt is made to induce a program which mimics the recorded behavior. As a result, primary emphasis is not placed on development of detailed representations of the relationships between concepts and operational definitions or on the independent validation of models. In the extreme case, the final goal of the research is the construction of a program which will mimic behavior with little concern for principles of reproducibility, parsimony, and discriminability.

This latter orientation may lead accounting researchers to become so involved in building the computer program that the contribution to basic theory or an applied problem is easily forgotten. Productive accounting research requires a well-defined research problem and explicit consideration of the prospective contribution to the field. Direction and structure are as necessary here as in the experiments described in prior chapters. It cannot be overemphasized that *process tracing is not a substitute for theory or a well-defined purpose.*

Payne (1976) provided an excellent example of how these two traditions can be combined. While the theory and method of problem solving were used, a deductive, experimental approach to testing was also used. Observable measures of behavior indicative of different well-specified models were developed in advance, and the variables hypothesized to influence the choice of models were systematically manipulated.

Methodological Problems

Einhorn, Kleinmuntz, and Kleinmuntz (1979, p. 470) summarize the attractive features of the type of computer model that normally results from this research:

> (a) It apparently captures the ongoing problem-solving, since it is based on the person's own report; (b) since the verbal report is usually made on representative stimuli, the natural environment or problem space of the person is preserved; (c) the computer model is a sequential step-by-step set of rules, and, since we generally seem to process information sequentially, the model has greater face validity than the regression approach; and (d) the computer model seems configural in that the patterns of information are conditional on one another. This fits our preconceived ideas about how we make complex judgments.

However, the authors suggest that any initial enthusiasm should be tempered by two caveats. First, even though the resulting data may provide more specific sequential information relating to process, this does not imply a perfect matching of data and process. Second, the resulting increase in the level of detail of a model does *not* make it any more or less a process model. Unfortunately, this misunderstanding is fostered by the inappropriate label "process tracing" often used when referring to these techniques. Protocols at best provide an *incomplete record* of the contents of short-term memory. The relationship between these incomplete measures of attention and mental processes is less obvious than it might first appear. This problem is illustrated by the difficulty in inferring the importance of a particular cue to the judgment from simple measures of the frequency and timing of their verbalization.

Given the relatively short history of their use, it is not surprising that process-tracing techniques are less developed than their counterparts in lens model and decision-theory research. While the usefulness of the techniques is well illustrated by the examples presented in this chapter, the researcher considering their use should be aware of the major methodological problems faced in such an endeavor. One should note that virtually all the methodological warnings concerning case construction, representative design, and performance measurement discussed in Chapter 2 are as applicable to this type of research as they were to the research in Chapter 3. Unfortunately, though, they often receive less complete treatment, as the process-modeling portion of the study receives the major emphasis. Some of the problems specific to process-tracing methods are briefly discussed next.

The specific benefits of these research methods relate to their ability to provide more *detailed time-dependent* models of process. The unique problems associated with the techniques also relate to these benefits. Four of the problems are briefly discussed: (1) the validity of verbal report data, (2) the objectivity of data-coding methods, (3) the objectivity of related tests, and (4) the difficulty in communicating results.

The question of the validity of verbal reports of mental processes has been the subject of recent heated debate (see, e.g., Nisbett and Wilson, 1977; Ericsson and Simon, 1980; and Simon, 1979). Two major questions are raised in this regard. First, people may not be aware of or have access to their higher-order cognitive processes. Second, requiring subjects to think aloud is obtrusive and may significantly alter the behavior under study. It is likely that there is some validity to both issues, and their potential impact is of sufficient magnitude to warrant further study. Taking care not to overstate the meaning of protocol data will effectively deal with part of the first problem. The second can be remedied in part through use of no-protocol control groups and multiple measurement methods, as suggested by Payne, Braunstein, and Carroll (1978) and Einhorn, Kleinmuntz, and Kleinmuntz (1979). When multiple methods are used, each acts as a control for possible effects of the other experimental methods.

Questions concerning the objectivity of data-coding methods, in particular those related to verbal protocols, are often so severe as to question the scientific status of the research. In fact, practitioners of the technique admit that this portion of protocol analysis is more of an art than a science. The choice of coding categories, the choice of the "short phrases" which serve as the unit of analysis, and the assignment of each phrase to a category are highly subjective and are often not even described in the research writeup. Those researchers who present examples of complete protocols and resulting programs provide illustrations of the fact that the relationship between the two can be less than obvious. Even the most objective computer-aided coding techniques require only that the coder (usually the researcher or assistant) be able to force the protocols into a predetermined general framework. This can lead to selective attention to certain protocols and lack of reproducibility of results. Furthermore, alternative coding schemes which could as easily "fit" the data are usually readily available. Attempts to measure agreement between different coders using the same scheme do *not* effectively address this issue. A comparson with competing coding schemes more closely approaches a solution to this problem.

Closely related to this issue is the validity of tests of the goodness of fit of the resulting model. In most situations, the ability of the computer model to account for the verbalizations is seen as a sufficient test of the validity of the model. The weakest form requires only that most protocols be "easily" coded within the coding scheme. More stringent tests require predictions of protocols and final choices. However, even in these latter cases, competing models are rarely used for comparison purposes. Clarkson (1962) presents an initial attempt to use control models. When combined with the fact that good statistical descriptors of protocol data have not been developed, tests of fit or comparisons across groups or treatments are usually ad hoc at best. The researcher is often left with the option of providing a seat-of-the-pants comparison of two "typical" subjects whose similarity to other group members is determined in the same fashion. Others choose to "let the data speak for itself," despite the fact that this speech is often garbled and subject to varying interpretations. The lack of a definition of error, as provided in the regression and ANOVA models, contributes to problems of comparison. Since systematic and random components of behavior cannot be distinguished, both receive equal attention in the resulting model.[9]

Finally, the sheer volume of data produced in protocol studies, combined with the lack of objectivity in coding and the lack of adequate descriptive statistics, usually presents tremendous problems for the researcher attempting to communicate the results to a reader. Reports of protocol studies are usually quite long and difficult to read, even when the results from relatively few subjects are presented.

None of these problems is insurmountable, but they do represent the price that one pays for more detailed data. In general, the best approach to these problems is adherence to basic tenets of scientific method and, in particular, experimental design and use of multiple measurement methods. The recommendations of Campbell and Stanley (1963) are as applicable here as in the prior two chapters.

---

[9]In fact, the test-retest reliability of verbal protocols (agreement of protocols on two iterations of the same subject completing the same problem) is rarely, if ever, even measured.

CONCLUDING COMMENTS

The discussions in this chapter have attempted to emphasize that the analysis of predecisional behavior is complementary to the other research we have discussed. As Einhorn, Kleinmuntz, and Kleinmuntz (1979) emphasize, the approaches differ mainly in the level of detail or the generality of the resulting models. These authors show how protocols with different surface structures can be generated from the same rule, and that different general rules cannot be discriminated in many situations. Accountants will be interested in an earlier illustration in a financial context.

In Clarkson's (1962) study, detailed observation of a trust officer using numerous process-tracing techniques resulted in a series of portfolio selection models. The author describes the models as discrimination nets involving a series of binary decisions that are primarily conjunctive in nature (see Clarkson, 1962, p. 50). Securities that meet all the minimum criteria are selected. However, a close look at the segment of Clarkson's "yield" portfolio selection model presented in Figure 4–1 will illustrate the difficulty in making this interpretation. Note that a dividend yield of less than 4% (T_2) but greater than 3.5% can be compensated for by an appropriate mean yield (T_4) and prior selection of a security with greater than 4% yield (T_5). In the same fashion, a security lacking in earnings growth (T_6) will still be acceptable if both the forecasted earnings (T_{11}) and dividends (T_9) are positive. While this model suggests that dividend yield and earnings growth are weighed heavily in the process, the *general decision rule* includes a strong compensatory element. The fact that the rule is *operationalized* in a sequential branching structure does not change the compensatory nature of the rule.

Furthermore, fewer researchers are aware of an earlier paper by Clarkson and Meltzer (1960) in which the identical process is modeled as an additive process (an additive difference model, to be exact) and the predictive results are approximately equal. The principal part of this second model involves scoring each cue for each security as low, medium, or high (1, 2, 3, respectively), subtracting the resulting vector of each security from another, summing the differences, and choosing the security with the highest score. The question of which model actually underlies the process is clearly problematic. Conclusions about alternative models will depend on which attributes of the data are emphasized. Furthermore, Einhorn, Kleinmuntz, and Kleinmuntz (1979) note that the search for *the* correct model, whether algebraic or process tracing, tends "to obscure rather than clairify some of the important conceptual problems in decision making" (p. 482) that both are attempting to investigate. It is hoped that the approach taken in this book highlights this complementary nature of the three research approaches that we have discussed.

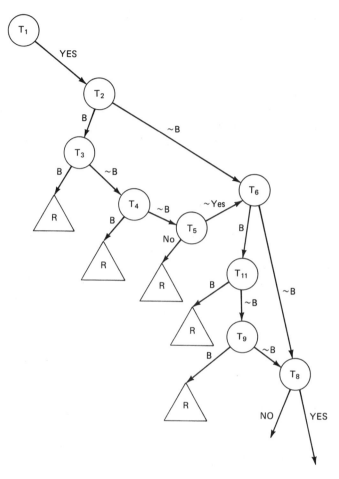

Dictionary
Yield portfolios
discrimination net

T_1 — Defensive characteristics	T_8 — Is forecasted dividend > 0
T_2 — Dividend yield ⩾ 4%	T_9 — Mean growth in working capital
T_3 — Dividend yield ⩾ 3.5%	T_{10} — Is industry depressed-marked "hold"
T_4 — Mean yield (past)	T_{11} — Are forecasted earnings > 0
T_5 — Have we selected a stock with ⩾ 4%	T_{12} — Is forecasted dividend = 0
T_6 — Mean growth in earnings per share	T_{13} — (y) on Relative Value List
T_7 — Stability of earnings	T_{14} — Is price 10% below high
B — "Below"	~A — "Not above"
~B — "Not below"	Ⓐ — Accept
A — "Above"	Ⓡ — Reject

FIGURE 4–1

Segment of yield portfolio model

Source: Clarkson [1962, Appendix B, p. 110]

Attempts to apply the theory and methods from the problem-solving literature to questions of decision making under uncertainty are fairly recent phenomena. As a result, many unresolved methodological problems exist. The studies reviewed in this chapter demonstrate that, when an experiment is conducted with much forethought and attention to the tenets of scientific method, an important contribution can be made. However, the reader should be aware that good science in a developing area requires greater effort than similar research in more mature areas. Accounting researchers who aspire to make a contribution to the study of predecisional behavior must be prepared to make this effort.

DISCUSSION QUESTIONS

1. Provide a brief discussion or description of each of the following:
   a. Predecisional behavior
   b. Bounded rationality
   c. Verbal protocol
   d. Information search
   e. Causal models
   f. Prototypes
2. Attempt to "think aloud" while answering the following two questions:
   a. In what year did Columbus discover America?
   b. If $2X + 16 = 20$, what does X equal?
   Did you have greater difficulty verbalizing your thoughts for question a or b? What characteristics of the two tasks caused this difference? What implications does this difference have for evaluation of the completeness of the mapping of verbal protocol data to mental processes?
3. Chase and Simon's chess masters appeared to be able to increase their "memory capacity." Is this an accurate interpretation of their result? Describe how memory capacity is "increased."
4. Explain the relationship between the *representativeness* and *availability* heuristics discussed in Chapter 3 and the hypothesis generation process discussed in Chapter 4.
5. In their study of medical diagnosis, Elstein, Shulman, and Sprafka (1978) found evidence of a tendency for a decision maker to select a hypothesis, seek confirming evidence, ignore disconfirming evidence, and ignore alternative hypotheses. What types of errors are likely to result from this strategy? Give examples of accounting situations where this strategy might be employed.
6. In their neurology diagnosis experiment, Elstein, Shulman, and Sprafka (1978) found that the correct diagnosis was arrived at if the correct hypothesis was generated at some point in the process. If auditors perform the analytical review process in the same fashion, what methods might help ensure that the auditors will generate the correct hypothesis?

7. Auditing situations are different in some ways from the medical study of Elstein, Shulman, and Sprafka (1978). Differences include the following:
    a. Information is usually not costless to an auditor, whereas it was to the doctors in the study.
    b. Whereas the patient was definitely ill in the medical study, auditors frequently face a substantial chance that nothing is wrong.
    How might these differences alter the decision-making process?

8. Einhorn (1976) characterizes many accounting situations as follows:

    > (1) the task is ill defined; (2) information must be searched for—it is not given; (3) data are rarely perfectly reliable; (4) hypothesis formation, as well as hypothesis confirmation/disconfirmation, occurs within a broad range of possibilities.

    Describe an accounting situation with these characteristics (which has not been mentioned in this book) in (a) management accounting, (b) financial accounting, and (c) auditing.

9. Many studies of predecisional behavior attempt to induce models of process by observing protocols or information search produced while completing some realistic problems. Payne (1976) took a different approach to testing for use of alternative decision rules. Describe these differences and their costs and benefits.

10. If verbal protocols provide an incomplete record of the contents of short-term memory, do differences in verbal protocols between subjects necessarily imply different decision processes? Explain.

11. If a cue is mentioned in a protocol or selected from an information board, does this imply that the cue influenced the final judgment? Explain the relationship between cue usage coefficients in the lens model and cue importance measures based on verbalizations or information search.

12. How might protocol or information search data explain findings of poor self-insight in the lens model literature discussed in Chapter 2 (refer to question 11 for hints)?

13. What criticisms have been leveled at the objectivity of data resulting from protocol analysis?

CHAPTER FIVE

Characteristics of Human Judgment and Decision Aids

Until recently, research in each of the three categories discussed in this book was conducted independently with little recognition of mutual interests and goals. This fact makes the consistent picture of human decision making which evolves from the literature all the more surprising and convincing. All three emphasize the difficulties humans face in drawing inferences from multiple sources of data. Such difficulties appear to stem from the small capacity of short-term memory, which limits the quantity of data that may simultaneously be considered. On the other hand, the decision maker's principal strength appears to lie in (1) a complex associative memory where small cue patterns can lead to retrieval of complex associations which guide the judgment process, and (2) the ability to code nonquantitative information. These basic characteristics lead to the use of simplifying rules or heuristics which ease the strain on short-term memory and also take advantage of the capacity of long-term memory (e.g., representativeness).

While the use of heuristics is often effective, unaided human judgment is in many instances imperfect. For example, judgment is frequently less than perfectly reliable, and important cues are often ignored or misweighted. Furthermore, in some cases, decision makers are unaware of both the judgmental rules they apply and the accuracy of their judgments. Significant evidence of decision error in important situations has been presented in each of the last three chapters, and the importance of these errors in accounting contexts has been illustrated. While the strengths and weaknesses of human judgment have been outlined in detail, it is valid for the reader to note that, except in parts of Chapter 2, few methods for correcting these weaknesses have been presented.

In Chapter 1, it was emphasized that accountants' interest in their own or users' decisions was motivated by interest in *improving* these decisions. The purpose of this chapter is to address this final issue. Decision aids have been suggested in the behavioral decision theory literature which improve one's ability to solve complex decision-making problems. These aids are demonstrated and, where available, examples of the many significant accounting applications will be presented.

DECISION IMPROVEMENT OPTIONS

In Chapter 1, three basic options for improving decisions were outlined (see Figure 1–1):

1. Changing the information.
2. Educating the decision maker to change the way she or he processes information.
3. Replacing the decision maker with a model.

Some combination of these may also be employed. All these options have been investigated, although option 3 has received the greatest attention. A sample of these methods will be discussed in the remainder of the chapter. The discussion will be organized on the basis of the stage in the decision process which is addressed. First, methods for aiding *hypothesis generation and information search* will be examined. Second, the more extensive literature on aids to *information integration* will be reviewed. Finally, methods for aiding *action choice* will be discussed.

HYPOTHESIS GENERATION
AND INFORMATION SEARCH

The importance of the cognitive representation of a problem to the approach taken to its solution was established in Chapter 4. It guides initial information search and the formation of hypothesized solutions based on the initial information. The hypotheses then guide further information search, which usually involves attempts to confirm the most likely hypothesis. The research suggests that the principal advantage of humans over machines lies in the ability to use a complex associative long-term memory to focus on likely problem solutions and to guide information search. However, two potential biases related to this decision stage have been suggested. The first involves the failure to consider a sufficient number of alternative hypotheses. The second relates to the failure to search for evidence which contradicts the likely solution or neglecting such information once it has been gathered. Like the basic research in predecisional behavior, the decision aids designed to address these biases are in an early stage of development. Most involve relatively simple pencil-and-paper methods for augmenting short-term memory.

Generating the correct hypothesis

Elstein, Shulman, and Sprafka's (1978) most crucial finding was that *every* physician who at any time considered the correct solution to the diagnostic problem selected this solution as the final diagnosis. This finding emphasizes the critical nature of the hypothesis-generation stage of decision making. The human propensity to narrowly define the set of possible solutions results in efficient information search, but it also may lead to significant error. Two approaches to avoiding this problem have been suggested: *standard workups* and *fault trees.*

Elstein and Bordage (1978) suggest that the standard clinical workups commonly used in medicine serve to ensure that certain hypotheses (or data related to them) are considered and also act as a hedge against prematurely restricting the range of hypotheses considered. At the same time, they serve as a labor-saving device, eliminating the need to make certain information selection decisions for each case. The use of standard workups also has a long history in auditing, where they serve the same purposes. Standard audit programs which prescribe a list of tests to be conducted on virtually all opinion audits are commonplace at most large CPA firms. As more formal methods for evaluating audit information have been developed (which are discussed later), these programs have become more detailed and all-encompassing.

The second method, fault trees, is a problem-organizing method commonly used in determining malfunctions in mechanical systems. The Rasmussen Report (Atomic Energy Commission, 1975) and Fischhoff, Slovic, and Lichtenstein (1978) describe the technique and its application to such complex systems as nuclear power plants and more simple systems such as automobiles. A fault tree organizes a problem or complaint and its possible causes into a branching structure. When complex mechanical systems are analyzed, subsystem failures which may cause the overall system failure are first listed, and then individual component failures related to each subsystem failure are listed along with their interrelationships. Recognition of interrelationships between components highlights necessary and sufficient conditions for system failure. The construction of a fault tree forces the problem solver to specify all *conceivable* causes for the complaint of interest before extensive data collection is completed and can help avoid premature hypothesis restriction. When completed, the tree can guide the troubleshooter by indicating an efficient approach to eliminating alternative explanations.

The most obvious accounting application of fault trees would be as an extension of flow-charting techniques which are currently used for designing and analyzing internal control systems. A basic difference between fault trees and flow charts is the former's organization around possible *system failures,* as opposed to the latter's emphasis on *transaction flows.* In the course of an audit, fault trees could be constructed to indicate important potential errors and the controls designed to detect them. These trees would highlight the key controls and also focus on their interrelationships. If compliance tests indicate that a control is not functioning properly, the fault tree would suggest any potential errors that might result, whether overlapping controls are available, and if the effectiveness of related controls should be examined. This information would direct the auditor to *specific* substantive tests aimed at detecting these errors. In this fashion, the fault tree may allow audit effort to be concentrated on potential problem areas. When combined with probability theory, fault trees also show promise for providing more exact estimates of the probability of error, which may become necessary as internal control reporting requirements change. Both standard workups and fault trees take advantage of a person's ability to recognize problems and potential solutions and, at the same time, augment her or his limited short-term memory to allow simultaneous consideration of a greater number of potential solutions and more complex problem interrelationships.

Searching for the correct information

Because hypotheses play such a major role in directing information search, the hypothesis-generation aids discussed previously also assist information search. For example, in the internal control case just discussed, the fault trees guided the alteration of planned substantive tests in response to negative results from compliance tests. In addition to these approaches, other techniques have been recommended which help avoid the tendency to selectively search for confirming evidence (see e.g., Elstein and Bordage, 1978, and Koriat, Lichtenstein, and Fischhoff, 1979). Two very simple methods have strong intuitive appeal. First, deliberate consideration of alternative hypotheses would effectively make contradictory evidence more salient and may eliminate some of the bias toward the search for confirming evidence. Similarly, the second approach simply requires that both confirming *and* contradictory signs related to a hypothesis be listed and equal portions from each category be considered. Both "methods" only direct the decision maker's attention to this potential bias and simple ways of avoiding it. Joyce and Biddle's (1981b) results suggest that many biases might be eliminated if the decision maker's attention were directed toward important evidence (e.g., base rates).

The aids in these categories are not particularly sophisticated nor has their effectiveness been rigorously tested. Furthermore, most of these aids actually *increase* the amount of information the individual must process. For this reason, strong recommendations for their use must await evidence indicating that the costs of processing the additional information are outweighed by the benefits of increased accuracy. The state of development of these techniques, as indicated earlier, reflects the state of basic research on predecisional behavior. However, these simple "paper and pencil" and "rule of thumb" approaches benefit from the simplicity of their application and, given the importance of these early stages of the judgment process, may prove effective. Methods designed to help people evaluate information that has already been acquired are more well developed and have been tested and applied in many situations. These techniques are the next topic for discussion.

COMBINING MULTIPLE SOURCES OF INFORMATION

The limited ability of people to integrate information from different sources appears to be the most consistent finding of the literature reviewed in this book. Inconsistency in judgment and misweighting of cues resulting from, among other factors, the failure to consider cue redundancies and a tendency to overweight unimportant cues and overlook important cues was extensively documented in the regression literature. Inattention to base rates and sample sizes and other biases which result in misweighting of information were the most significant source of error discovered in the probabilistic judgment literature. Errors due to neglect of disconfirming evidence and misinterpretation of noncontributing data were found in the problem-solving literature. While some experimental results may overstate the magnitude of this problem, Dawes's (1979, p. 573) and others' conclusion that "experts are much better at selecting and coding information than they are at integrating it" appears applicable to accountants and users of their information. The validity of the statement is further attested to by recent market interest in decision aids aimed at alleviating these problems. Fortunately, this important area of decision aiding is the most developed. A variety of methods that are applicable in different circumstances will be discussed in this section. The majority involve *replacing the decision maker with a model* in a portion of the decision process. These methods are discussed first. Then some preliminary research involving *changing the report format* is presented.

Replacing the decision maker with a model

The prospect of replacing human judges with a model in at least part of the decision process has intrigued many since computers came into common use. However, early predictions of radical changes in organizational decision making were not borne out. Attempts at change in a variety of professional settings including accounting, banking, medicine, and psychology were initially met with virtually identical objections concerning (1) technical problems with the models, (2) resistance to perceived attacks on decision makers' prized judgmental ability, and (3) moral issues relating to "dehumanizing" aspects of mathematical models (see Elstein, 1976, and Dawes, 1979, for a discussion). The author's early efforts with bankers and auditors sometimes met with similar defensive responses by those whose judgmental procedures were being scrutinized. In many business applications, these objections have been eliminated by both technological improvements and the weight of additional evidence. Again, the profit motive appears to be a most effective motivator.

A variety of methods have been developed to help judges combine large volumes of data. The techniques are aimed at improving the consistency of judgment and/or eliminating misweighting of cues. They also often provide significant cost savings. Each method is appropriate for decision situations with different characteristics. The specific aids to be discussed include (1) environmental regression models, (2) expert measurement and mechanical combination, (3) the composite judge, and (4) social judgment models.

ENVIRONMENTAL REGRESSION MODELS

In Chapter 2, a regression (or discriminant analysis) model, constructed by regressing the criterion event on the available cues, was shown to outperform human judges. Unlike the judge, these models make perfectly reliable predictions and optimally weight the available cues (in the least-squares sense). A fairly stringent set of environmental conditions is necessary for construction of this type of model. Quantitative specification of both the decision-relevant cues *and* the criterion event is required, as is a sufficient number of cases to estimate the parameters of the model. These conditions limit applications to a subset of *repetitive* decisions.

This decision aid was the first to gain wide acceptance in the business community. Its most comprehensive application has been to consumer-credit decisions (see Foster, 1978). In many major consumer-credit-granting institutions, including credit-card companies and retail chains, *credit-scoring models* have for the most part, replaced the human loan officer. Some models not only make credit-granting decsions, but automatically notify the applicant of the good or bad news. Their use is now so widespread that they have received much attention in the popular press (e.g.,

Wiener, 1977, and Main, 1977) and from regulators (see Bettner, 1980). Based on past loan experience, regression models are constructed that include the factors which maximally discriminate between those who do and do not pay back their loans. The credit scores which result from the model are combined with data on the relative costs of rejecting good credit risks (type I errors) and accepting poor credit risks (type II errors) to determine whether applicants should be accepted or rejected. Significant reductions in bad-debt losses and loan-processing costs have been widely reported by organizations using the models. The models provide the additional benefit of allowing rapid implementation of changes in credit policies through simple adjustments in either prior probabilities, cue weights, or error costs. At the same time, the statistical analyses have put to rest many inaccurate but widely accepted rules of thumb which had led to unjust credit discrimination in the past (e.g., relating to age and sex; see Main, 1977).

The major criticism leveled by decision makers against credit-scoring and other statistical models is that they eliminate the human judge's ability to use intuition and "gut feel," which they believe would improve on the accuracy of the models. However, results at Sears (reported in Main, 1977) and other organizations which allow credit managers to overrule the model suggest that, when a credit manager employs "gut feel" and accepts an applicant which the model rejects, 95% of the loans are difficult or impossible to collect. Furthermore, the author is aware of no reported case where adding intuition to the recommendations of the models improved predictive accuracy.

The widespread adoption of environmental models in consumer-credit scoring has led to their application in a variety of other tasks. In commercial lending, Altman's ZETA *bankruptcy prediction* model reportedly is being marketed successfully (see Altman, Haldeman, and Narayanan, 1977). This model is of particular interest because it not only combines readily available accounting and market data, but also makes numerous accounting adjustments, such as capitalization of leases, consolidation of finance subsidiaries, and elimination of goodwill. Altman, Haldeman, and Narayanan (1977) report prediction accuracy ranging from 91% in the first year before failure to 77% fully 5 years before failure. They also attempt to consider both the prior probability of occurrence and the relative costs of the two different types of misclassification errors in the model. Auditors have also become interested in using these models to aid in evaluating a company as a going concern for both reporting and engagement acceptance decisions (e.g., Arthur Andersen & Company).

The application of environmental models which is probably of greatest practical import to the reader is the *Discriminant Function System* used by the Internal Revenue Service to *select tax returns* for audit. The IRS first randomly selects a sample of returns for audit, the results of which provide the data base for construction of a model which discriminates between taxpayers who are and are not in compliance with the law. The model is used to select the majority of taxpayers who are subsequently audited. Each year, additional data are gathered to update the model. Annual updating of the model adjusts for structural changes in the underlying process.

Other agencies of government are also using models in *regulatory activities.* For example, the Federal Deposit Insurance Corporation uses a model to allocate examiners and the Comptroller of the Currency uses a model in the process of classifying "problem banks." In all these applications, relevant cues were easily quantified. However, in many important situations, only the expert judge can collect and code some of the necessary data. For example, evaluations of management abilities which play a major role in commercial lending are based on human observation and consultation with industry experts. In auditing, the effectiveness of controls not subject to statistical testing must be measured by expert judges. If appearance, speaking ability, and demeanor are relevant to CPA firm recruiting decisions, these factors must be measured by the expert interviewer. As suggested earlier, experts' abilities to select and code information are their principal advantage over machines. Yet the existence of unquantified cues does not mean that data combination must also be left to the expert.

EXPERT MEASUREMENT AND MECHANICAL COMBINATION

Einhorn (1972) developed a decision aid which is useful in situations where the lack of quantification of some cues precludes the use of simple models. He demonstrates how considerable increments in accuracy can be gained by combining the expert's comparative advantage in selecting and coding cues with the superior ability of a mechanical combination rule. His method employs the human to measure cues and then uses a model to combine them into a global judgment. He illustrates the use of expert measurement and mechanical combination in a judgment situation with life and death consequences where a criterion for measuring accuracy was available. His test involved the prognosis for patients suffering from Hodgkin's disease (a form of cancer of the lymph system).

In the experiment, three expert pathologists made two types of evaluations from biopsy slides taken from 193 patients who subsequently had died from the disease.[1] Each slide was first evaluated as to the relative amount of nine histological characteristics (or cues) chosen as relevant to the diagnosis by the physicians themselves. Second, a global disease severity rating was made in terms of a classification scheme developed by ex-

[1] At that time, Hodgkin's disease had an extremely high mortality rate.

perts in this field. To test his hypothesis, Einhorn compared the accuracy of the doctors' global judgments (the result of expert measurement and *clinical* combination) with the validity of judgments formed by regressing the patients' survival time on the nine component scores (the result of expert measurement and *mechanical* combination), the difference being due to the differential validity of clinical versus mechanical combination. The results were startling. In each case, mechanical combination of the component ratings outperformed the global judgments. The results strongly support Einhorn's hypothesis and should be particularly convincing to accountants, because the subjects in the task were highly trained and the experiment was highly realistic. The technique was able to eliminate both unreliability and misweighting in the human combination rule.[2] This approach is often referred to as a "divide and conquer" strategy based on the assumption that, if a complex problem is divided into components, it can be more easily solved.

Einhorn's application required that criterion data and a large number of cases be available for estimation of cue weights. In situations where these conditions are not met, weights may be estimated from the related research literature and from expert judgments. In these cases, use of the model for cue combination will still eliminate unreliability and, if the experts have been accurately designated, may eliminate misweighting. Expert measurement and mechanical combination based on human-determined *policy* weights have found numerous applications in a variety of business settings. These weights often reflect company policy as determined by members of senior management. The policy combination rules can be applied either through equations or simple decision tables.

As Joyce (1976) points out, auditors have become increasingly concerned with the fact that different staff members make widely differing decisions in the same circumstances. Given the lack of criteria for judging the accuracy of many audit decisions, many firms appear to be adopting Einhorn's (1974) view of consensus as a necessary condition for existence of professional expertise. This view is based on the earlier stated fact that consensus between judges places a limit on maximum accuracy. While consensus does not ensure accuracy, when lacking it may be taken as prima facie evidence of inaccuracy. Steadily increasing emphasis on quality control and the development of more detailed procedure manuals is evidence of concern over this issue. The most recent trend in building consensus in audit judgments is the use of expert measurement and mechanical combination models using weights determined by firm policy-makers.

---

[2]Readers will be interested in noting that a business application of the same technique predates Einhorn by 9 years. Unfortunately, the task involved the selection of "undervalued" securities based on human estimates of future growth rates, dividend payouts, and the standard deviation of earnings (Whitbeck and Kisor, 1963).

Two major types of applications have been developed. The first are *diagnosis systems*. The auditing profession has followed the same pattern as other professions in attempting to build judgmental consensus across experts. In particular, the parallel between developments aimed at promoting consensus in the evaluation of internal control and the diagnosis of psychiatric problems is startlingly close. For example, Spitzer, Endicott, and Robins (1975) review the history of attempts to increase between-judge consensus of psychiatric diagnoses and discuss the three steps that have been taken. In 1952, the American Psychiatric Association issued the first "Diagnostic and Statistical Manual of Mental Disorders" (DSM-I). This simple manual contained only standardized names and very general descriptions of the features of each of a variety of illnesses. This was followed in 1968 by DSM-II, which contained listings of specific symptoms "normally" associated with each illness, but did not indicate which conditions were necessary or sufficient for diagnosis of an illness. The next advance involved the development of the *Research Diagnostic Criteria* by the same authors, which indicated which specific combinations of symptoms should lead to each diagnosis. The same general approach has been adopted in the new DSM-III.

Auditors have followed an almost identical pattern[3] in developing methods for "diagnosing" the adequacy of internal control systems. A review of different editions of several auditing texts and CPA firm procedure manuals also indicates a series of three approaches. Before about 1950, like DSM-I, guides to internal control evaluation only included general discussions of "good" practices, such as separation of duties and hiring of competent personnel. Occasionally, specific procedures (e.g., periodic balancing of the cash account) would also be mentioned (see, e.g., Montgomery, 1940, and Committee on Auditing Procedure, 1949). Around 1950, detailed internal control questionnaires were developed which listed the *specific* attributes normally associated with good internal control (see Montgomery, Lenhart, and Jennings, 1949). Over time, more detailed questionnaires were developed for particular accounts. Like the DSM-II psychiatric diagnosis manual, these questionnaires did not indicate which conditions were necessary or sufficient for a system to be judged to contain a material weakness. Use of these procedures remained virtually unchanged until the late 1970s. However, during the 1970s, an extensive body of behavioral decision theory research in auditing contexts had documented considerable lack of consensus in audit judgments and decisions (see Appendix A and Holstrum, 1980). In response, a number of firms have developed new techniques which include, like DSM-III, a specification of "critical" combinations of control conditions that are sufficient to classify part of a system as weak (see, e.g., Deloitte, Haskins, &

---

[3]It is interesting to note that both psychiatrists and auditors faced increasing attention from the courts over the same period, which suggests possible similarities in motivation.

Sells, 1979). The decision-table format used in these models appears most appropriate for this situation. A number of firms are also using expert measurement and mechanical combinations in a second type of judgment: determining the extent of audit tests.

The same concern over the consensus of audit judgments extends to *decisions* concerning the *extent of audit tests.* A number of CPA firms have recognized that the principal strength of auditors on the job is their ability to use expert judgment to assess numerous characteristics of the client. But, as the research literature has indicated, their ability to combine information, and in particular to intuitively apply probability concepts (see Chapter 3), is weak. These firms have concentrated their efforts on developing expert measurement and mechanical combination methods for determining audit sample sizes which take advantage of the auditors' judgmental strengths and augment their weaknesses. Both decision tables and equation systems have been used to implement these systems. Some specific examples follow.

A simple but intriguing method for implementing explicit policy guidelines for determining statistical reliability levels in year-end substantive tests was developed by Touche Ross & Co. (1977, p. 96) for an *experimental* field manual.[4] This technique is closely associated with the ANOVA method of policy capturing discussed in Chapter 2. It sets forth specific guidelines for relating different levels of three variables, (1) required overall level of assurance, (2) results of the evaluation of internal control and compliance tests, and (3) the results of the analytical review, to the choice of statistical reliability to determine sample size. A table specifies statistical reliability levels for all combinations of two levels of results of analytical procedures (positive and not positive) and three levels of the other two variables (low, moderate, and high assurance and excellent, good, and not-good control). This table forms a 2 × 3 × 3 factorial ANOVA design and, like the experimental data discussed in Chapter 2, can be analyzed to determine the cue-weighting policy implicit in the guidelines. Such an analysis is presented in graphical form in Figure 5–1. It suggests that internal control system evaluation has the potential of having over twice the effect on statistical reliability as either analytical review results or required level of assurance, which were weighted approximately equally. The effects of interactions were quite small. Of particular interest is the fact that the model is one of the first to *explicitly* consider *audit risk* in determination of the extent of audit tests. While inconsistencies between auditors in the assessment of the three variables undoubtedly will exist, the table will eliminate inconsistencies in combining the factors into the global judgment. The graphical analysis presented in Figure 5–1 also supplies a simpler basis for discussing policy issues than case

---

[4]Note that this table was substantially revised and shortened in the adopted version. However, the experimental version is of greater interest to this discussion.

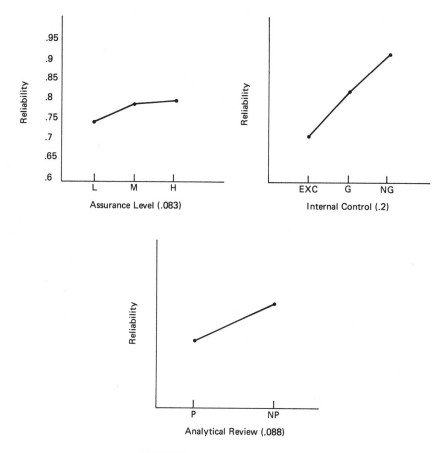

FIGURE 5–1

Cue weights implicit in decision table

by case consideration of each of the 2 × 3 × 3 alternatives. Furthermore, the table provides a much simpler way of communicating firm policy on setting sample sizes, which should result in greater adherence to the policy.

Peat, Marwick, Mitchell & Co. (1980) have recently developed and implemented a highly sophisticated system of expert measurement and mechanical combination for determining sample size for substantive testing. The method provides a combination of decision tables and equations which mechanically combine the expert's component judgments of (1) the size of aggregate errors in the account for which assurance is to be provided (called "gauge"), (2) the results of internal control review and compliance tests, (3) the existence of overlapping substantive tests, and (4) the prior probability of error, with (5) the level of stratification of the sample, and (6) characteristics of the distribution of dollar values, to determine sample size. The mechanical combination rule was derived from a study of actual sample size decisions. The associated worksheet is presented in Figure 5–2. In addition a separate decision table for computing audit gauge is provided. This method appears to be simple to apply, yet it ensures the inclusion of a wide variety of factors relevant to sample-size judgments. Of particular interest is the direct consideration of related audit tests and the auditor's prior expectations. The research in Chapter 3 suggests that auditors would have difficulty in integrating these factors intuitively. This example also illustrates how quantitative cues can be combined in the same model with cues requiring expert measurement.

Supporters of unaided intuitive judgment often criticize similar techniques on the grounds that there is some arbitrariness in the consensus rules implicit in the decision table. However, they fail to consider the fact that there is at least as much arbitrariness in the individualistic rules previously applied. More importantly, this new approach ensures that the key decision variables are attended to and the directions of their effects are correct. The evidence in Chapter 2 suggested that selection of the correct variables and assignment of the proper sign are the major determinants of judgmental accuracy. Furthermore, by promoting consistency (lessening variance), this method reduces the chance of an extreme error, simplifies the combination of audit results produced by different audit teams, and eases implementation of changes in firm audit policies. Finally, the method does not reduce reliance on professional judgment, but refocuses it on the important tradeoffs such as those between level of assurance provided, reliance on internal control and other tests, and substantive testing levels.

Expert measurement and mechanical combination would also be particularly useful in the earlier mentioned CPA firm employment decision, where quantitative data such as grade-point average and school quality could be combined in a mechanical model with expert measured cues such as appearance and professional demeanor. This same method is applicable in a variety of business situations where policy prescriptions must be applied by a large number of agents of an enterprise. Finally, it should be noted that when the levels of differential weights are particularly difficult to determine, the equal-weighting scheme discussed in Chapter 2 may provide a useful substitute (see Einhorn and McCoach, 1977).

THE COMPOSITE JUDGE

Both environmental regression models and expert measurement and mechanical combination require explicit specification and measurement of the decision-relevant variables. However, in many important decisions, relevant cues cannot be easily identified or measured. The typical

Client _____ W.P. No. _____

Year end _____ ACCOUNTANT _____

                                         DATE _____

SUBSTANTIVE TEST OF DETAILS WORKSHEET

Test of account: _____

Test objective(s): _____

Audit procedure(s): _____

Definition of error(s): _____

- SELECT RELIANCE CLASS

Planned restriction of sub-stantive test based on internal control (cross reference to related Compliance Test of Details Worksheet(s) or Inquiry and Observation Compliance Test Worksheet(s))	Reliance class if	
	There are other significantly effective substantive tests (than that planned on this worksheet) directed to the same test objective(s)	There are no other significantly effective substantive tests (than that planned on this worksheet) directed to the same test objective(s)
Maximum	A	A
Moderate	A	B
Little or None	B	C

- SELECT SAMPLE SIZE FACTOR

For reliance class selected above, planned sampling method, and expected amount of monetary error, select sample size factor from table below, and enter on line (2) below.

Reliance Class	Stratified[1] sample with expected error		Unstratified sample with expected error	
	Small[2]	Large[2]	Small[2]	Large[2]
A	2	4[3]	5	10[3]
B	4	8	10	20
C	6	12	15	30[4]

(1) Any stratification plan below the minimum should be considered an unstratified sample

(2) "Small" in this context means the auditor judgmentally assesses that the most probable total monetary error in the account being tested does not exceed 1/3 the audit gauge. Otherwise, select "Large"

(3) If "large" error expected, "maximum" reliance on internal control is not warranted. Therefore, this factor will be used where there is moderate reliance on internal control with significantly effective other substantive tests related to the same objective

(4) If "Large" error expected and internal controls cannot be relied upon an unstratified sample is generally inappropriate

- COMPUTE SUBSTANTIVE SAMPLE SIZE

Enter:			
	AUDIT GAUGE (From Audit Gauge Worksheet)	(1)	$ _____
	Sample size factor (from table above)	(2)	$ _____
	Dollar total of population being sampled (may be estimated)	(3)	$ _____
	One third of line (1)	(4)	$ _____
	Dollar total of all items in population greater than line (4) (enter -0- if unknown)	(5)	$ _____
	Number of population items in amount on line (5)	(6)	_____ *
Compute:	(3) − (5)	(7)	$ _____
	Sample size = (7) x (2) − (1)	(8)	_____ **

*Audit all items in line (6) plus the sample determined in line (8).

**If the actual sample size varies from the computed sample size by more than 20%, the workpapers contain an indication of the rationale for using the different sample size.

FIGURE 5—2

Peat, Marwick, Mitchell & Co. decision table

approach to aiding human judges in these situations involves the use of interactive groups, which is extremely expensive. Libby and Blashfield (1978, p. 122) note that

> they require many judges, more than one decision iteration, and time consuming meetings where the numerous group members are forced to find mutually convenient times and locations to meet. In addition, in situations where the negative effects of pressures for conformity outweigh the positive effects of information exchange, the validity of group judgments may be lower than that of the average individual. The Delphi technique has been developed in reaction to this latter problem. However, even this technique requires numerous judges and many decision iterations.

Many others have demonstrated that equal-weighted *composite judgments,* which are formed by taking the mean judgment of a large group of individuals, are significantly more valid than the average individual judge.[5] However, the use of large aggregates is still expensive. Libby and Blashfield (1978) demonstrated that the majority of the increment in accuracy gained by aggregating large numbers of judges can be obtained by aggregating only three judges. In Libby's (1975b) business-failure prediction task, median validity rose from $r_a = .48$ for individual judges to .57 for three-judge composites. The 43-judge composite scored only .64. This technique should prove particularly useful in situations such as commercial lending, where many decisions are currently made by either individuals or senior loan committees whose membership includes a large number of senior officers. Employing a three-member composite judge as a middle level of analysis between these two should prove more efficient than the interactive committee, be more accurate than the individual loan officers, and possibly be *more* accurate than the interactive committee. In situations where decisions must still be made in a committee or other social process, mechanical methods can still be used to aid judgment.

SOCIAL JUDGMENT THEORY

Kenneth Hammond has suggested that, in social judgment situations, it is difficult to eliminate disagreement if the source of the disagreement is unknown (see e.g., Hammond and Adelman, 1976). He uses the regression methodology associated with the lens model to describe differences of opinion on judgment policy in terms of the differences in weights placed on different attributes. He recommends (like Einhorn) that cue values be measured empirically or by experts, and that the determination of compromise weights be left to those active in the choice process. When

---

[5]Dawes (1970) proves that when the correlation between any pair of individual judgments is less than 1, the equal-weighted aggregate will be more valid than the average individual.

this process is complete, the expert-determined cue values can be mechanically combined with the socially determined cue weights to evaluate alternative solutions.

Hammond suggests that the usefulness of this approach lies in the fact that making sources of disagreement explicit eases the process of developing compromise solutions. The normal approach of concentrating on outcomes clouds the basic policy issue being debated. He has demonstrated the usefulness of the approach in a number of interesting applications. For example, Hammond and Adelman (1976) used social judgment theory to satisfactorily resolve intergroup conflict in a major social dispute. The issue addressed was the type of handgun ammunition to be used by the Denver police. The police preferred to use soft-nosed bullets because of their greater stopping effectiveness and *lesser* threat to bystanders. Opponents argued that they created excessive amounts of injury and *greater* threats to bystanders. Opinions of different groups of citizens ranged widely on this inflammatory issue. When the different groups met to discuss the issue, the community rapidly became polarized, and they were not able to reach a compromise agreement. Meetings often degenerated to name-calling and insults. Over time, this developed into a highly charged, emotional issue. Hammond and Adelman volunteered to aid in the development of a compromise solution. They first analyzed the arguments of the different groups to determine which were the relevant attributes of ammunition. They discovered the three mentioned: the degree of injury, stopping effectiveness, and the threat to bystanders. The disagreement between the groups could be then conceptualized in the following manner. The police were primarily concerned with stopping effectiveness and threat to bystanders, while other groups were concerned with the degree of injury and threat to bystanders. Clearly, there were disagreements as to the facts about the ammunition's characteristics *and* about values. To resolve the dispute over facts, a group of ballistics experts were called in to rate alternative ammunition on the three factors to provide "objective" cue values for each bullet. The political question of appropriate cue weighting was then left to the elected representatives of the people, the city council. They decided to weight the cues equally. It was then possible to use a simple equation to choose the bullet with the highest expected utility. As it turned out, the type chosen caused a lower degree of injury, had greater stopping effectiveness, and was a lesser threat to bystanders than the bullets presently in use. No group was perfectly happy with the solution, but everyone was more satisfied than they had been with the original ammunition. It is not clear that this type of process will always produce this result. There may be cases where knowledge of sources of disagreement actually adds to the conflict. But in this case, before Hammond entered the scene, the possibility of the final outcome was not even imagined.

This same technique has been applied to labor-management disputes, regional planning, and in developing land-use policies (see Hammond and others, 1977). It also could be employed in situations such as FASB policy decisions and in faculty recruiting and evaluation. A basic principle underlying this approach is to split the political question from the scientific question. Measurements of cues are provided by the experts. The appropriate group utility function is determined through the political process, which is aided by making the sources of disagreement explicit. One reason the bullet study was so successful was that everyone could agree on who the experts were. In most accounting situations, this will be more difficult as experts are usually selected according to the kind of testimony that they will give. Joyce, Libby, and Sunder (1981) have investigated use of a similar approach combined with *Statement of Financial Accounting Concepts No. 2* in accounting policy making. However, application is still a long way off. Social judgment theory has already been used in faculty evaluation procedures and in particular in a search for sex discrimination. Roose and Doherty (1978) found that, although male faculty on average earned over $2,200 more than female faculty, when a faculty evaluation model was built based on evaluations of sex-blind achievement profiles (containing age, publication record, etc.) and actual salaries were then predicted using the model, the discrepancy became inconsequential. Given the current regulatory environment, other similar applications are likely to follow. All the techniques discussed so far have aimed at helping the decision maker combine information from multiple sources by replacing the decision maker with a model in at least part of the process. The literature describing these different approaches is quite extensive, and we have only sampled a few of the available techniques. A much smaller literature addressing the second option, *changing the report format,* also presents many possibilities for accountants.

Changing the report format

The impact of the method of displaying data on the accuracy of human judgment has received surprisingly little attention from financial accountants, managerial accountants, information system designers, and auditors. For example, managers must monitor a set of complex financial controls using data printed out in almost random format by the computer. To the contrary, decision makers responsible for the control of many mechanical systems are often presented with data whose format was determined by extensive research by human factors engineers and engineering psychologists. Two examples include airplane control panels and nuclear reactor control displays. Great care is taken in the design and placement of the multitude of gauges and dials which make up an airplane control panel. They are designed to maximize the pilot's ability to recognize problems and respond with appropriate corrective action. Even these well-designed analog indicators will be replaced in the near future with digital readouts on computer screens, which will further ease the pilot's task. The importance of the method of displaying data was recently brought home to the residents of the Harrisburg, Pennsylvania, area, where a faulty gauge resulted in a near meltdown of a nuclear reactor, even though backup gauges accurately indicated the problem. Unfortunately, the control panel was not designed in such a way to bring this discrepancy to the operator's attention. While the inaccurate display of accounting information will not likely result in such disastrous consequences, accounting reports could be better designed to take advantage of human abilities as pattern recognizers. Two such options will be addressed in this section: *improving tabular presentations* and *multidimensional graphics.*

IMPROVING TABULAR PRESENTATIONS

The art of presenting statistical data in a readable form has received little attention in accounting and other disciplines. A look at many complex tables suggests they are poorly prepared and difficult to interpret, even for an expert in the field. One look at the typical auditor's spread sheet often used for analytical review will suggest that some trends, changes, and interrelationships that exist will likely be missed and spurious ones discovered. Many tables presented in internal and external financial reports are similarly prepared, though there is wide variance across firms. In a particularly insightful article, Ehrenberg (1977) suggests that a good table should make patterns and exceptions obvious when the probable pattern is known beforehand. While the development of approaches to improving specific tables may at first seem complex, he presents and demonstrates the effectiveness of four basic rules or guidelines: (1) round to *two* significant digits, (2) use row and column averages (or totals if appropriate), (3) present the main pattern of data in the columns, and (4) order the rows and columns by some measure of their size. He suggests that rounding to two significant digits seems severe, but appears necessary for mental arithmetic; averages help one keep important relations in mind, such as above and below average; columnar presentation allows one to compare individual digits by running the eye up and down the column; and ordering by size aids in interpreting a figure by seeing the general pattern of the surrounding ones. These principles are demonstrated in a simple table of data adapted from the United States Steel Corporation 1978 Annual Report and presented in Table 5–1. Part A contains segmental sales data substantially as presented in the actual report, and in Part B the four rules have been applied. The reader will be more accustomed to the traditional presentation in Part A. However, if one attempts to quickly determine segmental trends over time and changes in relative contribution and to evaluate the current year's performance, Part B should be more understandable, even though the original table is well constructed. The effect should be more dramatic in the case of more complex tables.

MULTIDIMENSIONAL GRAPHICS

The simple tables just discussed and traditional line and bar graphs are useful for presenting the relationship between only two financial variables. Moriarity and Roach (1977) and Moriarity (1979) suggest the use of multidimensional graphics for displaying relationships between multiple financial variables to allow decision makers to identify trends and changes. These graphics can serve the same purpose as organizing gauges to highlight malfunctions on airplanes. The authors suggest that if multidimensional graphics are used, human skills at pattern recognition may even allow them to outperform statistical models in tasks such as analytical review and financial analysis. The particular technique suggested is Chernoff's (1973) schematic faces. These faces are constructed by assigning each variable of interest to a feature of a face. For example, one variable

TABLE 5–1

Application of the Principles of Table Construction

PART A: FROM ANNUAL REPORT

Sales	Millions of Dollars				
	1978	1977	1976	1975	1974
Steel manufacturing	$ **8,989**	$ 7,736	$6,969	$6,577	$ 7,684
Chemicals	**808**	700	648	656	733
Resource development	**396**	386	359	353	349
Fabricating and engineering	**1,536**	1,459	1,334	1,225	1,034
Transportation and utility	**549**	446	446	379	,411
Total Segment Sales	**$12,278**	$10,727	$9,756	$9,190	$10,211

PART B: AFTER APPLICATION OF RULES

Year	Steel	Fabricating and Engineering	Chemicals	Transport and Utilities	Resource Development	Total
1974	$7,700	$1,000	$730	$410	$350	$10,000
1975	6,600	1,200	660	380	350	9,200
1976	7,000	1,300	650	450	360	9,800
1977	7,700	1,500	700	450	390	11,000
1978	**9,000**	**1,500**	**810**	**550**	**400**	**12,000**
Average	$7,600	$1,300	$710	$450	$370	$10,000

controls the size of the eyes, one the length of the nose, and so on. The faces may be constructed by hand or with the aid of a computer.

Figure 5–3 contains an example from Moriarity and Roach (1977) where the 13 *Dun and Bradstreet Key Financial Ratios* of W. T. Grant and Co. are presented for years 1965 through 1974. This example demonstrates Moriarity's (1979) contention that schematic faces have particular potential because (1) people are familiar with faces, so they can easily distinguish change, (2) they are rich enough in detail to represent a large number of variables, (3) there is a significant amount of psychological research indicating the saliency of various facial features, which may provide a simple method to assign weights to features, and (4) inexpensive technology for their construction is available. Unfortunately, the cartoon

FIGURE 5–3

Faces for W. T. Grant, 1965 to 1974

Source: Moriarity and Roach [1977, Figure 1]

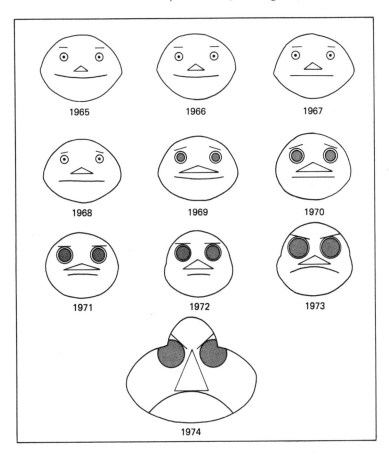

faces are themselves so funny looking that it may be difficult for most accountants to take them seriously. However, they provide an excellent example of the possibilities of multidimensional graphics for accounting. Consider the auditor conducting a routine analytical review. The purpose of these tests is to detect changes in accounts which are not consistent with changes in other accounts. For example, if sales rise, we would expect cost of goods sold and sales commissions to also rise. An unexpected change in sales commissions would alert the auditor to a potential problem area worthy of extra audit effort. Multidimensional graphics may provide a simple method of presenting these relationships to auditors. Of course, these methods are relatively untested and should be examined in future research.

Many of the techniques for helping decision makers to combine multiple sources of data into global judgments, which were discussed in this section, appear to have practical value for accountants. But, like most of the research on which their development was based, very few aid in combining the judgments with the costs of error to determine a final choice. Some limited research in this area is discussed next.

ACTION CHOICE

As discussed in detail in Chapter 3, a complete model of decision making requires not only specification of the probabilities of future outcomes associated with each action, but also specification of the utility of each outcome. The importance of doing so is best illustrated in a medical context in recent articles by Pauker (1976), McNeil, Weichselbaum, and Pauker (1978), and McNeil and Pauker (1979). They point out that surgical procedures are usually chosen based on survival rates, and diagnostic tests are usually chosen depending on information content and health outcomes. However, when the patient's utilities for the many possible outcomes (e.g., immediate death, death in 5 years, pain) were considered, often different treatments for heart disease and other ailments and different diagnostic tests would be prescribed.[6] Fryback and Thornbury (1978) suggest that both the nonmonetary and monetary costs to patients can be reduced if physicians are simply instructed to *explicitly* consider each possible outcome and all its consequences. Informal methods such as checklists of cost factors should prove useful in this regard. A second approach, often used in auditing, is to require a rationale memo for each decision which requires the decision maker to lay out relative costs and benefits of the selected auditing procedures. Making the important factors explicit appears to be the key to these methods. This issue is addressed in an auditing context by Turner and Mock (1980). More formal

[6]They also note the importance of the surgeon's past record to these choices.

quantitative methods for eliciting and combining probabilities and utilities have also been developed, but are beyond the scope of this book. The interested reader is referred to Keeney and Raiffa (1976).

THE NEED TO EVALUATE JUDGMENT

The goal of this book is to present a descriptive theory of decision behavior in accounting contexts and to illustrate how this theory can aid accountants in *improving* their own decisions or the decisions made by users of their data. Each of the first four chapters developed general principles of human decision making. The positive orientation of these chapters provided the basis for the normative recommendations made in this final chapter. The decision-aiding methods discussed have the potential for improving the quality of judgments in accounting contexts. It is appropriate to conclude this discussion by noting that, like unaided human judgment, the effectiveness of decision aids must be evaluated empirically. While this evaluation process may at first appear to be simple, this is clearly not the case. Einhorn and Hogarth (1978) illustrate the difficult problems faced when judging the quality of judgment, even in simple binary classification problems such as the graduate-admissions or bank-lending decisions often used in this book as examples. In these situations, evidence about outcomes concerning both selected and rejected applicants is necessary for assessing the quality of judgment. As was suggested in Chapter 2, it is often difficult or impossible to determine outcomes for rejected applicants. For example, admissions officers cannot easily track applicants who do not enter their programs, and loan officers usually have little information about the future success of rejected loan applicants. In these situations, most individuals evaluate their own judgment from the success rate of accepted applicants (the positive hit rate).

Einhorn and Hogarth (1978) point out that the positive hit rate is affected by four factors: (1) the correlation between the judgment and the attribute being judged (judgmental accuracy), (2) the portion of applicants selected (the selection ratio), (3) the base rate or unconditional probability of success, and (4) the impact of the act of being selected on future success (treatment effects). Small selection ratios and high base rates of success tend to produce high positive hit rates but many unobserved false negatives. If the act of selection also increases an applicant's chances for success, the positive hit rate will be high even if judgmental accuracy is very low. In these circumstances, reliance on the positive hit rate can lead to overconfidence in the quality of our own judgment, whether it be formed through intuition or by mechanical means. Regardless of the judgmental strategy one follows, greater care in the evaluation of the quality of judgment may be the most important decision aid.

A FINAL NOTE

It is appropriate to conclude this book with a discussion of methods for improving decisions. Back in Chapter 1; we began by demonstrating that accountants' concern for *improving* their own decisions and those of users motivates research aimed at describing decision behavior in accounting contexts. The following chapters presented an integrated picture of this behavior. Now we have returned to this initial topic to fulfill the initial promise by suggesting decision-improvement aids which closely fit this picture of human decision-making strengths and weaknesses. The literature relied upon in these chapters is extensive and drawn from a variety of disciplines. However, accounting research and practical applications of its results have barely scratched the surface of available opportunities. For example, most accounting problems in managerial accounting and management information systems have hardly been touched on. Even the relatively extensive literature in auditing and financial accounting has addressed only a small portion of important decision-related problems. The developing psychological theories and accountants' growing interest in improving decisions should motivate an increasing number of research opportunities limited only by our imaginations.

DISCUSSION QUESTIONS

1. Provide a brief discussion or description of each of the following:
   a. Standard workup
   b. Fault tree
   c. Search for confirming evidence
   d. Environmental regression models
   e. Expert measurement and mechanical combination
   f. Composite judge
   g. Social judgment model
   h. Chernoff faces
   i. Selection ratio
   j. Positive hit rate
2. Explain the similarities and differences in the role played by standard clinical workups in medical practice and by standard audit programs in public accounting.
3. Take a portion of a sample flow chart from an auditing textbook and try to construct a fault tree for the subsystem. What problems did you encounter in your attempt? What types of data would you gather to estimate the necessary probabilities? To what degree would you have to rely on subjective probability estimates? How might the fault tree be used by auditors? [*Note:* It is suggested that students review the summary of the Rasmussen Report (Atomic Energy Commission, 1975) before answering this question.]

4. Consider a manager investigating the cause of a significant materials price variance. How might the bias toward search for confirming evidence lead to incorrect conclusions? (*Note:* Consider the fact that a number of changes may be reflected in the variance, some of which may offset one another.)

5. Explain the situational characteristics necessary for implementing each of the alternative methods discussed in the chapter for replacing the decision maker with a model (e.g., number of cases, quantitative cues). Construct an accounting situation (not mentioned in the chapter) where each might be employed and indicate the potential costs and benefits of each application and why you chose the specific method over others.

6. What causes of lack of consensus does expert measurement and mechanical combination eliminate? What causes still remain?

7. How might multiple judges with varying areas of expertise assist in managerial planning decisions through the use of expert measurement and mechanical combination? Present a specific example and evaluate the costs and benefits over other strategies, such as interactive groups.

8. Touche Ross & Co. eliminated "assurance level" from the final version of its expert measurement and mechanical combination model (see Figure 5–1). This change may have resulted from one of the costs of making decision rules explicit. Using this or other examples, discuss these costs in terms of political activity, potential litigation, or other problems. Does the fact that the variable was eliminated from the table necessarily imply that this variable is no longer considered in decisions? (*Note:* A reading of the Committee on Auditors' Responsibilities Report may shed light on this question.)

9. Evaluate the argument made by opponents of mechanical models that they are "arbitrary."

10. Explain the potential benefits of using the composite judge in place of interactive groups. Suggest an accounting situation where their use might be appropriate.

11. How might social judgment theory actually make the development of compromise solutions more difficult? (*Note:* Consider how knowledge of your opponent's opinions might increase animosity.)

12. Both improved tabular presentations and multidimensional graphics have been suggested as changes in report format. What characteristics of the judgment situation would lead you to choose multidimensional graphics over tabular presentations? (Use examples.)

13. What problems are faced when attempting to examine the accuracy of judgment in the following situations?
    a. Cost variance investigation
    b. Capital budgeting
    c. Audit work allocation
    d. Commercial lending

APPENDIX A

Accounting Research Using Regression, ANOVA, and Multidimentional Scaling

In the short period of 7 years, a significant body of accounting research using regression-related approaches has been produced. These studies have examined many significant accounting policy issues in a number of decision contexts. This literature is reviewed in detail in this appendix. The research is classified in the same three categories as in Chapter 2 (clinical versus statistical prediction, multiple cue probability learning, and policy capturing) to facilitate comparison of the results. Each accounting issue addressed is also presented under a separate subheading. The research is summarized at the end of the Appendix in Table A–2 which is keyed to the information processing variables listed in Figure 1–3.

CLINICAL VERSUS STATISTICAL PREDICTION

Accountants' interest in serving the needs of users has motivated the study of the accuracy of judgments made from accounting data. Thus far, the accuracy of human judgment has been investigated in two accounting contexts: business-failure prediction and stock-price prediction.

[1]This section is based largely on Libby and Lewis (1977, 1982), with permission of *Accounting, Organizations and Society* and Pergamon Press.

Business-failure prediction

Libby's (1975a, b) study of the accuracy, consistency, consensus, and predictability of loan officers' business-failure predictions was described in Chapter 2. The participants received rather high marks on all attributes. The accuracy of many subjects approached environmental predictability (74% correct on average), they were consistent over time 89% of the time, they agreed with one another 80% of the time, and the linear model predicted 88% of their responses. Libby (1976a) also reported that his subjects' accuracy could not be improved by "bootstrapping" with linear "models of man." This finding may have resulted because the loan officers more nearly approached optimal accuracy in their predictions than did subjects in prior investigations, and the cue distributions were highly skewed. We would expect that in most situations similar to the ones studied (repetitive decisions based on a small number of numerical cues in an unchanging environment), models of man will perform *at least as well* as humans themselves. A composite judgment formed by combining all 43 judgments was almost as accurate as the *best* individual judge.[2] In general, the loan officers' predictions were more accurate and exhibited greater consensus than those of most judges previously studied.

Two independent studies conducted on different continents made almost identical extensions of Libby's (1975a, b) failure-prediction study. The results of all three studies are compared in Table A–1. Casey (1980) asked 48 experienced loan officers to evaluate financial ratio profiles representing 30 firms, half of which had failed within 3 to 5 years of the financial statement date. The cases were represented by six accounting ratios (Libby's five plus total liabilities/owner's equity) for three consecutive years (instead of one, to increase realism of the task). The environmental predictability of the cue set (based on the *original* sample) was 80%, 83.3%, and 73.3% for the third to fifth year before failure, respectively. A major difference between the two studies was that the subjects in the Casey study were not apprised of the highly unrealistic priors (50-50). While interrater agreement was high (80% on average), average accuracy of the individuals (56.7%) and accuracy of the composite judgment formed by averaging all the subjects' responses (60%) were not very high. The fact that, on average, 86.7% of the nonbankrupt firms and only 26.7% of the bankrupt firms were accurately predicted suggests that the use of inaccurate priors may have overpowered the validity of their cue combination rules. Consistent with the traditional financial analysis literature, highest subjective weights were placed on measures of leverage, liquidity, and profitability.

This issue of inaccurate priors was assessed in an independent yet

---

[2]The correlation between the mean judgment and the criterion must be at least as large as the average correlation of the responses and criterion.

surprisingly similar study by Zimmer (1980) of Australian bankers' ability to predict failure for Australian firms. The major difference between this study and Casey's was that Zimmer's subjects were told in advance that half of the firms had failed. Forty experienced Australian loan officers and a group of part-time third- and fourth-year financial accounting students evaluated 42 firms, one-half of which had failed within 3 years of the financial statement date. Judgments based on 3-year, five-ratio profiles were made on a fail-not fail scale and a three-point confidence scale. The five cues (earnings/total assets, quick assets/quick liabilities, dividends/earnings, debt/gross cash flow, and long term debt/equity) for 3 years predicted 88.1% of the cases based on the *original* sample and 83.3% based on the Lachenbruch cross-validation technique. Unlike Casey's bankers, the participants averaged 77% accuracy, and all but two produced greater than random accuracy. Like Libby (1976a), Zimmer found that subjects were more accurate for judgments in which they had greater confidence. Consensus and response linearity were also high (average 72% and 90%, respectively), and the composite judge outpredicted the average judge (86% to 77%) as expected. The results suggest that the differences between Libby's (1975b) and Casey's (1980) results are probably due to the question of specification of priors. Of additional interest is the fact that the part-time students' performance was very similar to that of the bankers. This result is consistent with Ashton and Kramer (1980).

TABLE A-1

Results of Bankruptcy Prediction Studies

Attributes	Libby %	Casey %	Zimmer %
Accuracy	74	56.7	77
Consensus	80	80	72
Linear predictability	88	*	90
Composite judgment	82	60	86

*Not reported.

One additional study of failure prediction is of particular interest. Abdel-khalik and El-Sheshai (1980) have taken a step toward separating the impact on achievement of information choice and its use. The literature reviewed above has evaluated the accuracy of human judgment by comparing three types of processors: (1) human processors (HP); (2) "models of man," where mathematical representations of the subjects (from the right side of the lens) replace the subjects themselves (MP$_s$); and (3) environmental or optimal mathematical models from the left side of the lens (MP_e). However, in all studies examined, either a small number of cues were preselected for the subjects (e.g., Libby, 1975a) or the selection from a larger set was left to the subject but not recorded by the experimenter (e.g., Ebert and Kruse, 1978). To disentangle these separate subprocesses, Abdel-khalik and El-Sheshai considered two potential selection techniques, human (HS) and mechanical (MS). By examining the validity of the six combinations of selection and processing, conclusions concerning the contribution of both subprocesses can be drawn.

In this initial study, four of the combinations are investigated. Twenty-eight commercial lenders evaluated 32 firms, one-half of which had defaulted on debt. Subjects first purchased up to four cues from a list of 18 ratios and trends (based on an explicit cost function), and then evaluated the 32 cases. The participants were then given the opportunity to purchase up to four more cues before being asked to evaluate the firms a second time. On average, 3.5 cues were purchased in the first round and an additional 1.5 in the second. The most frequently purchased items in the first round were earnings trend, current ratio, cash flow to total debt, and the trend in the last ratio. Even though additional cues were purchased, there was no difference in accuracy between the two evaluations. The average subject responses were highly predictable (84%). The average accuracy for the four information choice/use combinations were: HS/HP = 62.5%, HS/MP_s = 62.5%, HS/MP_e = 67.5%, and MS/MP_e = 90.6%. The fact that the change in *processing* strategies increased accuracy by only 5%, while switching from human to mechanical *selection* (given optimal processing) increased accuracy by 23.1%, suggests that the choice of cues is crucial while the weighting is of lesser consequence. This conclusion is consistent with that of Dawes and Corrigan (1974) and others. Although the complete six-celled matrix was not analyzed and is necessary to confirm these conclusions, this is the first study known to the author to directly test how well individuals choose cues.

Stock price prediction

Two studies of the linear predictability, consensus, and accuracy of students' predictions of stock prices made from accounting and market indicators are reported by Wright (1977, 1979a). In the first experiment, students predicted prices from five cues. Linear regression models were used to predict subjects' estimates of change in price and percentage price change. The linear models predicted the responses, averaging $\overline{R}_s$ = .70 and .67 for the two responses. Subject accuracy was $\overline{r}_a$ = .16 and .20 on the average for the two responses. Subjects exhibited accurate linear and nonlinear use of the information, as measured by the matching index (G) and the correlation between the nonlinear variance in the response and criterion (see Tucker, 1964). Little interjudge consensus was reported. Many subjects also tended to overprice low-priced stocks.

In his second experiment, Wright (1979a) modeled a different group of students' percentage price change decisions from four accounting and market-based cues. Similar analyses indicated similar results, with more advanced students outperforming their less educated counterparts. The incremental accuracy of the composite of all judges previously reported by Libby (1975b) was also in evidence.

Ebert and Kruse (1978) investigated whether security analysts' predictions of rate of return could be "bootstrapped." Bootstrapping occurs when linear models of the decision maker outperform the decision maker. Five security analysts estimated the 12-month rate of return on 35 securities (and 15 repeats) on the basis of 21 cues related to the economy, the industry, and the firm. Stepwise regression models of the analysts' judgments were built on the basis of five different random samples of 20 cases and validated on the remaining 15. Bootstrapping again was the norm (four of five judges). The linear models captured the judges' policies well, and consistency over time was high. Where the average achievement of the analysts, $\bar{r}_a$, was .23, the average model of man, $\bar{r}_m$, was .29.

MULTIPLE CUE PROBABILITY LEARNING

Studies of the effects of characteristics of the information set and task environment on judgmental achievement are becoming of increasing interest to accountants. Three of these issues have been addressed in accounting contexts: (1) the impact of changes in the algorithm used to produce cue values, (2) the effects of different types of feedback on learning, and (3) the impact of numerical cue presentation versus use of multidimensional graphics.

Impact of accounting changes

Ashton (1976) investigated whether judges learn to adjust cue-weighting rules when the algorithm used to produce the cue values is changed. The change in cue weighting was measured by comparing the ability of a regression model built from responses to an initial set of cases to predict later responses in two conditions: (1) where an accounting change had been made, and (2) where a change had *not* been made. Presumably, if subjects adjust their cue usage in response to an accounting change, the predictability of the model over time would be reduced. The experimental task involved the setting of product prices on the basis of three cues (elasticity of demand, competition, and unit cost). The accounting change was from variable- to full-cost data for unit cost. The change did result in a decline in predictability, as hypothesized. One of two moderating variables, whether the change increases or decreases the importance of the data, also had an effect. However, Libby (1976b) suggested numerous confounding variables which also could have decreased predictability.

Again, two very similar but independent replications of a prior study, in this case Ashton's (1976) study of functional fixation, were conducted at the same time on two continents. Swieringa, Dyckman, and Hoskin (1979) and Marchant (1979) investigated whether judges learn to change cue-weighting rules when the algorithm used to produce the cue values is changed. They modified Ashton's (1976) experiment in light of Libby's (1976b) suggestions. Swieringa, Dyckman, and Hoskin asked 228 undergraduate introductory accounting students to determine two sets of 30 selling prices based on Ashton's three cues (elasticity of demand, competition, and unit cost) in one of six conditions related to the change in the method used to compute the product cost cue (variable cost no change, full cost no change, and a 2 × 2 design: variable-to-full versus full-to-variable and two levels of information about the change). Three different measures of changes in decision rule were used: average difference scores, the numer of subjects identified by the Chow test as having changed decisions, and the F values from the Chow test. While the average difference scores indicated greater change than in the control groups, the other two scores were generally nonsignificant. Linear predictability of the subjects, as usual, was high ($\overline{R}_s^2 = .85$) .

In Marchant's (1979) study, 180 second- and third-year accounting students were asked to set selling prices for two sets of 15 products on the basis of Ashton's three cues. The subjects were split into the same six groups. Again, linear predictability of the responses was high ($\overline{R}_s^2 = .925$). The majority of subjects did not change their cue-weighting scheme according to the Chow test, and no between-group differences in F ratios from the test were significant. The small difference between the findings and those of Swieringa, Dyckman, and Hoskin (1979) may have been due to one or both of two causes: (1) the decreased power of the tests resulting from smaller case sample size, and (2) the fact that Swieringa, Dyckman, and Hoskin's less experienced subjects were still in a learning stage, which might make them more sensitive to the change.

Feedback methods

The effectiveness of various forms of feedback was investigated in three studies. The first is a particularly novel experiment. Harrell (1977) investigated the impact of two vehicles for management control: organizational policies and feedback given by immediate superiors. In the real world, these may or may not conflict with one another. In his research, Harrell recognized the parallel between these two motivational techniques and two forms of feedback that have been studied in the multiple cue probability learning literature: (1) task properties or policy feedback, where "optimal" or company policy weights for multiple cues are directly presented and, (2) outcome feedback, where the superior's actual preferred judgment in each case is presented as feedback. In the experiment, 75 Air Force officers evaluated the performance (on an eight-point scale) of 32 training wings (2^5 factorial) described by five dichotomous (satisfactory–unsatisfactory) cues (cost per pilot, quality of pilots graduated, highly competent all-volunteer force, compliance with regulations, and aircraft maintenance). Each of the 75 participants evaluated the 32 cases twice, both before and after receiving one of five different feedback combinations: (1) no feedback, (2) policy feedback only, (3) policy feedback and *consonant* outcome feedback, (4) policy feedback and *dissonant* outcome feedback, and (5) policy feedback and *random* outcome feedback. The participating Air Force officers turned in an excellent performance, indicating that they were highly skilled at learning from both types of feedback. Judgments of group 2 (policy only) were more like the policy than were judgments of group 1 (no feedback). Group 3 judgments (policy plus *consonant* outcome feedback) were even more like the policy than were the judgments of group 2. Group 4 judges (policy plus *dissonant* outcome feedback) appeared to ignore the policy and follow their superior's preferences. Group 5 participants (policy plus *random* outcome feedback) were able to discern the random nature of the outcome feedback and to ignore it, performing the same as group 2. While no subject followed the policies exactly, this would be expected as these experienced officers would have priors as to the appropriate responses, and all types of feedback would be considered in a sequential revision process which would be unlikely to result in ignoring the priors. These results conflict sharply with the results of psychological studies.

In addition, this research is of particular note because it is one of the initial efforts to investigate information-processing issues in managerial accounting. It is also one of the few such studies to go beyond an exploratory description of behavior to investigate a theory or set of hypotheses developed on the basis of prior research in the accounting and psychology literature. As in other studies, the repeated-measures ANOVA was used to develop the experimental cases. However, a between-groups experimental design was also used to test the hypotheses of interest.

Two additional studies investigated learning. They analyzed the effects of different types of feedback on the learning of environmental relationships. The general purpose of the studies was similar to that of Harrell (1977), but they did not directly address an accounting problem. Ashton (1981) expanded Ashton (1976) to examine the effects of two different types of feedback and three levels of environmental predictability (R_e) on the learning of an equal-weighting decision rule in the three-cue product pricing paradigm. Thirty-six undergraduate students, 56 first-year MBA students, and 46 doctoral consortium fellows set prices in the following procedure. First, 30 cases with predetermined prices were presented. This can be thought of as initial *outcome feedback*. Then each subject set prices for 30 new cases. One of two types of feedback (task properties indicating equal weights versus a general description of the cues) followed, after which 30 more cases with predetermined prices were presented. Finally, subjects set prices for an additional set of 30 products. The participants were assigned to one of three levels of environmental predictability (R_e = .01, .82, .98). The *linear predictability* of the subjects' responses (R_s) and the relationship between the subjects' model and the environmental model (G), called *matching*, were measured and compared between groups. Average R_s and G were .879 and .937, respectively, for the prefeedback cases. No difference was indicated between the pre- and postfeedback cases. Both G and R_s increased as the environmental predictability (R_e) increased. The Ph.D. candidates turned in the highest performance, and the type of additional feedback had no effect. The results suggest that the initial outcome feedback produced the significant learning. This finding is inconsistent with the psychological literature; however, it is open to question because (1) a control group receiving no form of feedback was not employed and (2) the default decision rule, equal weights, was optimal for the task. Lack of environmental predictability, which indicates the amount of "error" or randomness in the environment, was again shown to be a detriment to learning.

Kessler and Ashton (1981) analyzed the effectiveness of four types of feedback on the learning of a more realistic financial analysis task. Unlike much of the psychological research and Ashton's (1981) study, this analysis utilized a meaningful task where both theoretical and empirical relationships exist. Thirty-four bond issues with stable Moody's ratings from 1972 to 1975 were classified into the six rating categories on the basis of three ratio profiles (net operating income/sales, price/earnings, and long/term debt/total assets). Environmental predictability (R_e) based on the derivation sample was .74 and there was little intercue correlation. Each of the 69 participating first-year MBA students evaluated the same set of cases four times, three to four days apart, after receiving feedback in between. The subjects received one of four types of feedback: (1) summary hit rates, (2) univariate correlations between cases and subject responses plus summary hit rates, (3) univariate correlations between the cues and the actual event (task-properties feedback) plus summary hit rates, and (4) both types of correlations plus summary hit rates. While the first two types of feedback had no effect, the other two types resulted in an increase in achievement (r_a) and matching (G) in session 2, which leveled out in the later sessions. Predictability of subject responses remained high ($\overline{R}_s$ = .8 to .9) and unchanged through all four trials. A ceiling effect appeared to set in early, as subject achievement approached environmental predictability. The results concerning the effectiveness of task properties feedback are consistent with Harrell (1977) and the psychological literature. Note that the effectiveness of *outcome* feedback was not addressed in this study.

Data presentation

Questions concerning data presentation, though a natural concern for management accountants and information systems designers, have received little attention from researchers. Emphasis has been given to the simpler task of making marginal improvements in the accuracy or timeliness of data or in decision models which theoretically could be applied to the data. The final study discussed in this section is the first accounting study to address the important issue of the relationship of data presentation to prediction accuracy. Furthermore, it demonstrates the potential importance of this whole area to accountants in an original and humorous fashion.

Multidimensional graphics have been suggested as an aid to the human's ability to follow trends in related variables (such as financial statement data). In two experiments, Moriarity (1979) evaluated the use of multidimensional graphics in place of standard financial statement presentations. In the first, 277 introductory accounting students at Oklahoma predicted the failure of 22 discount retail firms (half of which had failed) on the basis of one of four presentations of 6-year data: (1) schematic faces with no explanation; (2) schematic faces with an explanation of what the features represented; (3) selected financial statement balances needed to calculate the Dun and Bradstreet key ratios; and (4) the key ratios themselves. The schematic faces were based on simple transformations; that is, one financial variable controlled the length of the nose, another the width, and so on. Financial variables were assigned to features on the basis of author's judgment of their importance. Average errors out of 22 were 7.3, 7.09, 7.49, and 8.62, respectively. The only significant difference was that the "key ratio" group was less accurate than the other three. However, response times were all significantly different, increasing with each of the four treatments in the order listed.

A second experiment compared the judgments of 20 practicing accountants based on the ratio and faces presentations. Each participant evaluated half of the firms on the basis of each presentation. The order was reversed for half of the subjects. The subjects judged an average of 6.5 cases incorrectly using the ratios and only 4.7 using the faces. The results using the faces also outpredicted Altman's (1968) mathematical model.

POLICY CAPTURING

Studies of the relative importance of different cues in the judgmental process account for over half of the accounting literature which uses regression-related approaches. These attempts to make explicit the mysteries and folklore of professional judgment are becoming increasingly popular as members of the accounting profession attempt to analyze their own judgmental performance. Studies of internal control evaluations and materiality judgments have tended to dominate this group, but other types of judgments have been analyzed in more recent research. Most of the studies have made use of ANOVA to build the algebraic models.

Portfolio selection

Two studies have used ANOVA to measure the present state of cue usage, decision rule form, and decision consistency and consensus of stockbrokers' judgments. Slovic (1969) and Slovic, Fleissner, and Bauman (1972) examined stockbrokers' judgments of the likelihood that the price of a company's stock would increase. In the Slovic (1969) research, two young stockbrokers analyzed a set of 128 hypothetical companies represented by 11 dichotomous financial factors normally available in Standard and Poor's reference reports, including market-derived and accounting information. The cue combinations were constructed according to a 1/16 fractional replication of a 2^{11} factorial ANOVA design. Each case was evaluated on a nine-point "recommendation to buy" scale. Agreement between brokers, as measured by the correlation between their judgments, was only .32. The linear additive components (main effects) accounted for 71.7% and 79.9% of the total response variance of the two subjects, and interactions accounted for only 7% and 5% of total response variance.

A substantial replication of the Slovic (1969) experiment was performed by Slovic, Fleissner, and Bauman (1972). Thirteen stockbrokers and five MBA students participated in the study. The number of dichotomous financial factors presented was reduced to eight, and 64 cases were constructed using a ¼ fractional replication of a 2^8 factorial ANOVA design. Evaluations were made on a nine-point capital appreciation scale with a time horizon of 6 to 18 months. There was very little consensus between brokers. Agreement was higher between the students than between the brokers. The weights attributed to the cues computed from the linear model revealed substantial individual differences. Main effects accounted for 50% of broker 2's and 70% of broker 10's response variance. Interactions accounted for 0% and 13% of the two brokers' response variance, respectively. Subjects' estimates of their cue usage bore little relation to the weights in the linear models measured by ω^2. On the average, the earnings-per-share trend was the most important variable in the cue-weighting schemes of both groups of subjects.

Internal control evaluation

Ashton's (1974a) study, which was discussed in Chapter 2, used ANOVA to assess cue usage, decision rule form, subjective cue usage, and the decision consistency and consensus of auditor's judgments of internal control. In this study, 63 practicing auditors from four firms of various sizes judged the strength of a payroll internal control subsystem on a six-point scale. Thirty-two cases represented by six dichotomous indicators of internal control were presented to each subject. The cases were constructed using a ½ fractional replication of a 2^6 factorial design. A second administration of the experiment followed 6 to 13 weeks later. The auditors' judgments were highly consistent over the period between the two administrations, averaging $r = .81$. There was also considerable agreement or consensus among the auditors. The average correlation between pairs of auditors' judgments was .70. Main effects accounted for over 80% of judgmental variance on the average. Few interactions were found, indicating that the internal control factors did not interact in their effects on perceived quality of internal control. Two-thirds of the subjects made significant use of at least five of the six factors. The two most important factors in the subjects' decision models dealt with separation of duties. The auditors also had an extraordinarily high level of self-insight into cue usage.

In an attempt to reconcile Ashton's (1974a) findings of high degrees of consensus between auditors in internal control judgments with other researchers' reports of lack of consensus in sample selection behavior, Joyce (1976) studied auditors' consistency, consensus, cue usage, subjective cue usage, and decision rule form in audit program planning. Thirty-five practicing auditors evaluated either 20 or 36 cases (including four repeat cases) by indicating how many hours would be allocated to five categories of audit work related to accounts receivable. The cases differed on three dichotomously defined internal control variables and two related accounting ratios, and were constructed on the basis of a ½ replication of a 2^5 factorial design and a full replication of the same factorial design in the experiments. The complete design was included to allow tests for interactions. ANOVA and MANOVA were used to model the subjects.

Joyce hypothesized substantially lower interrater reliability than that reported by Ashton (1974a) as a result of similar judgments of internal control quality being combined with dissimilar utilities for different types of audit work. Interrater reliability was much lower when measured by the combined number of hours of audit work assigned to the cases, averaging only $r = .37$. The mean for test-retest reliability was .86, with a median of .98. Similar studies in other contexts report lower test-retest reliability.

In the models, the linear additive components or main effects accounted on the average for 74.7% of the reliable judgment variance, while interactions accounted for 3.3%. However, two judges heavily weighted interactive components. As in Ashton's study, separation of functions was the most important variable in determining judgment. The MANOVA results suggested that some subjects followed simplifying heuristics in allocating time to categories, including keeping some items constant and applying constant ratios of time to two or more categories. The auditors overestimated the importance of minor cues and underestimated the importance of major cues. This finding is consistent with the majority of previous research. All findings were similar to Ashton's, except for the hypothesized difference in consensus and lower self-insight into decision rules.

Three studies substantially replicated Ashton (1974a). Major issues addressed were experience effects and the generality of results. Hamilton and Wright (1977) made minor modifications in the Ashton paradigm to investigate the impact of different experience levels on internal control judgment. Seventeen practicing auditors of varying levels of experience from a single office of a national CPA firm each evaluated a set of 32 payroll internal control cases on Ashton's six-point scale. The cases were formed by a completely-crossed factorial design combining five dichotomously-scaled internal control factors (cues). The authors omitted two of Ashton's six cues and split his two separation-of-duties factors into three. Results substantially mirrored Ashton's. There was considerable consensus ($\bar{r} = .66$, Spearman); however, subjects with more than 3 years of experience exhibited consistently greater consensus. A simple main effects regression accounted on average for 79% of the variance in subject responses, and cue weights again indicated the primacy of separation of duties in these evaluations. Self- insight into their judgmental policies, as measured by the correlation between their subjective weights and those of the regression models, was also very high. No differences based on experience were in evidence for these latter variables.

Ashton and Kramer (1980) and Ashton and Brown (1980) also replicated Ashton (1974a). Ashton and Kramer (1980) compared the judgments of students and auditors in the same task. They hypothesized differences based on age, experience, and wealth. Thirty undergraduate student volunteers completed a single replication of Ashton's (1974a) payroll internal control instrument (six cues in a 2^6, ½ fractional replication design). The students were less predictable (74% versus 86.6%), placed less emphasis on separation of duties (36.9% versus 51.4%), and had less self-insight than the auditors. The results were consistent with the direction of the nonsignificant differences found by Hamilton and Wright (1977). However, the differences may all have been caused by decreased test-retest reliability, which was not measured in the study.

Ashton and Brown (1980) modified Ashton's instrument to include two additional cues in hopes of making the task more complex and thus more realistic. In this study, 31 auditors (most with 1 to 3 years of experience) evaluated 128 cases produced by a ½ replication of a 2^8 design plus 32 repeat cases. The two additional cues related to the rotation of duties and the use of background inquiries for new employees. The order of cue presentation was also varied. Again, the results were almost identical to Ashton (1974a). Main effects accounted for 71.3% of the variance, while interaction effects were small. Separation of duties was by far the most important factor, but the rotation-of-duties cue was given little weight. Self-insight and consistency over time were again high ($\bar{r}$ = .86 and .91, respectively), and cue order made no significant difference. They concluded that the added complexity of the task had no effect.

In addition to the preceding three replications, Mock and Turner (1979) attempted to substantially modify the Ashton paradigm by making it more representative of real-world internal control evaluations. In this study they investigated the effects of *changes* in internal control and differences in guidance on sample-size judgments for four audit tests. This multivariate audit work allocation judgment is similar to that used by Joyce (1976). Within the context of an extremely thorough set of background data, the authors manipulated the size of the change (weak to fair and weak to strong) and the level of detail in the instructions related to internal control. Unlike most studies in this area, a repeated measures design was not used. Each of the 71 seniors and 2 supervisors from the participating "Big 8" firm evaluated only one case. This resulted in confounding the effects of changes in the different individual internal control cues (note that this was purposefully done). Furthermore, the manager's recommendation as to reliance on internal control was also confounded with the actual changes in control. This leaves open the possibility that the manager's recommendation, and not the change in control, caused the behavior. The degree-of-change variable was significant for all four procedures, including the procedure which was seemingly unrelated to the change (though probably interrelated with the other items in real life). The level of guidance concerning reaction to the change had no effect, suggesting that the participants were already aware of the firm's guidelines. A number of demographic variables were also unrelated to the responses. Note that most of the findings in all four of these studies are very similar to those of Ashton (1974a) and Joyce (1976).

Materiality judgments

Boatsman and Robertson (1974) used discriminant analysis to model the materiality judgments of 18 CPAs and 15 security analysts and to measure and compare their cue usage. On the basis of simulated values of eight factors whose interrelationships matched the environment, each subject classified 30 cases into three disclosure categories: none, footnote, line item. An aggregate discriminant analysis model was built. The model predicted 63% of the three category classifications and 84% of all disclose-no disclose decisions. The percentage-of-net-income factor accounted for 73% of the predictive power of the model. Whether or not the item of interest was a gain or loss on disposal of fixed assets, as opposed to an accounting change or an uncertainty, accounted for 24% of predictive power. Individual differences existed, but their degree could not be accurately assessed as no interrater reliability statistics were reported. In addition, no difference was found between the two groups of subjects in cue usage. However, the lack of power of the statistical tests caused by small sample size may have produced this result.

Hofstedt and Hughes (1977) studied factors affecting the disclosure decision in an experiment where 19 students acting as auditors evaluated losses from the write-off of an unconsolidated subsidiary in terms of its probability of disclosure on a scale of 0 to 100. Three materiality factors were varied systematically in a $3 \times 3 \times 3$ factorial design. The size of the loss relative to operating income was more important than the size relative to total investments in unconsolidated subsidiaries or to the book value of the subsidiary being written off. One interaction was significant for nine subjects. However, addition of this interaction only increased average linear predictability from $\overline{R}^2 = .70$ to .73. Significant individual differences were noted in cue usage. The same self-insight biases noted in Joyce (1976) were reported.

Two studies by Moriarity and Barron (1976, 1979) attempted to illustrate the use of conjoint measurement techniques (see, e.g., Green and Wind, 1973) to extend the earlier study by Boatsman and Robertson (1974) of auditors' materiality judgments. Conjoint measurement techniques first categorize *ordinal* judgments by decision rule form (e.g., additive, multiplicative, distributive) and then determine cue weights (usually called part worths). In practice, results normally are close to the ANOVA model, which analyzes *interval* judgments and assumes an additive or combination additive-multiplicative model. In the first (1976) study, 15 partners from eight large CPA firms *ranked* 18 cases formed by a $3 \times 3 \times 2$ factorial ANOVA design according to materiality of an error in estimate of depreciable life causing a decrease in earnings of $500,000. The cases were represented by financial statements, and the net income earnings trend and asset size were varied. Eleven of the subjects were classified as additive or nearly additive, and the remaining four appeared to use a number of cues interactively. This finding is consistent with the computationally simpler ANOVA studies. As in all prior studies, the net income effect was by far the most important. Moriarity and Barron also point out a number of problems faced in using the technique, including the large number of cue values necessary to accurately determine functional form, failure to use cross-validated measures of model fit, and the assumption of error-free data. It appears as though, *in practice,* the conjoint measurement approach does not provide benefits over the simpler ANOVA approach, which is in much greater favor among decision researchers.

This was made even more clear in the second study, which assumed an additive model (like the main effects ANOVA model). An attempt was made to determine the size of the effect and the shape of the function of five cues in *overall preaudit materiality* judgments. In the study, no background information was presented to the subjects, and the judgment of interest, overall preaudit materiality, was left undefined (as it is in the auditing literature). Five audit partners from one firm completed the 30 experimental cases. Each indicated varying degrees of unfamiliarity with the task. When combined with questions concerning the cue levels chosen and subject heterogeneity, these problems severely limit the interpretability of the data. However, it is interesting to note that the income effect was again strongest.

Litigation risks

Two studies used the ANOVA methodology in new contexts. Schultz and Gustavson (1978) studied the factors that contribute to the risk of litigation against CPAs. Because of the shortage of empirical data, the authors turned to the expert judge for insight. They studied the cue usage, consensus, and self-insight of five actuaries representing five of the six U.S. insurers of accounting firms. Each actuary judged 36 cases formed by a 2^5 factorial design plus four repeat cases. The five dichotomous cues included the number of accountants in the firm, the percentage of "write-up work" performed, the rotation of accountants among clients, the size of clients, and the financial condition of clients. These cases were presented in the context of extensive background information concerning the firm, its practice, and the other terms of the insurance. Judgments were made on a nine-point "probability of a valid claim" scale. Consensus among the five actuaries was surprisingly poor. Mean interrater reliability ($\bar{r}$) was only .12. More striking is the fact that all five could agree only on the more risky level of *one* cue—client condition. On the other hand, the responses were highly predictable, and the subjects exhibited a high degree of insight into their cue weightings.

Internal audit competence

In the second new application, Gibbs and Schroeder (1979) studied the relative importance of various factors to the expert evaluation of the competence of an internal audit staff and the consensus of their judgments. The major contribution of the study is a detailed list of 54 criteria developed from an extensive survey. In the experiment reported, 146 partners and managers judged 32 cases, formed from a 2^5 factorial design, on a four-point competence scale. The cues which varied across cases were continuing education, educational background, knowledge of company operations, knowledge of new trends and techniques in auditing, and the amount of supervision. The third and fifth cue were most important on average. Unlike most such studies, only a group model (as opposed to individual models) was constructed. The high proportion of group variance accounted for (68.5%) indicates substantial agreement across participants. However, the conceptualization of the judgment as having three independent parts, the use of only 5 cues where 54 had been identified, and the presentation of cues as uncorrelated when they are likely to be correlated in the world (e.g., continuing education and knowledge of new trends and techniques in auditing) cast doubt on many of the conclusions of the study.

Uncertainty disclosures

Libby (1979b) tested a set of hypotheses concerning the effect of uncertainty disclosure and the incremental effect of the auditor's qualification on lending decisions. These hypotheses were based on the findings of Libby's (1979a) study (discussed in Chapter 2) of the message communicated by different audit reports. While the earlier study indicated that the uncertainty qualification increased perceived risk and motivated the search for additional information about the uncertainty, it made no attempt to separate the effect of the uncertainty disclosure from that of the auditor's qualification. Thirty-four commercial loan officers from four money center banks participated in the study. On the basis of extensive background data and case-specific information, they evaluated a $2 million term loan request from a medium-sized, family-owned paperboard fabricating company. While ANOVA was used as the method of case construction, a number of modifications were made to achieve a more representative design. First, four basic cases were formed by combining two levels of financial statements and verbal management evaluations. The financial statements were constructed to mirror the 75th and 25th percentile statistics reported in *RMA Annual Statement Studies*. These four cases were then combined with uncertainty disclosure-supplemental data combinations. Consultation with the participating banks suggested that the litigation disclosure was *always* followed by a supplemental in-house investigation. In light of this, three initial levels were chosen: (1) no disclosure, (2) disclosure combined with a supplemental report predicting a positive outcome, and (3) disclosure with a supplemental report predicting a negative outcome. Although this design results in confounding the effects of the disclosure and the supplemental report, it was thought necessary to accurately portray the environment. The basic 12 cases were formed by combining the two financial statements, the two management evaluations, and the three uncertainty conditions. The subjects were split into two groups, depending on the type of audit report issued when an uncertainty was disclosed (unqualified or "subject to" qualification). In a departure from prior studies, this factor was made a *between-subjects* factor to mask the principal purpose of the study, the test of the audit report variable. The resulting lack of relationship between the audit report and the supplemental in-house report was thought to be realistic, given the lack of agreement on disclosure decisions discovered in prior research. The subjects evaluated their 12 cases by indicating whether they would recommend the loan and what interest premium they believed would be charged for such a loan. While the uncertainty disclosure-supplemental report variable had a large significant effect on their judgments, the type of audit report seemed to have no effect. Furthermore, the subjects appeared to estimate the expected outcome of the uncertainty and treat it as certain. These initial conclusions were based on the assumption that the loan officers would *not* change their information search behavior as a function of the form of the audit report—an assumption in need of further research. In addition, other levels of supplemental information should be studied.

Accounting policy preferences

Libby's (1979a) study using multidimensional scaling to uncover cue usage in the evaluation of different types of audit reports was described earlier. The other two studies employing MDS attempted to model the accounting policy preferences of major participants in the policy-making process. Rockness and Nikolai (1977) analyzed APB voting patterns in a search for similarities associated with affiliation and possible client pressures. They compiled the voting records of all members and transformed them into similarity measures between each pair of members. The three-dimensional solutions computed using the ALSCAL algorithm suggested few systematic patterns, except what appeared to be a conceptual-pragmatic dimension with academics and a few similarly inclined practitioners on the conceptual side and a compromise and pragmatic group on the other. Over time, placement of firm representatives in the patterns shifted quite drastically. No groupings based on "Big 8" affiliation or other obvious patterns emerged.

Brown (1981) performed a significantly more detailed analysis of the accounting policy preferences of respondents to FASB discussion memoranda. He identified nine major issues resulting in standards, and 27 respondents (including mainly the sponsoring organizations of the FASB, large CPA firms, and large industrial companies) who commented on seven or more of the issues. The FASB position was also used to generate a hypothetical respondent. From the discussion memoranda, 51 individual policy questions were derived and similarity measures based on answers to these questions were computed for each pair of respondents. The ALSCAL method was used to generate an overall two-dimensional map. The sponsoring organizations of the FASB (AICPA, FEI, AAA, NAA, and FAF) were spread to all four corners of the map. There appeared to be a strong separation between the preparer and attestor respondents. Only one cluster, which included four of the "Big 8" firms and the New York Society of CPAs, was evident. Not only did the FASB not side with the "Big 8" firms, as has been alleged in Congress, but the FASB often took an outlier position, highly similar only to the position of the Financial Analysts Federation. This suggests that the FASB pays more than lip service to a user orientation. Furthermore, when individual issue maps were produced, they indicated major changes in coalition from issue to issue.

TABLE A-2

Summary of Lens Model Studies in Accounting Contexts

Study	Type of Decision Maker	Task	Modeling Technique	Variables of Interest	Results
Libby (1975a)	43 commercial loan officers	Classify 5 ratio profiles into fail or not-fail	Discriminant analysis, 60 real cases	Decision rule form (IIB1) Predictability (IIIA5) Stability (IIB3)	Highly linear High (88%) Stable over 1 week and response thresholds
Libby (1975b)	43 commercial loan officers	Classify 5 ratio profiles into fail or not-fail	Discriminant analysis, 60 real cases	Accuracy (IIIA1) Consistency (IIIA3a) Consensus (IIIA3b) Composite judge (IIA2)	High (74%) High (89%) High (80%) More accurate than average judge
Casey (1980)	46 loan officers	Classify 6 ratio profiles for a 3-year period into fail or not-fail (not told priors)	Discriminant analysis, 30 real cases	Decision rule form (IIB1) Accuracy (IIIA1) Consensus (IIIA3b) Composite judge (IIA2)	Highly linear 56.7% versus Libby (1975) 74% 80% versus Libby (1975) 80% 60% versus Libby (1975) 82%
Zimmer (1980)	40 Loan officers and part-time accounting students	Classify 5 ratio profiles for a 3-year period into fail or not-fail (told priors)	Discriminant analysis, 42 real cases	Decision rule form (IIB1) Accuracy (IIIA1) Predictability (IIIA5) Composite judge (IIA2) Consensus (IIIA3b)	Highly linear 77% versus Libby 74% 90% versus Libby 88% 86% versus Libby 82% 72% versus Libby 80%
Abdel-khalik and El-Sheshai (1980)	28 commercial lending officers	To purchase up to a maximum of 8 cues with which to discriminate between firms that	Discriminant analysis, 32 real cases	Human-mechanical (IIIA1) Accuracy (IIIA1)	A change in processing strategies increased accuracy by 5%; a change in selection strategies increased

TABLE A-2 *(continued)*

Summary of Lens Model Studies in Accounting Contexts

		failed or did not fail		Cue usage (IIB2)	accuracy by 23.1% On average 3.5 cues purchased in first round and 1.5 cues in second; most frequently purchased were earnings trend, current ratio, and cash flow to total debt; cues added in 2nd round made no difference in accuracy
				Predictability (IIIA5)	High 84%
Wright (1977)	39 2nd-year MBA students	Predict Δ in stock price and %Δ in stock price from 5 accounting and market indicators	Regression, 60 real cases	Decision rule form (IIB1)	Partly nonlinear
				Predictability (IIIA5)	High ($\bar{R}$ = .7 and .67)
				Consensus (IIIA3b)	Low
				Accuracy (IIIA1)	Low ($\bar{r}$ = .16 and .2)
Wright (1979a)	35 1st-year and 12 2nd-year MBA students	Predict %Δ in stock price from 4 accounting and market cues	Regression, 60 real cases	Decision rule form (IIB1)	Partly nonlinear
				Predictability (IIIA5)	Medium ($\bar{R}$ = .53 and .62)
				Consensus (IIIA3b)	Low ($\bar{r}$ = .38 and .54)
				Accuracy (IIIA1)	Low ($\bar{r}$ = .2 and .31)
				Composite judge (IIA2)	More accurate than average judge; 2nd-year students more predictable, accurate, and consensual
				Prior experience (IIA4a)	
Ebert and Kruse (1978)	5 security analysts	To estimate the returns of 35 securities on the basis of 22 information cues plus 15 repeat cases	Regression	Model of man (IIA1)	Average model of man outperformed average man
				Composite judge (IIA2)	More accurate than 4 of the 5 analysts
				Consistency (IIIA3a)	High

TABLE A-2 *(continued)*

Summary of Lens Model Studies in Accounting Contexts

Study	Type of Decision Maker	Task	Modeling Technique	Variables of Interest	Results
Ashton (1976)	106 1st-year MBA students	Set product prices from 3 cues	Regression, 60 simulated cases	Information about cue attributes (IE2c) Uniformity over cases (IE3d) Stability (IIB3)	No effect for amount of information about cue attributes but increase in importance had greater effect; change reduced predictability; % of average difference between model and man, 20.95% for those receiving change and 5.59% for no change
Swieringa et al. (1979)	228 introductory accounting students	Set product prices from 3 cues	Regression, 60 simulated cases	Information about cue attributes (IE2c) Uniformity over cases (IE3d) Stability (IIB3) Predictability (IIIA5)	No effect for amount of information about cue attributes Chow test indicated that there was no significant change in decision rule after change in the accounting method $\overline{R}_s^2 = .85$
Marchant (1979)	180 undergraduate accounting students	Set product prices from 3 cues	Regression, 30 simulated cases	Information about cue attributes (IE2c) Uniformity over cases (IE3d) Stability (IIB3) Predictability (IIIA5)	No effect for amount of information about cue attributes Change in accounting method had no effect on the decision rules of a majority of subjects $\overline{R}_s^2 = .925$
Harrell (1977)	75 Air Force officers	Evaluate the performance of 32 training wings	ANOVA (2^5 factorial)	Feedback (IE4)	Task-properties feedback and outcome feedback were highly effective

Summary of Lens Model Studies in Accounting Contexts

		represented by 5 dichotomous cues before and after receiving one of five different feedback combinations			
Ashton (1981)	36 undergraduate students, 56 MBA students, and 46 consortium fellows	To estimate product prices based on 3 cues, with varying feedback on task and accuracy	Feedback (IE4) Information content (IC)	Regression, 60 simulated cases	Initial outcome feedback effective, supplemental task-properties feedback no effect Both G and R_s increased as R_e increased
Kessler and Ashton (1981)	69 MBA students	To classify bonds into 6 rating categories based on 3 ratio profiles	Feedback (IE4) Accuracy (IIIA1) Predictability (IIIA5)	Regression, 34 real cases	Two treatments, (1) univariate correlations between the cues and actual event and summary hit rates, (2) univariate correlations between cases and subject responses; univariate correlations between cues and actual event and summary hit rates, increased achievement and matching in session 2, then leveled out; the other 2 types had no effect; no effect on predictability
Moriarity (1979)	A. 277 introductory accounting students	A. To predict the failure of 22 discount retail firms, half of which had failed, based	Format (ID1) Accuracy (IIIA1)		Subjects were more accurate using the schematic faces as opposed to financial balances or ratios

TABLE A-2 *(continued)*

Summary of Lens Model Studies in Accounting Contexts

Study	Type of Decision Maker	Task	Modeling Technique	Variables of Interest	Results
	B. 20 practicing accountants	on 4 presentations of data B. To predict the failure of 11 discount retail firms		Information about cue attributes (IE2c) Speed (IIIA2)	Explanations had no effect Faces produced faster responses
Slovic (1969)	2 young stockbrokers	Recommendation of stocks from 11 pieces of market and accounting data on 9-point scale	ANOVA (1/16 fractional)	Decision rule form (IIB1) Predictability (IIIA5) Consensus (IIIA3b)	Highly linear High (82% of variance) Low ($\bar{r}$ = .32)
Slovic et al. (1972)	13 stockbrokers, 5 MBA students	Estimation of capital appreciation from 8 of above 11 cues on 9-point scale	ANOVA (¼ fractional)	Decision rule form (IIB1) Predictability (IIIA5) Cue usage (IIB2) Consensus (IIIA3b) Prior experience (IIA4a) Subjective cue usage (IIIB1)	Highly linear High EPS trend most important Low Students greater self-insight and consensus and emphasized accounting data more Low self-insight and overestimate less important cues
Ashton (1974a, b)	63 auditors	Rate payroll internal control from 6 cues on 6-point scale	ANOVA (½ fractional)	Decision rule form (IIB1) Predictability (IIIA5) Cue usage (IIB2) Consistency (IIIA3a) Consensus (IIIA3b)	Highly linear High (86.4% of variance) Separation of duties most important High ($\bar{r}$ = .81) High ($\bar{r}$ = .7)

TABLE A-2 *(continued)*

Summary of Lens Model Studies in Accounting Contexts

Study	Subjects	Task	Method	Subjective cue usage (IIIB1)	High self-insight ($\bar{r} = .89$)
Joyce (1976)	35 auditors	Plan hours of 5 categories of audit work from 5 internal control and related accounting cues	ANOVA (½ fractional and complete) MANOVA	Decision rule form (IIB1) Predictability (IIIA5) Cue usage (IIB2) Consistency (IIIA3a) Consensus (IIIA3b) Subjective cue usage (IIIB1)	Highly linear High (78%) Separation of duties most important High ($\bar{r} = .863$) Low ($\bar{r} = .37$) Low self-insight and overestimate less important cues
Hamilton and Wright (1977)	17 auditors	Rate payroll internal control from 5 cues' on a 6-point scale	ANOVA (2^5 factorial)	Decision rule form (IIB1) Cue usage (IIB2) Consensus (IIIA3b) Subjective cue usage (IIIB1) Prior experience (IIA4a)	Highly linear Separation of duties most important High ($\bar{r} = .66$) High self-insight No effect
Ashton and Kramer (1980)	30 undergraduate auditing students	Rate payroll internal control from 6 cues on a 6-point scale	ANOVA (½ fractional)	Prior experience (IIA4b) Decision rule form (IIB1) Predictability (IIIA5) Cue usage (IIB2)	Suggested that differences with Ashton (1974a,b) due to these characteristics of subjects Highly linear Lower than Ashton (1974a,b) (74% versus 86.6%) Separation of duties highest but less important (36.9% versus 51.4%)

TABLE A-2 (continued)

Summary of Lens Model Studies in Accounting Contexts

Study	Type of Decision Maker	Task	Modeling Technique	Variables of Interest	Results
				Subjective Cue Usage (IIIB1)	Less self-insight than auditors (.77 versus .89)
Ashton and Brown (1980)	31 auditors	Rate payroll internal control from 8 cues on a 6-point scale	ANOVA (½ fractional) plus 32 repeats	Decision rule from (IB1)	Highly linear
				Predictability (IIIA5)	High (71.3% of the variance)
				Cue usage (IIB2)	Separation of duties most important, rotation of duties least important
				Consistency (IIIA3a)	High ($\bar{r} = .91$)
				Consensus (IIIA3b)	High ($\bar{r} = .67$)
				Subjective cue usage (IIIB1)	High self-insight ($\bar{r} = .86$)
				Sequence of cues (ID2)	Different sequences had no effect
				Number of cues (IB1)	2 additional cues had little effect
Mock and Turner (1979)	71 seniors and 2 supervisors	Adjust planned sample size for 4 specific auditing procedures based on improvement in internal controls from extremely thorough case materials	ANOVA	Cue usage (IIB2)	Change in control had significant effect
				Instructions (IE2)	Specificity had no effect
				Consensus (IIIA3b)	Low: sample sizes for "strong" controls varied less than for "fair" controls
Boatsman and Robertson (1974)	18 auditors, 15 analysts	Classify into 3 disclosure categories based upon 8 factors	Discriminant analysis, 30 simulated cases with realistic statistical properties	Decision rule form (IIB1)	Highly linear
				Predictability (IIIA5)	High (63%)
				Cue usage (IIB2)	% of net income effect strongest, type of item important

TABLE A-2 (*continued*)

Summary of Lens Model Studies in Accounting Contexts

Hofstedt and Hughes (1977)	19 MBA students acting as auditors	Probability of disclosure of loss from 3 materiality factors on 100-point scale	ANOVA (factorial)	Prior experience (IIA4a) Decision rule form (IIB1) Predictability (IIIA5) Cue usage (IIB2) Consensus (IIIA3b)	No difference between groups Highly linear High (74% of variance) Relative income effect most important Low
Moriarity and Barron (1976)	15 audit partners	Ranking materiality of error in estimate of depreciable life	ANOVA (factorial)	Decision rule form (IIB1) Cue usage (IIB2)	11 subjects classified as additive or nearly additive; 4 subjects classified as configural Net income most important
Moriarity and Barron (1979)	5 audit partners	Estimation of preaudit materiality based on five financial variables	Conjoint analysis	Consensus (IIIA3b) Cue usage (IIB2)	Low Income effect was the strongest
Schultz and Gustavson (1978)	5 actuaries	To assess risk of litigation against CPA firms from 5 cues (characteristics of practice and clients)	ANOVA (factorial) + 4 repeats	Cue usage (IIB2) Consensus (IIIA3b) Subjective cue usage (IIIB1)	All cue weights were significant Low ($\bar{r} = .12$) High self-insight
Gibbs and Schroeder (1979)	146 partners and managers from "Big 8" accounting firms	Evaluate the competence of an internal audit staff as required by S.A.S. No. 9	ANOVA (factorial)	Cue usage (IIB2) Consensus (IIIA3b)	Knowledge of company operations and techniques in auditing were the most important cues High

TABLE A-2 (continued)

Summary of Lens Model Studies in Accounting Contexts

Study	Type of Decision Maker	Task	Modeling Technique	Variables of Interest	Results
Libby (1979b)	34 commercial loan officers from 4 money center banks	To evaluate a $2 million term loan request from a medium-sized company with varying degrees of uncertainty disclosure	ANOVA (factorial)	Cue usage (IIB2)	Uncertainty disclosure, supplemental report was significant, whereas type of audit report had no effect
				Heuristics (IIB4)	Subjects appeared to estimate the most likely outcome of the uncertainty and then treat it as certain
•Libby (1979a)	30 "Big 8" audit partners and 28 "money center" commercial lenders	Perception of messages communicated by different audit reports	MDS (INDSCAL) experimental data	Experience (IIA4a) Perception of characteristics of information set (IIIB3)	Perceptions of auditors and lenders appeared to be the same
				Cue usage (IIB2)	Two dimensions were identified and described as "need for additional information" and "amount of audit judgment required"
Rockness and Nikolai (1977)	Members of APB	Make accounting policy choices	MDS (ALSCAL) actual data	Personal characteristics (IIA3) Prior experience (IIA4a) Consensus (IIIA3b)	Three-dimensional solution suggested few systematic patterns except on a pragmatic-conceptual dimension
Brown (1980)	27 respondents representing sponsoring organizations of FASB, large CPA firms, and large industrial companies	Assessment of 51 policy issues to determine policy preference of respondents to FASB discussion memoranda	MDS (ALSCAL) actual data	Prior experience (IIA4a) Consensus (IIIA3b)	Strong separation between preparer and attestor respondents; only one cluster was evident; there were major changes in coalitions from issue to issue; FASB not dominated by sponsors

APPENDIX B

Accounting Studies
of Probabilistic Judgment [1]

The idea of using normative decision theory in auditing (Ward, 1976; Kinney, 1975), management control (Dyckman, 1969), and information system selection (Demski, 1972) has prompted a considerable volume of accounting research into the human processing of probabilistic information. This literature is reviewed in detail in this Appendix. Most models suggested for the accountant's use involve selection of an action which will maximize the decision maker's expected utility under circumstances in which the payoff or consequence to the decision maker is conditioned upon her or his action choice and the occurrence of some state of nature. Such models conceptually require the decision maker to (1) specify all possible states of nature and feasible alternative actions, (2) define the payoffs or consequences and assign utility measures to them, (3) evaluate information and form a subjective probability distribution over the possible states, and (4) choose the optimal action. The decision maker is assumed to be an expected utility maximizer and a Bayesian processor of information. Although these models are conceptualized as sequential, in practice we may be able to observe only the final action

[1]This Appendix is based largely on Libby and Lewis (1977, 1982), with permission of *Accounting, Organizations and Society* and Pergamon Press. The author would like to thank Barry Lewis who contributed most of the material in this apendix.

choice. To avoid the apparent confounding problems, most research in this area has attempted to separately study specific components of the models. Probability estimation has received by far the most attention.

The research reviewed in this Appendix is classified into four categories. Studies in the first section use Bayes's theorem as a criterion for evaluating intuitive judgments made from accounting information. The second section deals with the choice of techniques used to elicit subjective probabilities. The third section reviews studies of the role of heuristics and biases in accounting contexts. The final section includes studies of the ability of decision makers to perform the role of information evaluators, as well as those that use the expected utility framework in a purely descriptive fashion. This research is summarized at the end of the Appendix in Table B–1 which is keyed to the information processing variables listed in Figure 1–3.

INTUITIVE JUDGMENT AND THE BAYESIAN MODEL

Early accounting studies of probabilistic judgment used the Bayesian model as a criterion against which to compare human performance. Three accounting issues which were investigated included data aggregation, the impact of dual versus single information systems, and the accuracy of business-failure predictions.

Data aggregation

In the Barefield (1972) study the findings from the Bayesian literature were used to formulate the hypothesis that subjects would perform better with aggregated data than with the sequential presentation of disaggregated data. The hypothesis was constructed on the basis of prior psychological research studying the effect on conservatism of sequential presentation and of the number of data items. Barefield found no overall significant effect of aggregation, but did note that subjects using disaggregated data were slightly less able to discern the optimal criterion (as determined by statistical decision theory), but were more consistent in applying their actual criteria than those subjects using the aggregated data.

Dual information systems

Dickhaut (1973) used the average absolute difference between subjects' probability estimates and the Bayesian probability estimate as the dependent measure in an experiment designed to consider the possible disadvantage of resolving the problem of choosing between alternative information systems by presenting both alternatives. At the same time, several variables that could affect the subjects' probability estimates were systematically manipulated. In the experiment, subjects estimated the probability that an object was a member of one of two mutually exclusive subsets. Estimates were based on a message which an information system associated with that object.

The experimenter manipulated the number of information systems, the setting, and the type of subjects. Drawing from the literature on the concept of information reduction, Dickhaut hypothesized that subjects would perform better with a single information system than with a joint information system, because the latter system requires a greater amount of information reduction and hence represents a more difficult task. Dickhaut also reviewed research dealing with the effect of task familiarity on performance and research examining the interaction of age and the ability to handle abstract concepts. As a result, Dickhaut hypothesized that undergraduate students would perform better in an abstract setting dealing with cubes and algebraic identities and that older businessmen would perform better in a business setting dealing with profits and stock market changes. The results indicated (1) that the single information system did produce higher performance, but, as hypothesized, the type of subject and experimental setting interacted in their effect on performance, and (2) that task difficulty affected the interaction of subject and setting. The finding of numerous contextual effects and differences between types of subjects should suggest caution in the interpretation of studies aimed at choosing between alternative accounting information systems.

Business failure prediction

Kennedy (1975) used Bayes's theorem in a descriptive role to measure cue usage in loan officers' predictions of bankruptcy from four financial ratios. Twenty-four loan officers sequentially examined four financial ratios and total asset size for each of 12 companies, half of which had later become bankrupt. Recognizing that the items of information were not statistically independent, Kennedy randomized the order of presentations within and across subjects. Prior probabilities of bankruptcy were elicited on the basis of industry classification only. After each piece of information, subjects gave revised estimates of the probability of bankruptcy. Using the ratio form of Bayes's theorem, Kennedy computed the inferred likelihood ratio for each piece of information. The likelihood ratios were interpreted as an index of data diagnosticity or cue usage, since they determine the degree to which the prior odds change upon receipt of the new information. This is quite similar, then, to the interpretation of regression coefficients or ω^2 weights in the lens model approach. Kennedy defined usefulness as a combination of magnitude of impact and accuracy of direction.

All ratios had a statistically significant impact. The debt-to-equity ratio had the greatest positive effect on probability estimates and was U-shaped, showing high diagnosticity at extreme values. Although Kennedy emphasizes the measurement of usefulness, the key contribution of the experiment may have been the demonstration of the usefulness of Bayes's theorem in measuring cue usage. The technique also shows promise as a method of studying the impact of information set variables on cue usage.

ELICITATION THEORY

To study the probability component of the judgment process, we must elicit from the decision maker quantified representations of his or her subjective probability estimates. Since we are attempting to measure an unobservable state of belief, we are concerned with how good the measurement is. Reviews of the psychology literature by Chesley (1977), Lichtenstein, Fischhoff, and Phillips (1977), and Slovic, Fischhoff, and Lichtenstein (1977) have identified two major research directions. The first has been the investigation of various definitions of "goodness." Normative goodness refers to the extent that the elicited probabilities conform to probability axioms and correspond to the decision maker's state of belief; substantive goodness reflects the amount of knowledge of the topic area contained in the elicited probability; and calibration refers to the long-run appropriateness of levels of confidence. In general, the results of this research indicate (1) that most decision makers are overconfident, (2) that training seems to improve performance, and (3) that experts sometimes perform very well. The other research direction has been examination of the effect of different elicitation methods on the "goodness" of the measurement. This line of research has failed to identify a best method for eliciting probabilities.

Since several accounting studies have dealt with the comparison of different elicitation methods, and since terminology in the literature does not appear to be consistent, it might be useful to describe briefly some commonly used methods. Methods can be conveniently classified as either direct or indirect. The most common direct methods include (1) fractile estimation, in which subjects assign values of the continuous variable to predetermined probability levels or fractiles of the cumulative density function (CDF) or the probability density function (PDF); (2) bisecting techniques, in which subjects repeatedly bisect a range of the continuous variable into equally likely subdivisions; (3) fixed-interval methods, in which subjects assign probabilities to fixed partitions of the continuous variable in either the CDF or PDF; and (4) curve-fitting methods, where subjects draw a graph of the PDF. Indirect methods, where probabilities must be inferred from responses, include (1) mean-variance method, in which subjects must specify the mean and variance of a normal distribution; (2) equivalent prior sample (EPS), where subjects relate their feeling of uncertainty to having seen r occurrences in n trials; (3) odds estimation, where subjects give the ratio of the likelihood of two events; and (4) behavioral methods, where probabilities are inferred from the betting behavior of subjects in standard lotteries.

Convergence of different assessment methods in auditing

Three related accounting studies attempted to assess the convergent validity of different elicitation methods. Convergent validity is the degree to which we obtain similar responses from two or more different elicitation techniques. Corless (1972) examined two necessary conditions for using Bayesian revision to combine statistical sampling evidence with qualitative evidence. These conditions were that an auditor can specify information from which a prior probability distribution can be constructed and that the distribution thus obtained accurately reflects the auditor's beliefs. In the study, auditors were presented with case descriptions about the internal controls in payroll preparation. Two methods of elicitation were used to assess their belief about the error rate in payroll preparation: (1) a beta distribution was constructed from responses to the bisecting method, and (2) a discrete distribution was constructed from the responses to the fixed-interval method. For each auditor, these distributions were compared on their medians and interquartile ranges. Although auditors were apparently quite capable of providing the necessary information, the considerable discrepancy between the two distributions for most auditors led Corless to conclude that neither distribution should be relied upon as accurately reflecting the beliefs of the auditors.

Felix (1976) compared a bisecting method and the EPS technique. After a brief training session on probability, auditors assessed prior probabilities for error rates in two attributes of an order-receiving, shipping, and billing system. His choice of methods was based on several factors. The bisecting method was used to provide some comparison with the Corless study; the EPS method was chosen as a logical tool for auditors who have some experience in obtaining sample evidence in the form of error rates. Since responses to the EPS technique uniquely identify a beta distribution, and a beta distribution can be constructed from responses to the bisecting method, Felix felt he had a more reasonable basis of comparison than did Corless. When two distributions were compared on the basis of quartile values, the results indicated somewhat smaller differences than those found by Corless. Although Felix allowed the possibility of a positive training effect, there were enough differences between the two studies to make the question indeterminable.

Both Corless (1972) and Felix (1976) compared distributions on the basis of the average *difference* of quartile values as a percentage of the average quartile value. Crosby (1981) improved this design with statistical tests of significance. Information was presented in a case study designed to enable auditors to develop beliefs about the strength of internal control over sales and billing. Using direct estimation of fractiles and the EPS technique, Crosby assessed probability distributions for their beliefs about the error rate for one attribute in the system. Although no training was given to the auditors, explanations of the methods were provided, and consistency checks were incorporated to encourage participants to reexamine their fractile estimates for conformity to their beliefs. A beta distribution was constructed from the estimated fractiles, and the goodness of the fit was assessed by a chi-square test. Note that prior studies merely assumed a good fit. Again, the responses from EPS completely specified its own beta distribution. The two distributions were compared with respect to their central tendencies and dispersions. Using both a paired *t*-test and a signed rank test, the null hypothesis of no difference in means, medians, variance, and 90% credible intervals could not be rejected. The hypothesis of no difference in the 50% credible interval, however, was rejected.

These results are not as encouraging as they might first appear. As Crosby noted, the range of possible error rates is small, from 0% to about 10%; hence we would not expect much difference in the 90% credible interval. Also, the case material provided the previous year's compliance testing error rate, which apparently became the mean estimate for the current year's estimate by participants. This was probably a problem with the Felix study, as well, although Felix did not report the error rate provided to subjects. Finally, a quick calculation from Crosby's data indicates relative percentage differences even larger than those found by Felix.

The studies reviewed thus far have merely examined the consistency of responses from different elicitation methods. We must recognize, however, that in the absence of objective criteria, convergence cannot provide a basis for determining which method to use. Two methods which yield poor normative and substantive probability responses may, nonetheless, have high convergent validity. Lack of convergence is even more difficult to interpret. Two approaches have been taken to solve this problem.

Accuracy studies in auditing

In an extensive series of experiments, Chesley (1976, 1977, 1978) developed an accuracy measure to objectively compare methods. His studies are also distinguished by the use of joint, nondichotomous distributions and by the fact that he tested hypotheses developed from psychological theory. In each of the experiments, subjects were asked to assess a joint probability distribution for the weights of acceptable steel plates produced from a drill-press operation. They were given marginal distributions for machine operator performance, distributions of machine performance conditioned on level of operator performance, and information from which they could specify a marginal distribution of input plate weights from a new supplier. This marginal input distribution was elicited from the participants and was used, along with the given distributions, to calculate a joint probability distribution for the weight of steel plate produced in the operation. This calculated joint distribution, which was individual-specific, became the standard against which the elicited joint distributions could be compared. In all the experiments, detailed instructions, descriptions of the elicitation methods, and practice questionnaires were provided.

The main thrust of the three experiments was to examine certain theories which would explain why one elicitation method might be better than another. Torgerson (1958) described scale difficulty as a function of the number of cognitive scale elements (i.e., units, origin, distance). This theory would predict that a bisecting technique would be easier to use than direct estimation of fractiles. Chesley (1976, 1977) found the direct method to be superior in performance. Slovic (1972) suggested that the ease of a response mode is a function of its congruity with the way the information is mentally stored by the subject. Chesley (1977) found, however, that congruency of data presentation and response mode had no significant effect on performance. One last possibility, familiarity with the response mode, was tested (Chesley, 1978). Using five different response modes, Chesley was unable to find differences among them. This last experiment was hampered by small sample sizes and lack of an effective way of blocking by measures of familiarity. Other interesting findings in this series include indications that multiple stage elicitations with reconciliation points improve performance; that engineering and accounting students were indistinguishable, both normatively and substantively; that performance in an embedded figures task was correlated with probability assessment performance; and that assessing subjective likelihood distributions is not significantly more difficult than assessing prior distributions.

Impact of differences on audit decisions

Even if objective criteria for judging probability estimates are available, we need some idea of the effect of assessment differences on decisions in order to determine if observed differences are significant in a practical sense. Two studies approached the question of the effect of different elicitation techniques on audit judgments. Crosby (1980) compared Bayesian sample sizes using input from both EPS and direct fractile methods. The subject auditors and the case materials were those described in Crosby (1981). Results of this study indicated that the normatively derived sample sizes were significantly dependent upon which method of elicitation was used. EPS generated smaller sample sizes than the fractile method. Both methods, in turn, provided smaller samples than judgmental and classical sample sizes. Although there was no real benchmark by which to decide if a sample size was "too small," the results may suggest that the overconfidence (tight distributions) found by Lichtenstein, Fischhoff, and Phillips (1977) could lead to insufficient sample sizes and increased risk for auditors.

Kinney and Uecker (1979) examined the effects of different methods of eliciting subjective evaluations on compliance sampling results. Their methods differed only in the form of questions used to assess fractiles. Using methods similar to Tversky and Kahneman (1974), they asked auditors to evaluate one of four sample results and to assess either the 95th percentile population error rate or the probability that the population error rate was greater than 8%. Results of prior studies in psychology predict that the first method will yield confidence intervals that are too narrow, while the second method will yield intervals that are too broad, presumably because the implied anchor points are different. In an audit context of evaluating sample results, these judgmental "errors" would be equivalent to increasing beta and alpha risk, respectively. For comparison purposes, Kinney and Uecker used classical evaluations of the sample results and counted the number of times subjects accepted the results (given an upper acceptable limit and confidence level) when they were not justified by classical evaluation. A chi-square test indicated significant dependence on the elicitation method. The direct fractile method was more likely to accept results more often than justified. One problem with this analysis, however, is that the accept-not accept decision is dichotomous, while the assessment is continuous. It is not clear, for example, that very slight overconfidence is normatively better than gross underconfidence.

HEURISTICS AND BIASES

One possible reason that different elicitation methods yield different distributions is that the methods induce subjects to use different simplified processing rules, or heuristics. This explanation prompted the study by Kinney and Uecker (1979) cited previously. It is becoming increasingly apparent that heuristic use is also dependent on task characteristics. In a review of the literature of heuristics and biases, Biddle and Joyce (1981) laid a base for an extensive series of experiments with the ultimate goal of suggesting to practitioners the conditions under which specific heuristics are likely to be employed, when errors in audit judgment will result from the use of a heuristic, and methods of avoiding these situations. Other studies have investigated management-control and financial-analysis tasks. This section includes studies aimed toward that goal.

Representativeness

The representativeness heuristic (Kahneman and Tversky, 1972) generally posits that an assessment of the likelihood that *A* comes from population *B* will often be based on the extent to which *A* is similar to *B*. Frequently, this process will lead decision makers to ignore normatively relevant data, such as base rates, data reliability, and predictability.

Swieringa and others (1976) extended Kahneman and Tversky's work to a general business context and tested the generality of their results to alternative methods of posing questions in the experiments. Using students, they performed five experiments testing the effects of the predictive significance or diagnosticity of information, operationalized as prior probabilities and sample size, on judgments of likelihoods. A sixth experiment examined the effect of cue intercorrelation and consistency. In general, the replications tended to confirm prior findings of representativeness. However, there was significant variation in the magnitude of the effect, depending upon how the questions were posed and the particular judgment context. These extensions suggest that representativeness may be a contingent rather than a general method of processing information.

AUDITING APPLICATIONS

Joyce and Biddle (1981b) tested for auditors' neglect of base rates and insensitivity to reliability in situations in which this heuristic could lead to systematic departure from normative responses. In one test for neglect of base rates, auditors were asked to estimate the probability of management fraud when a key manager's personality profile matches a master profile of fraudulent managers. Positive and negative hit rates for the procedures, as well as the base rate of management fraud in the population, were also given. Although neglect of both base rates and false positive rates would lead to an estimate equal to the positive hit rate, most auditors estimated a lower probability. There was a significant main effect for the base-rate manipulation (but not for the false positive manipulation). While auditors performed better than subjects in previous studies, they still underweighted base-rate information in arriving at estimates exceeding Bayesian probabilities.

In a second experiment, auditors judged the probability of management fraud, given base rates and a nonconclusive description of a company. Since subjects in the different base-rate cases received the same description, the normative ratio of posterior odds should be equal to the ratio of prior odds (i.e., the base rates). Subject deviation from this normative result indicated once again that the auditors were underweighting the base-rate information. In addition, in both experiments, lack of appreciation of base-rate information is more pronounced when base rates are low. The potential impact on auditing is quite serious in certain areas where base rates are typically low and consequences are high (e.g., management fraud).

In experiments aimed at testing the effect of source reliability, Joyce and Biddle (1981b) asked auditors to judge the probability of collection of an overdue account on the basis of a credit report from either a credit agency or the credit manager of the client. Results indicated that in a between-subjects design, the auditors did not differentially weight the source of information. In a within-subjects design, however, where each subject was sensitized to the two sources, the auditors weighted the credit agency as more diagnostic. The authors suggest that explicit comparisons of the credibility of different sources could be built into audit programs.

Bamber (1980) developed a formal probabilistic definition of source credibility in an experiment to test whether audit managers differentially weight the work of different audit seniors. A normative Bayesian model was expanded to include measures of sampling error and judgmental error (source credibility). Audit managers were given a case description representing a realistic audit situation. After reading the description, which included the previous year's audit results, they were asked to assess the likelihood that the control system for sales and receivables was sufficient to justify substantial reliance on it. After reading the result of compliance tests conducted by a senior and his recommendation, the managers revised their estimates of likelihoods. Source credibility was indicated by explanations of the senior's technical ability (90%, 80%, or 70% reliable). The log likelihood ratios inferred from the managers' responses were compared with the log likelihood ratios of the Bayesian model. Results from a repeated measures ANOVA indicated a highly significant main effect for source credibility. These results are consistent with the within-subjects findings of Joyce and Biddle (1981b), but provide no information on a between-subjects basis. Again, the idea of making source credibility explicit in the judgment process is recommended.

Another related aspect of representativeness is insensitivity to the relationship between sample size and sampling error. Uecker and Kinney (1977) searched auditors' judgmental evaluations of random sample results for insensitivity to sample size and for the opposite behavior, insensitivity to error rate. One hundred and twelve practicing CPAs participating in a state society continuing education program completed an audit case involving a test of compliance of internal control. From each of five pairs of sample outcomes they chose the sample result which provided the better evidence that at the 95% confidence level the population error rate is less than 5%.

Subjects utilizing the representativeness heuristic would choose the sample result showing the lower sample error rate, regardless of sample size. To test for this heuristic, three of the five pairs were constructed in such a way that the sample with the larger error rate provided the better evidence of compliance. Insensitivity to error rate would result in subjects' choosing the larger sample size as long as the sample error rate were less than the actual rate of 5%. The other two pairs were designed so that the smaller sample sizes provided the better evidence of compliance to allow testing for "conservatism." In all cases, the sample error rate was lower than the critical rate.

The results showed that the CPAs outperformed subjects in similar prior research, responding correctly nearly 70% of the time. Only 9 CPAs consistently selected the lower error rate, indicating consistent representativeness, while 17 consistently selected the larger sample, suggesting conservatism. However, nearly 75% of the CPAs made at least one error and 56% made at least two errors. This indicates either a poor understanding of basic statistical concepts or lack of interest in the experiment. Since few subjects consistently exhibited the hypothesized heuristics, modifications of the theory may be in order. The apparent interaction between sample size and sample error rate suggests a contingent processing model. However, clarification of this issue requires a more sophisticated experimental design.

Biddle and Joyce (1979) ran a series of experiments to test auditors' appreciation of the role of sample-size information. Auditors were asked to (1) evaluate two samples from different-sized populations, (2) evaluate different-sized samples from the same population, and (3) evaluate sample results in isolation without population information. Results indicate that while more than half of the auditors performed normatively, a large number appear to have based their decisions on sampling fractions, or at least to have overemphasized sampling fraction information. Another large subset of the auditors conformed to neither the normative rule nor the representativeness heuristic. In the case of these experiments, we have to ask whether our expectations of the subjects were reasonable. In the first task, for example, the normative response required the auditor to intuitively sense the difference between standard errors of .021 and .022 for a binomial distribution with a finite correction factor. Even with a sophisticated knowledge of the relationship of sample size and sampling fraction to sampling error, would we expect auditors to compute this exactly? It is not too surprising, therefore, that a large number of auditors chose each of three available answers.

Anchoring

Another common heuristic cited by Tversky and Kahneman (1974) is referred to as anchoring and adjustment, in which decision makers choose some initial starting point (prior experience, a best guess) and then make adjustments from this anchor on the basis of additional information. Psychological research has shown that such adjustments are typically in the right direction but of insufficient magnitude. Again, since the audit process can be viewed as the updating of beliefs on the basis of current information, knowledge of whether, and in what situations, auditors make these kinds of errors is important. Several recent studies have addressed this issue.

AUDITING APPLICATIONS

Joyce and Biddle (1981a) conducted three experiments to detect the use of anchoring and adjustment by auditors. The first experiment was a replication of a typical Tversky and Kahneman (1974) task using auditors and audit words, but not using a realistic audit context. Given a normatively irrelevant anchor, auditors were asked to estimate the incidence of management fraud. Results showed that the estimates of the group with a high anchor exceeded those of the group with a lower anchor. It is not clear, however, that we can interpret this as a case of insufficient adjustment based on additional information, because no information was given. The fact that the anchor was relevant to the auditors is probably evidence of relative ignorance of the base rate of management fraud. A second experiment asked auditors to make extent-of-audit judgments, given information that controls are either weak, changing from strong to weak, or changing from weak to strong. The results showed some evidence of a contingent adjustment strategy. That is, subjects overadjusted when controls became weak and underadjusted when controls became stronger. As the authors note, this behavior is consistent with a conservative approach to auditing. Interpretation of this result is made difficult by a research design in which the dependent variable (an extent-of-audit decision) confounds a probability assessment with some unknown decision rule which combines probabilities and utilities. We cannot know whether the experimental manipulation affected the assessment, the utilities, the decision rule, or some combination of these. The authors recognized this problem in a third experiment in which auditors were told that successful introduction of a new product was necessary for a certain client to remain a going concern. The auditors were asked to judge the probability of successful introduction, given certain necessary elementary events. The experimental manipulation was to phrase the question in either conjunctive form (success requires all elementary events) or disjunctive form (failure results if at least one elementary event does not occur). The auditors were then asked to suggest an opinion on the client's financial statements. Results showed that the probability assessments were unaffected by the manipulations, but that opinions varied widely. For example, one subject recommended an unqualified report based on a probability assessment of .5, while another subject, who assessed the probability of success at .8, chose a disclaimer. Efforts to choose research designs that avoid confounding different elements of the decision process are necessary to clarify experimental results.

Kinney and Uecker (1979) reported evidence of anchoring by auditors in an analytical review application. Subjects were given audited sales, cost of goods sold, gross profit, and gross profit percentage information for the prior 2 years. They were also given unaudited book values for the current year and were asked to provide a range of values beyond which they would investigate a change in the gross profit percentage. For one group of subjects, book values showed a significant increase in this percentage; for the second group, there was a significant decrease. The mean upper and lower control limits set by subjects were significantly higher for the group with higher book values. This is consistent with the use of anchoring and adjustment only if the book values are normatively irrelevant. It seems just as likely, however, that subjects look at the book value, decide (on some basis) that it either should or should not be investigated, and then provide a range of values consistent with that decision. Regardless of the interpretation, however, the authors' recommendation of more objective variance investigation criteria may be entirely appropriate.

A second experiment by Kinney and Uecker (1979), discussed in the preceding section, recommended the use of a risk assessment elicitation method over a direct fractile approach in a compliance testing situation. This recommendation was based on prior research which indicated that overconfidence was a frequent result of the use of the fractile method. This difference in results is said to arise because the two methods provide different anchors for the decision maker. Although the results indicate that auditors using the fractile method might be more likely to accept sample results when they are not justified, we must consider several issues. As we have already noted, there are problems in interpreting dichotomous decisions based on continuous cues. We might also question the appropriateness of using a classical statistical evaluation as the benchmark, rather than a Bayesian model which accounts for differences in priors. If the classical benchmark is appropriate, then why not recommend the use of a sample evaluation table in place of *either* elicitation method? The data show that, if we define accuracy as percent of deviation from the statistical evaluation, the auditors using the fractile assessment were more accurate in three out of four cases. Are we sure that we want to recommend an elicitation technique that is less accurate? Finally, the data really present no evidence of insufficient adjustment. Since we can only guess what anchor subjects may have used, we can only guess as to the direction and magnitude of the adjustments. In fact, since some mean responses were greater than the standard and some were smaller, we might conclude that different anchors were used or that some groups overadjusted and some underadjusted.

FINANCIAL ANALYSIS

In assessing the accuracy of subjective probability judgments, Wright (1979b) had students generate probability distributions for the systematic risk of securities. For each of 15 firms, subjects received a measure of earnings variability and a debt-to-equity measure. At both the aggregate and the individual levels, there was evidence of conservative revision of probabilities (i.e., revision in an appropriate direction but to an inadequate degree). Subjects were more accurate for single-cue versus joint-cue distributions. In a postexperimental questionnaire, subjects reported that, in the joint-cue tasks, they focused on the variability-of-earnings cue and "adjusted" their estimate for the value of the debt-to-equity cue.

MANAGEMENT CONTROL

Brown (1980) assumed a specific anchor and adjustment strategy to generate hypotheses concerning the effect of situational variables and payoff structures on the bias arising from use of an anchor and adjustment heuristic. In a cost variance investigation case, Brown used an expected value maximization model as a normative standard. The assumed strategy was that the initial anchor would be the midpoint between the means of the two states of control, and the adjustment would be 50% toward the normative model's optimal investigation point. The process distributions and the payoff matrixes were constructed so that the distance between the assumed anchor and the optimal point was smaller in case I than in case II. It was hypothesized, therefore, that there would be smaller anchoring bias in case I. Experimental results, using students, showed a significant cost effect, but in the opposite direction. The anchoring bias was greater in case I, where the distance between the assumed anchor and the optimal point was smaller. The author suggested that this may have been caused by a subjective adjustment limit; that is, case I involved an adjustment *toward* the standard cost, while case II involved an adjustment *away* from the standard. An equally plausible explanation is that the hypothesis was based on an erroneous assumption of the initial anchor. Case I, which penalized type II errors, may have induced an initial strategy of investigating all variances (the standard cost became the anchor); case II, which penalized type I errors, may have induced a strategy of not investigating any variances (the mean of the out-of-control distribution became the anchor). Under these circumstances, given identical adjustment strategies, we would expect the anchoring bias to be consistent with that obtained in the experiment.

While most of the research in this area has searched for generalized heuristic use, Magee and Dickhaut (1978) hypothesized that decision makers choose heuristics on the basis of situational variables. In a cost variance investigation case, they predicted that subjects under different compensation plans would exhibit different problem-solving strategies. Graduate business students made 24 investigation decisions based on cost reports and knowledge of the means and variances of the in-control (state 1) and out-of-control (state 2) probability distributions, as well as the probability of state occurrence. Noting that the subjects lacked the means to solve dynamic programming problems or to explicitly perform Bayesian revisions, the authors predicted the use of a control-chart approach. Such an approach would involve a lower limit L, below which investigation would never take place; an upper limit U, above which one would always investigate; and an interval between L and U that would trigger an investigation only after some number, N, of repeated observations. Subjects were paired into two different compensation plans. Plan 1 (CP1) provided payment of Z_1 minus costs incurred; plan 2 (CP2) paid Z_2 if costs were less than or equal to standard, and nothing otherwise. In both plans, costs included the investigation costs. The authors used a decision-tree questionnaire to elicit heuristics used by the subjects. The experimental hypotheses were supported, in that (1) most subjects used a control-chart strategy and (2) the compensation plan significantly affected the specific strategies used. Under each plan, subjects tended to choose the control-chart strategy consistent with maximization of their own compensation. With CP1, this involved a strategy of choosing U somewhere between μ_1 and μ_2. With CP2, the best strategy was to investigate all variances, that is, to set U equal to μ_1. These results seem to support our analysis of Brown (1980).

Sequence effects

In a nonaccounting task, Ronen (1971) searched for heuristics in subjects' aggregation of joint probabilities. He studied whether decision makers would be indifferent between events with equal joint probabilities (expected values) but differing sequences of marginal probabilities. Ronen related the experiment to decision makers' abilities to use probabilistic reports or to make capital-budgeting decisions. He hypothesized that, in a two-stage process, despite the fact that the objective joint probability is identical for each action, subjects would choose the action with the higher probability of first-stage success because of some form of discounting of probabilities. In two separate experiments, graduate students and management program participants chose between set A and set B, where each set consisted of two bags of marbles, each containing certain proportions of two colors of marbles. The object was to pick set A or B in such a way that one could sequentially pick a blue marble from the first bag and a red marble from the second bag. Probabilities of success were manipulated by varying the proportion of marbles in each bag. The manipulated moderating variables were absolute magnitude of the joint probabilities and magnitude of the difference between first- and second-stage probabilities. In most trials, the joint probabilities of the two sets were equal. In the remainder, predetermined differences existed. The results strongly suggest that subjects did not simply combine the probabilities multiplicatively to form expected value; rather, there was a significant subject preference for higher initial probabilities. Absolute magnitude of joint probabilities did not have a significant effect on choices, but the levels of differences between initial probabilities did. Finally, there was some evidence to indicate that subjects would prefer lower expected value (joint probabilities) sequences, provided the first-stage probabilities are higher.

Two studies provided further insight into Ronen's (1971) finding of a sequence effect in problems involving disaggregated probabilistic information. Hirsch (1978) extended the Ronen study by using both a chance task and a business task, by manipulating more independent variables, and by incorporating a personality variable. Manufacturing managers were asked to decide between two specialty products which were identified by the probabilities of successful production in each of two production departments and by their joint probabilities of success. A factorial design manipulated the differences in initial probabilities, the joint probability magnitude, and the difference in joint probabilities. Results showed that in both tasks, when the joint probability difference was zero, the sequence effect existed at all levels of the other variables. As joint differences increased, progressively higher levels of the other variables were required to produce the sequence effect. The deviations from expected value maximization were much greater in the chance task than the business task. With joint differences as high as .12, subjects in the chance task showed a sequence effect with initial stage differences as low as .03. In the business task, subjects who scored as internals on a locus-of-control scale were significantly more prone to the sequence effect than externals, who were almost unanimously expected-value maximizers. Hirsch suggested that internals might subjectively alter the probabilities on the basis of believing they can "beat the odds."

Snowball and Brown (1979) also used a business context to examine bank trust officers' use of disaggregated probabilities. They noted that Ronen's choice sets were contructed in such a way that if the joint probability of A exceeded B, the first-stage probability of B exceeded A (Hirsch's design was basically the same). This data set automatically classified a deviation from expected values as a sequence effect. Snowball and Brown set up a business task capable of distinguishing expected value maximization, preference for high initial-step probabilities, preference for high second-stage probabilities, and anti-expected-value maximization. Manipulated independent variables were joint probability distribution (JPD) and both first- and second-stage probability differences. Although the data were presented to the subjects as an independent series-of-choice situation, the experimental design used paired-choice situations to allow discrimination of all four response strategies. A risk preference variable was also used. Although nearly two-thirds of the responses were consistent with the normative model, the next most preferred response (18.5) was a preference for higher initial-stage probabilities. Another 11% of the responses showed a preference for higher second-stage probabilities. As in Hirsch (1978), nonnormative behavior decreased as joint differences increased. Results also showed that suboptimal strategies were more prevalent among those subjects with a higher disposition toward risk.

Dickhaut and Eggleton (1975) researched the nature of materiality thresholds. They designed their experiment to test the analogy between the process of making comparative judgments of numerical information and the psychophysical process of judging the brightness or intensity of physical stimuli. This study was prompted by the Rose and others (1970) conclusion that such judgments reflected Weber's law, which suggests that a just noticeable difference is a constant ratio of the standard in which it was established. Graduate students judged whether a particular outcome was essentially less than, not essentially different from, or essentially higher than an expectation. The experimenter manipulated the type of task (accounting-oriented versus nonconnotative), the sequence of data presentation (random versus nonrandom), and the format of comparison stimuli (expectation and actual versus expectation, actual, and difference). In all conditions, half of the trials used a standard of 2,000 and half used a standard of 80,000. The resulting data appeared to be consistent with Weber's law and, of the manipulated variables, only the random presentation had a significant, but minor, effect. Plots of the subjects' judgments, however, did not resemble plots of psychophysical judgments where one normally finds that stimuli near the noticeable difference threshold have a higher probability of not being consistently classified. The results suggest that subjects form simple percent-of-expectation decision rules and apply them consistently throughout the experimental task. Dickhaut and Eggleton also introduced a decision-tree questionnaire which proved useful in eliciting the heuristics used by the subjects during the task. Similar questionnaires would seem quite useful in other heuristic experiments, as a tool for cross-methodological validation. It has the advantage of flexibility, which allows tailoring of the instrument to specific hypotheses.

INFORMATION EVALUATION AND THE NORMATIVE FRAMEWORK

The studies in the preceding section sought evidence of specific simplifying heuristics to explain departures from normative standards. In contrast, the studies in this section are concerned only with the question of whether or not decision makers have the ability or can learn to perform as required by normative decision models.

Information evaluation

Three related studies have dealt with the accountant's role as an information evaluator in choosing an information system for another decision maker who will make an action choice. Each of the three studies involved a number of urns which contained varying proportions of black and white marbles. A simulated decision maker was to guess the proportion of black marbles in an urn (selected at random), given the prior probability distribution and the results of a sampling of the marbles in the urn. The task required the subjects (all students) to choose an appropriate sample size (i.e., to choose an information system), knowing the payoffs. Subjects were monetarily rewarded in such a way as to encourage expected-value maximization.

Uecker (1978) used two different simulated decision makers, one Bayesian and one conservative-Bayesian, to test subjects' ability to learn the optimal information system to provide the decision makers. Using a fixed per-unit cost of sampling, each subject performed 50 trials with feedback with each decision maker. Results showed that the subjects were apparently able to distinguish between the two simulated decision makers (DMs), since average sample-size choices for the two DMs were significantly different. Moreover, on average, subjects were closer to optimal sample size for the Bayesian DM. Compared to a normative model, however, the subjects did not tend to converge toward the optimal sample sizes for either DM. In both cases, and regardless of the order in which the DMs were presented, no significant amount of learning occurred over 50 replications.

In another version of this experiment, Uecker (1980) described a simulated decision maker to half the subjects to see if explicit knowledge of the decision rule would increase their ability to choose an optimal information system. Results indicated no difference in performance between those who received information about the DM and those who did not. Consistent with the first experiment, neither group showed significant improvement over repeated trials. Subjects in the second experiment were also presented with a high or low anchor during the experiment and results showed a significant difference in average sample sizes between these two anchoring groups, although there is no apparent evidence of the classical adjustment bias. An important confounding feature in these two experiments was the fact that the actual curve relating sample size and expected net gain from sampling was rather erratic. This means that it is possible that subjects found themselves in a position from which either increases or decreases in sample size would make them worse off. They may have mistaken a local maximum for a global maximum. In fact, as the author points out, a sample size of 40 may have had a better payoff than a sample size of 24, even though the optimal sample size was 22.

Hilton, Swieringa, and Hoskin (1981) tested the extent to which subjects correctly perceive the effect of accuracy on information value. Subjects were given knowledge of the DM and were presented with a series of trials. For each trial they were offered a particular sample size at a specific price. By varying prices and sample sizes over time, they were able to compute a demand value of information for a set of sample sizes ($n = 5, 10, \ldots, 25, 30$) for each subject. The normative responses would show information value increasing in accuracy with declining marginal returns. A prior study in marketing showed that subjects tended to overvalue information consistently. The Hilton, Swieringa, and Hoskin study removed one confounding aspect of the prior study, however, by separating the information evaluator from the DM. On average, the subjects were very close to normative values, both in terms of absolute amounts and in recognizing the declining marginal value of increased sample sizes. None of the three groups formed by cluster analysis, and only one individual subject, however, exhibited monotonically decreasing marginal increments in information value. The three clusters represented those who were near normative, those who undervalue information, and those who overvalue information. Since the experiment assumed risk neutrality and since knowledge of wealth position could affect the demand values of non-risk-neutral subjects, the authors controlled for risk attitude and presence or absence of feedback. The interaction term was not significant. One variable missing from each of the three preceding studies, which could partially explain nonoptimal performance, is the processing effort variable included in Hilton's (1980) enriched information economics IE model. In repeated trials, subjects may have performed only to that point at which the effort required exceeded the potential rewards. By the standards of this experiment, such rational, maximizing behavior would be classified as nonoptimal.

Normative framework

The research dealing with heuristic processing of information and with the ability of students to perform the information evaluation functions have compared actual performance with some objective or normative standard. The three papers in this section represent a more descriptive approach to the study of decision making. In these studies, normative decision theory is used not as a standard of performance but as a framework for examining elements of the decision process. Coincidentally, all three papers deal with the materiality construct in auditing.

From the extensive history of conceptual and empirical research on materiality, Newton (1977) was the first to explicitly address the effect of uncertainty on materiality judgments. As an example of her approach, audit partners were presented with a case involving a decline in value of marketable securities. Each subject was asked for a dollar amount of decline which, if permanent and not written down by management, would be material enough in relation to net income to warrant a qualfied opinion. Note that this "certainty equivalent" is the end product of most prior materiality studies. Subjects were then presented with several dollar value declines and asked for the minimum probability that the decline would be permanent, which would justify issuance of a qualified opinion. The purpose of these standard lottery questions was to estimate a utility curve for each subject over the range of values in the case. A final question provided a specific dollar decline and a probability of decline, and asked whether the subject would qualify the audit report. Responses from the elicitation phase were used to predict the answers to the final question. Although some subjects would qualify without regard to probability, results indicated that most of the audit partners seem to use probabilities in their judgments. Other results indicate that most auditors were risk averse and that judgments were consistent with expected utility maximization. Some subjects exhibited invariance of probabilities over different dollar amounts, a result which Newton viewed as a violation of utility theory. But note that such behavior does conform with a model constrained by absolute aversion to risk of all losses in excess of some cutoff point (see Libby and Fishburn, 1977).

Most studies which have examined the degree of consensus among auditors have found significant individual differences in tasks ranging from internal control evaluation to extent of audit decisions (see, e.g., Joyce, 1976). Efforts to explain these individual differences have generally been conducted using a methodology which has confounded cue utilization with the form of the decision model. To avoid these problems, Lewis (1980) viewed the audit decision process within an expected utility framework and suggested that specific elements of the process could be examined in isolation. In a case where the states of nature and the feasible actions are completely specified, for example, Lewis noted that sufficiency conditions for consensus are homogeneous utilities and identical subjective probability distributions over the set of states. Both Lewis and Ward (1976), who implicitly used a similar model, investigated aspects of the homogeneous utility conditions.

To see if auditors considered the same factors in a materiality decision, Ward asked audit partners and managers to rank the importance of 24 factors in making materiality judgments. These factors included elements of the legal, technical, professional, personal, and environmental influences on the auditor. To ease the task of the subjects, Ward used a Q-sort in which the participants sort the items into five piles with a specified number of items to be placed in each pile. The result is a fixed, bell-shaped distribution from each subject. Results of this ranking indicated significant (Kendall's $W = .386$, $p \leq .01$), but not overwhelming, agreement among auditors as to their *cognitive* beliefs about the materiality construct. Ward also examined an *affective* aspect of materiality by asking subjects about the relationship between the size of an audit error and the expected loss to the auditor. The subjects could choose from six functional forms, or they could trace out their own relationship. There was little agreement about the functional form of the relationship. Although 12 of 24 subjects chose either logistic or exponential relationships, all the forms were chosen by at least one subject, and five subjects provided their own tracings.

Lewis (1980) chose an audit case involving disclosure of a contingent liability and in which both the states and the actions were given. The purpose of the study was to examine the degree to which auditors have homogeneous utilities. Practicing CPAs, mostly supervisors and managers, were asked to express their preferences for the outcomes associated with a two-state, three-action decision. The preferences, shown on an eleven-point scale, were used as interval scale utility measures. A between-subjects design was employed by assigning subjects to either a high or low materiality situation. Homogeneity was measured as the average pairwise correlation of the utility measures among all auditors in each case. Results suggested that the homogeniety condition is significantly more likely as the level of materiality increases. This bodes well for auditors, in that it suggests that judgmental consensus is more likely in "important" situations.

TABLE B-1

Summary of Probabilistic Judgment Studies

Study	Type of Decision Maker	Task	Variables of Interest	Results
Barefield (1972)	28 MSIA students	Classify process as in or out of control from two variance reports or a linear combination of the two reports	Accuracy (IIIA1) Interrelationships (IB3) Aggregation (ID3) Number of cues (IB1)	High No effect Disaggregation tended to promote consistency but retarded selection of optimal criteria (no significant overall effect)
Dickhaut (1973)	Undergraduates and businessmen	Estimate probability of subset membership from single or joint information system in business and abstract settings	Accuracy (IIIA1) Number of cues (IB1) Type of task (abstract or business setting) (IE3a) Prior experience (IIA4a)	Single system produced higher performance; significant setting × subject interaction; significant three-way interaction
Kennedy (1975)	24 loan officers	Estimate probability of bankruptcy of 12 firms in 3 industries from 4 financial ratios	Cue usage (IIB2) Accuracy (IIIA1)	All ratios had significant impact on estimates; debt to equity ratio had greatest impact and accuracy with highest diagnosticity at extreme values; accuracy of other ratios differed by industry
Corless (1972)	Practicing auditors	Respond to two different subjective probability elicitation methods in estimating error rate in payroll preparations	Response mode (IE3b) Convergence (IIIA3c) Consensus (IIIA3b)	Within subjects different techniques produced different distributions; between subjects, very little agreement
Felix (1976)	Practicing auditors	Receive brief training session and respond to two different elicitation methods in estimating error	Response mode (IE3b) Convergence (IIIA3c) Prior experience (training) (IIA4a)	Smaller distributional differences than Corless, measured by quartile differences; possible

TABLE B-1 *(continued)*

Summary of Probabilistic Judgment Studies

		rates in shipping-billing function	training effect
Crosby (1981)	42 audit seniors	Respond to two different elicitation techniques in estimating error rate in billing-collection function	Response mode (IE3b) Convergence (IIIA3c)	Statistical tests of central tendency and dispersion indicate no differences in 90% intervals, but significant differences in 50% intervals
Chesley (1976)	28 IE and 28 Accounting undergraduates	Respond to two elicitation methods to describe prior distribution or likelihood distribution based on manufacturing case material	Type task (IE3a) Response mode (IE3b) Prior experience (IIA4a) Accuracy (IIIA1)	Nature of task and background of student had no effect on accuracy; significant elicitation technique effect on accuracy in first trial, but subsequent trials showed no effect
Chesley (1977)	28 MBAs	Same as (1976), describing prior distributions	Response mode (IE3b) Format of data (ID1) Cognitive structure (IIA3c) Accuracy (IIIA1)	Ease of response mode not a function of congruity of data and response mode; contradicts theory that method requiring more scale elements would cause greater cognitive difficulty; significant correlation between performance on embedded figures test and elicitation task
Chesley (1978)	47 CA students and 42 MBAs	Respond to five elicitation methods to describe marginal likelihood and joint likelihood distribution using (1976) case materials	Response mode (IE3b) Accuracy (IIIA1)	No significant differences in performance using any of the five methods

TABLE B–1 (continued)

Summary of Probabilistic Judgment Studies

Study	Type of Decision Maker	Task	Variables of Interest	Results
Crosby (1980)	42 audit seniors	Priors elicited in Crosby (1981) were used to compute Bayesian sample sizes; subjects asked to provide judgmental sample size	Response mode (IE3b) Response bias (IIIA4) Convergence (IIIA3c)	Different elicitation methods for priors result in significantly different sample sizes; Bayesian samples smaller than classical or judgmental samples
Swieringa et al. (1976)	120 MBA students, 316 I&LR students	Judgments of likelihoods in varied experiments in business and nonbusiness tasks	Heuristics (IIB4) Information content (IC) Interrelationships (IB3) Accuracy (IIIA1) Type of task (IE3a)	Evidence of representativeness heuristic, but sensitivity to prior probability depends on (a) whether stereotypes are associated with alternatives, (b) whether information is representative of the stereotypes; sensitivity to sample size is sub optimal but highly contextual; consistency of cues, not intercorrelation, is cause of unwarranted confidence of estimates
Kinney and Uecker (1979)	179 audit seniors	Set up investigation region for analytical review; use one of two elicitation methods to evaluate sample results	Response mode (IE3b) Heuristics (IIB4) Response bias (IIIA4)	Book-value "anchors" affect size of investigation region; different elicitation techniques provide different evaluation of sample outcomes
Joyce and Biddle (1981b)	Large number of practicing auditors spread over three	Judgments of probability in a variety of audit settings ranging from management	Information content (IC1,2) Heuristics (IIB4)	Base rates are not ignored, but are typically underweighted, especially

174

Summary of Probabilistic Judgment Studies

Study	Subjects	Task		Results
	experiments	fraud prediction to collectibility of receivables		when base rates are low; reliability of source of data was ignored in between-subjects design; in within-subjects design, subjects were sensitized to the differential reliability
Joyce and Biddle (1981a)	Large number of practicing auditors spread over three experiments	Make probabilistic judgments in variety of audit decision settings	Information content (IC3) Type of task (IE3a) Heuristics (IIB4) Response bias(IIIA4)	Normatively irrelevant anchors affect judgments only in unfamiliar tasks; in more familiar tasks, anchor and adjustment strategy could not explain degree of adjustment
Bamber (1980)	35 audit managers	Judge likelihood that client controls are adequate; revise probability based on senior's report of compliance testing	Information content (IC1,2) Heuristics (IIB4)	Subjects were sensitive to changes in reliability of audit seniors as source of data
Uecker and Kinney (1977)	112 practicing CPAs	Judgmental evaluation of sample results	Accuracy (IIIA1) Heuristics (IIB4) Prior experience (IIA4a) Information content (IC)	Evidence of conservatism (preference for large samples) and representativeness (insensitive to sample size); 75% made one error; 56% made two or more; experience factor not significant
Biddle and Joyce (1979)	Large number of practicing auditors spread over three experiments	Evaluate sample evidence and make sample-size choices in audit settings	Information content (IC2) Heuristics (IIB4)	Large proportion of subjects tend to overemphasize the sampling fraction, ignoring sample size; on the other hand, subjects generally understood inverse relationship of sample size and sample error

TABLE B-1 (continued)

Summary of Probabilistic Judgment Studies

Study	Type of Decision Maker	Task	Variables of Interest	Results
Wright (1979b)	11 MBA and Ph.D. students	Estimate probability distribution for the systematic risk of a security given single or joint accounting risk measures	Number of cues (IB1) Form of decision rule (IIB1) Heuristics (IIB4) Accuracy (IIIA1)	In aggregate and individually, subjects appeared to be conservative Bayesian; self-report indicated sequential process for joint cues, anchoring on one and adjusting based on the other; subjects more accurate with single cue
Brown (1980)	86 senior undergraduate and graduate business students	Make variance investigation decisions	Distribution(IBS) Costs and rewards (IE2b) Heuristics (IIB4) Response bias (IIIA4)	Assuming a mid-point anchor, adjusting strategy not consistent with anchor and adjustment heuristic
Magee and Dickhaut (1978)	38 graduate business students	Make variance investigation decisions	Costs and rewards (IE2b) Heuristics (IIB4)	Nature of incentive system influenced choice of investigation strategy
Ronen (1971)	22 graduate students, 78 businessmen	Choose between sets of sequenced events where joint probabilities are equal or nearly equal and initial-stage probabilities differ	Sequence (ID2) Heuristics (IIB4) Accuracy (IIIA1)	Subjects chose sets with higher initial-stage probabilities even when expected value was slightly lower; magnitude of difference between initial-stage probabilities affected choice
Hirsch (1978)	48 manufacturing corporation managers	Choose between sets of sequenced events in business and nonbusiness settings	Sequence (ID2) Type of task (IE3a) Heuristics (IIB4) Cognitive structure (IIA3c)	Sequence effect (Ronen, 1971) was found; as joint probability difference increased, subjects required higher difference in initial stage probabilities; effect more pronounced in

Summary of Probabilistic Judgment Studies

			nonbusiness task and by subjects with internal locus of control
Snowball and Brown (1979)	37 trust officers	Choose between sets of sequenced events in business settings	Sequence (ID2) Cognitive structure (IIA3c) Heuristics (IIB4)	Nearly 2/3 subjects were normative; 1/5 showed preference for higher initial probabilities; sequence effect diminished as joint probability differences increased; risk-seeking subjects were more suboptimal
Dickhaut and Eggleton (1975)	Graduate students	Judge similarity of pairs of numerical stimuli in business and nonconnotative settings	Format (ID1) Sequence (ID2) Type of task (IE3a) Heuristics (IIB4)	*Judgments* consistent with Weber's law, but *process* apparently not psychophysical; subjects often form simple percent-of-standard decision rule, which is consistently used; small sequence effect in one experiment; no format or setting effect
Uecker (1978, 1980)	40 and 41 undergraduate students, respectively	Choose appropriate sample size for simulated decision maker (costly sampling) in colored marble and urn problem	Information about cue attributes (IE2c) Stability (IIB3) Heuristics (IIB4) Accuracy (IIIA1)	Subjects could discern difference in decision rule of DM, but did not converge toward optimal choice, even when decision rule was known; normatively irrelevant anchor affected sample-size choices; no significant learning over multiple trials
Hilton et al. (1981)	104 MBA students	Decide whether to purchase sample sizes at a given price for simulated DMs use in	Costs and rewards (IE2b) Accuracy (IIIA1)	On *average*, subjects perceived monotonic effect of accuracy on information

TABLE B-1 *(continued)*

Summary of Probabilistic Judgment Studies

Study	Type of Decision Maker	Task	Variables of Interest	Results
		Uecker (1978) type task		value and their perceptions approximated the normative model, although few *individuals* were that good
Newton (1977)	19 CPAs, partners	Decide whether to qualify opinions in three circumstances given dollar magnitudes and probabilities; standard lotteries were used to estimate utility curves	Form of decision rule (IIB1)	Most subjects used probabilities in their judgments; most were risk averse and were consistent with expected utility maximization
Ward (1976)	24 CPAs, managers and partners	Rank importance of 24 materiality factors; indicate perceived functional relationship between size of audit error and expected loss of auditor	Consensus (IIIA3b) Perception of characteristics of information set (IIIB3)	Statistically significant, but weak, agreement in rankings of materiality factors; half of subjects specified either logistic or exponential relationship
Lewis (1980)	72 CPAs, mostly supervisors and managers	Rate desirability of outcomes in disclosure decision	Consensus (IIIA3b)	Utilities for audit outcomes are more homogeneous across auditors as materiality increases

APPENDIX C

Accounting Studies
of Predecisional Behavior

Development of accounting research using this approach is in its early stages. The basic psychological theory and analytical methods are also in earlier stages of development. However, several promising studies concerned with financial statement analysis, performance evaluation, and audit planning have been completed. Some of these studies examined the information search and cue combination strategies used by experts, others have attempted to compare experts with novices to determine the unique elements in expert strategies, and one study has begun to investigate the impact of task characteristics on strategy choice. Like the early research using the lens model framework, these studies attempted to describe the state of the art in decision making in a number of accounting contexts. Most involved straightforward replications of studies in other contexts. The research is summarized at the end of the Appendix in Table C–1 which is keyed to the information processing variables listed in Figure 1–3.

Financial analysis

Four studies have been conducted aimed at modeling expert financial analysts. The first such study, which we referred to earlier, is Clark-

[1] This Appendix is based largely on Libby and Lewis (1977, 1982), with permission of *Accounting, Organizations and Society* and Pergamon Press.

179

son's (1962) attempt to construct a model of a bank trust officer's portfolio selection process. After gathering background information through interviews, observations of meetings, and examination of documents, verbal protocols were taken from one trust officer as he selected securities to be included in new client portfolios. Based on the protocols and prior evidence, a computer program was intuitively derived and tested. Separate models for income and growth portfolios were constructed. The security selection portion of the models primarily involved a conjunctive process in which each security was subjected to a series of up to 15 binary tests until one security in an industry was found to meet all the tests. Additional industries were then subjected to the same process until the available funds were invested. The data used in the model included financial statements, stock prices, and forecasts. The ability of the models to predict the portfolio selections was tested on four new accounts not used in construction of the models. The predictions were quite accurate and were superior to random and naive single-variable models. The accuracy of the underlying representation was tested by a rough comparison with the protocols produced while the subject evaluated the new accounts. While the author judged the fit to be good, alternative representations could easily be suggested.[2]

Based on Payne's (1976) research, Biggs (1979) attempted to develop and test more objective criteria for discriminating between models with different functional forms which might be used in a financial analysis task. Eleven experienced financial analysts thought aloud as they selected the company with the highest earnings power from a group of five. Each company was represented by extensive multiperiod financial statements (10-year income statements and balance sheets and 2-year statement of changes in financial position). The protocols were categorized as reflecting one of three types of operators: information gathering, task structuring, or choice process. The protocols were then separated into individual episodes, and the operator sequences were interpreted as evidence of one of four processing models: additive compensatory, additive difference, conjunctive, or elimination by aspects. At least one subject appeared to be using each of the rules. However, the different models usually led to the same conclusions. The additive compensatory and elimination by aspects models were most frequently observed. Subjects using the compensatory models took much more time to complete the task. An attempt to use a postexperimental questionnaire to validate the results was partially successful.

Bouwman (1980) compared expert and novice financial analysts in

---

[2]In fact, we would describe the process as involving a strong compensatory component as evidenced by the fact that positive scores on other variables can offset failure to meet a criterion value. See Clarkson and Meltzer (1960) for an alternative representation (additive difference) which fits the output decisions at least as well as this model.

an attempt to determine the differences that education and experience produce in their decision-making strategies. Fifteen accounting students and three professional accountants thought aloud while they analyzed four cases to determine any underlying problem areas. Each case contained five pages of financial information drawn from the prior 3 years. The protocols were converted into problem behavior graphs, which present knowledge states as nodes and operators as arrows between nodes. The difficulties in interpreting and summarizing protocol data and the small sample size precluded valid statistical comparisons. However, a comparison of the graphs of a single student and accountant provided some potentially useful insights. The student appeared to follow a simple undirected sequential strategy where the information was evaluated in the order presented until a single problem was uncovered. Information was frequently examined based on very simple trends (e.g., sales are up). The information was used to form a series of simple relations which were internally consistent but may have been inconsistent with one another. Instead of developing detailed causal explanations, a significant fact which explained the others was searched for. When an observed fact was identified as a "problem," little additional information was gathered. On the other hand, the expert seemed to follow a standard checklist of questions. Data were often examined in terms of complex trends. He appeared to develop a general overall picture of the firm and classify it under a general category, such as "expanding company," based on the initial information acquired. When the sterotype was violated, an in-depth examination to uncover significant causes would be initiated. The problems seemed to be recognized based on a set of common problems or hypotheses associated with patterns of cues in long-term memory.

In the final study of financial analysis, Stephens (1979) asked 10 bankers to think aloud while evaluating one of two commercial lending cases. He found that the lending officers spent a great deal of time computing and analyzing ratios and ratio trends. No evidence was available that adjustments were made for differences in inventory or depreciation method.

Management accounting

In managerial accounting, Shields (1979a, 1980) has begun to study the general strategies used by managers in performance report evaluation and the impact of certain attributes of task complexity on these strategies. Twelve executive MBA graduates with an average of 17 years of business experience thought aloud while they analyzed four performance reports in order to estimate the cause of the observed behavior and to predict future behavior. The four cases were formed by a 2 × 2 factorial design combining either 3 or 9 responsibility centers with 6 or 13 performance parameters, including standard accounting variances and nonaccounting data (e.g., absenteeism). Data were presented to the subjects on information boards which contained an envelope with data cards enclosed for each performance cue. By collecting the cards in the order chosen, an accurate measure of information search is also provided. The verbal protocols were coded into 15 categories. The time spent on the task by each subject was split into quarters, and category frequencies and cue selection frequencies were computed for each quarter. Goal statements appeared to direct information search during the first half of the process. This was followed by hypothesis generation, which organized additional information search in the third quarter. The fourth quarter primarily involved development of causal attributions and predictions. A smaller percentage of the data was searched as the number of responsibility centers and performance parameters was increased. The variability in the percentage of information searched increased with the number of responsibility centers but not with the number of cues. Ex post measures of cue importance and order of presentation both affected search order.

Audit sampling

The audit sample selection research of Mock and Turner (1979) discussed earlier was extended in the first protocol analysis in audit decision making. Biggs and Mock's (1980) goal was to describe auditors' sample-selection processes in terms of overall patterns and use of specific information and to make a preliminary comparison of the impact of experience on these patterns. In the experiment, two experienced and two inexperienced audit seniors thought aloud while they made sample-size selections for Mock and Turner's (1979) detailed sample-selection case. The recorded protocols were converted to flowcharts and abstracts for analysis. As in the case of Bouwman's (1980) study, the subject sample was too small for reliable comparisons. However, the authors suggest that the more experienced subjects employed a significantly different decision strategy than their less experienced counterparts. The experienced seniors appeared to build an overall picture of the company and then make the four required decisions. The two new seniors employed a serial strategy involving a separate search for information relevant to each decision. These results are similar to Bouwman's (1980) financial analysis study. All the subjects attended to a much greater proportion of the available information than was indicated in the decision rationale memos produced by Mock and Turner's (1979) subjects. This suggests a potential audit documentation problem relating to lack of self-insight. There were also major between-subject differences in the sample-size decisions and the proportion of the available information attended to.

TABLE C-1

Summary of Studies of Predecisional Behavior

Study	Type of Decision Maker	Task	Data Collection and Analysis Methods	Variables of Interest	Results
Clarkson (1962)	Bank trust officer	Portfolio selection for actual cases	Verbal protocols, flow charts	Form of decision rule (IIB1) Predictability (IIIA5)	Mostly conjunctive Accurately predicted later selections
Biggs (1979)	11 financial analysts	Selection of company with highest earnings power among a group of 5 from extensive financial data	Verbal protocols, operator classification	Form of decision rule (IIB1) Decision speed (IIIA2)	Of four models, the additive compensatory and elimination by aspects were the models most often observed; the compensatory models took more time
Bouwman (1980)	15 accounting students and 3 professional accountants	Analyze 4 cases containing extensive financial information to determine any underlying problem areas	Verbal protocols, problem behavior graphs	Prior experience (IIA4a) Heuristics (IIB4)	Student followed simple undirected sequential strategy; information was evaluated in order presented until a single problem was uncovered; expert followed directed strategy based on standard checklists, complex trends, and stereotypes; developed overall company picture
Stephens (1979)	10 bank loan officers	Evaluate one of two bank lending cases	Verbal protocols	Cue usage (IIB2)	Spent great deal of time computing and

TABLE C-1 *(continued)*

Summary of Studies of Predecisional Behavior

Study	Type of Decision Maker	Task	Data Collection and Analysis Methods	Variables of Interest	Results
					analyzing ratios and ratio trends; no adjustment made for differences in inventory or depreciation methods
Shields (1979, 1980)	12 executive MBA graduates	Analysis of 4 performance reports for attribution of cause of behavior and expectancy of future managerial behavior	Verbal protocols and information boards	Number of cues (IB1) Context (number of cases) (IE) Heuristics (search) (IIB4)	Goal statements directed information search during first half of process; followed by hypothesis generation, which led to further information search; followed by causal attributions and predictions; variability of search increased with number of cases
Biggs and Mock (1980)	2 experienced and 2 inexperienced audit seniors	To make sample selections for Mock and Turner's (1979) sample selection case	Verbal protocols, flowcharts	Prior experience (IIA4a) Heuristics (IIB4) Subjective cue usage (IIB1)	Substantial difference between experienced and inexperienced Experienced built overall picture of the company; then made four decisions; inexperienced followed serial strategy involving separate search for information for each decision Attended to more cues than indicated

REFERENCES

ABDEL-KHALIK, A. R., and EL-SHESHAI, K. Information Choice and Utilization in an Experiment on Default Prediction. *Journal of Accounting Research* (Autumn 1980), pp. 325–342.

AICPA Warning Signals of the Possible Existence of Fraud. *The C.P.A. Letter* (March 1979) *59,* no. 5.

ALTMAN, E. I. Financial Ratios, Discriminant Analysis and the Prediction of Corporate Bankruptcy. *Journal of Finance* (September 1968) *23*, pp. 589–609.

————, HALDEMAN, R. G., and NARAYANAN, P. ZETA Analysis. *Journal of Banking and Finance* (June 1977) *1*, pp. 29–54.

ASHTON, R. H. An Experimental Study of Internal Control Judgments. *Journal of Accounting Research* (Spring 1974a) *12*, pp. 143–157.

————. Cue Utilization and Expert Judgments: A Comparison of Independent Auditors with Other Judges. *Journal of Applied Psychology* (September 1974b) *58*, pp. 437–444.

————. Cognitive Changes Induced by Accounting Changes: Experimental Evidence on the Functional Fixation Hypothesis. *Studies on Human Information Processing in Accounting,* Supplement to *Journal of Accounting Research* (1976) *14*, pp. 1–17.

————. A Descriptive Study of Information Evaluation. *Journal of Accounting Research* (Spring 1981) *19*.

————, and BROWN, P. R. Descriptive Modeling of Auditor's Internal Control Judgments: Replication and Extension. *Journal of Accounting Research* (Spring 1980) *18*, pp. 1–15.

————, and KRAMER, S. S. Students as Surrogates in Behavioral Research: Some Evidence. *Journal of Accounting Research* (Spring 1980) *18*, pp. 269–277.

Atomic Energy Commission. *Reactor Safety Study: An Assessment of Accident Risks in U.S. Commercial Power Plants (Wash-1400).* Washington, D.C.: the Commission, 1975.

BAMBER, E. M. Expert Judgment in the Audit Team: An Examination of Source Credibility. Unpublished manuscript, Ohio State University, Columbus, Ohio, 1980.

BAREFIELD, R. The Effect of Aggregation on Decision Making Success: A Laboratory Study. *Journal of Accounting Research* (Autumn 1972) *10*, pp. 229–242.

BAR-HILLEL, M. The Role of Sample Size in Sample Evaluation. *Organizational Behavior and Human Performance* (October 1979) *24,* pp. 245–257.

————. The Base-Rate Fallacy in Probability Judgments. *Acta Psychologica* (1980) *44*, pp. 211–233.

BETTMAN, J. R. *An Information Processing Theory of Consumer Choice.* Reading, Mass.: Addison-Wesley, 1979.

————, and JACOBY, J. Patterns of Processing in Consumer Information Acquisition. *In* B. B. Anderson (ed.), *Advances in Consumer Research, Vol. 3,* 1976, pp. 315–320.

BETTNER, J. Fed's New Role on Computer Credit Screening Draws Fire from Both Borrowers and Lenders. *Wall Street Journal,* November 3, 1980, p. 46.

BHASKAR, R., and DILLARD, J. F. Human Cognition in Accounting: A Preliminary Analysis. *In* Burns, T. J. (ed.), *Behavioral Experiments in Accounting II.* Columbus, Ohio: College of Administrative Science, Ohio State University, 1979.

BHASKAR, R., and SIMON, H. A. Problem Solving in the Semantically Rich Domains: An Example from Engineering Thermodynamics. *Cognitive Science* (1977) *1*, pp. 193–215.

BIDDLE, G. C., and JOYCE, E. J. The Role of Sample Size in Probabilistic Inference in Auditing. Unpublished manuscript, University of Chicago, December 1979.

_____. Heuristics and Biases: Some Implications for Probabilistic Inference in Auditing. In *Symposium on Auditing Research IV.* Urbana, Ill.: University of Illinois, 1981.

BIERMAN, H., and DYCKMAN, T. R. *Managerial Cost Accounting* (2nd ed.). New York: Macmillan, 1976.

BIGGS, S. F. An Empirical Investigation of the Information Processes Underlying Four Models of Choice Behavior. *In* Burns, T. J., *Behavioral Experiments in Accounting II.* Columbus, Ohio: College of Administrative Science, Ohio State University, 1979.

_____, and MOCK, T. J. Auditor Information Search Processes in the Evaluation of Internal Controls. *Working Paper 2-80-6,* University of Wisconsin, Madison, February 1980.

BLUME, M. E. Betas and Their Regression Tendencies. *Journal of Finance* (June 1975) *30*, pp. 785–795.

BOATSMAN, J., and ROBERTSON, J. Policy Capturing on Selected Materiality Judgments. *Accounting Review* (April 1974) *49*, pp. 342–352.

BOUWMAN, M. J. The Use of Accounting Information: Expert versus Novice Behavior. Unpublished manuscript, University of Oregon, Eugene, Ore., April 1980.

BOWMAN, E. H. Consistency and Optimality in Managerial Decision Making. *Management Science* (November 1963) *9*, pp. 310–321.

BREHMER, B. Social Judgment Theory and the Analysis of Interpersonal Conflict. *Psychological Bulletin* (November 1976) *79*, pp. 985–1003.

BROWN, C. Human Information Processing for Decisions to Investigate Cost Variances. Unpublished manuscript, University of Illinois, Urbana, Ill., 1980.

BROWN, P. R. A Descriptive Analysis of Select Input Bases of the Financial Accounting Standards Board. *Journal of Accounting Research* (Spring 1981) *19*.

BRUNSWIK, E. *The Conceptual Framework of Psychology.* Chicago: University of Chicago Press, 1952.

_____. Representative Design and Probabilistic Theory in a Functional Psychology. *Psychological Review* (May 1955) *62*, pp. 193–217.

_____. *Perception and the Representative Design of Experiments.* Berkeley: University of California Press, 1956.

CAMPBELL, D. T., and STANLEY, J. C. *Experimental and Quasi-Experimental Designs for Research.* Chicago: Rand-McNally, 1963.

CARROLL, J. D., and CHANG, J. J. Analysis of Individual Differences in Multidimensional Scaling via an N-Way Generalization of "Eckart-Young" Decomposition. *Psychometrika* (September 1970) *35*, pp. 283–319.

CASEY, C. J. Additional Evidence on the Usefulness of Accounting Ratios for the Prediction of Corporate Failure. *Journal of Accounting Research* (Autumn 1980) *18*, pp. 603–613.

CASTELLAN, N. J. Decision Making with Multiple Probabilistic Cues. *In* N. J. Castellan, D. B. Pisoni, and G. R. Potts (eds.), *Cognitive Theory*, Vol. 2, pp. 117–147. Hillsdale, N.J.: Erlbaum, 1977.

CHAPMAN, L. J., and CHAPMAN, J. P. Illusory Correlation as an Obstacle to the Use of Valid Psychodiagnostic Signs. *Journal of Abnormal Psychology* (June 1969) *74,* pp. 271–280.

CHASE, W. G., and SIMON, H. A. The Mind's Eye in Chess. *In* W. G. Chase (ed.), *Visual Information Processing.* New York: Academic Press, 1973, pp. 215–281.

CHERNOFF, H. The Use of Faces to Represent Points in k-Dimensional Space Graphically. *Journal of the American Statistical Association* (June 1973) *68*, pp. 361–368.

CHESLEY, G. R. The Elicitation of Subjective Probabilities: A Laboratory Study in an Accounting Context. *Journal of Accounting Research* (Spring 1976) *14*, pp. 27–48.

_____. Subjective Probability Elicitation: Congruity of Datum and Response Mode. *Journal of Accounting Research* (Spring 1977) *15*, pp. 1–11.

_____. Subjective Probability Elicitation Techniques: A Performance Comparison. *Journal of Accounting Research* (Autumn 1978) *16*, pp. 225–241.

CLARKSON, G. P. E. *Portfolio Selection: A Simulation of Trust Investment.* Englewood Cliffs, N.J.: Prentice-Hall, 1962.

_____, and MELTZER, A. H. Portfolio Selection: A Heuristic Approach. *Journal of Finance* (December 1960) *15*, pp. 465–480.

Committee on Auditing Procedures. *Internal Control.* New York: AICPA, 1949.

CORLESS, J. Assessing Prior Distributions for Applying Bayesian Statistics in Auditing. *Accounting Review* (July 1972) *47*, pp. 556–566.

CROSBY, M. Implications of Prior Probability Elicitation on Auditor Sample Size Decisions. *Journal of Accounting Research* (Autumn 1980), pp. 585–593.

_____. Bayesian Statistics in Auditing: A Comparison of Probability Elicitation Techniques. *Accounting Review* (April 1981) *56*.

DAWES, R. M. An Inequality Concerning Correlation of Composites vs. Composites of Correlations. *Oregon Research Institute Methodological Note,* (1970) *1,* No. 1.

DAWES, R. M. A Case Study of Graduate Admissions: Application of Three Principles of Human Decision Making. *American Psychologist* (February 1971) *26*, pp. 180–188.

————. The Robust Beauty of Improper Linear Models in Decision Making. *American Psychologist* (July 1979) *34*, pp. 571–582.

————, and CORRIGAN, B. Linear Models in Decision Making. *Psychological Bulletin* (January 1974) *81*, pp. 95–106.

DEGROOT, A. D. *Thought and Choice in Chess*. The Hague: Mouton, 1965.

DELOITTE, HASKINS, & SELLS. *Internal Accounting Control: An Overview of the D.H. & S. Study and Evaluation Techniques*. New York: Author, 1979.

DEMSKI, J. Information Improvement Bounds. *Journal of Accounting Research* (Spring 1972) *10*, pp. 58–76.

DICKHAUT, J. Alternative Information Structures and Probability Revisions. *Accounting Review* (January 1973) *48*, pp. 61–79.

————, and EGGLETON, I. An Examination of the Processes Underlying Comparative Judgments of Numerical Stimuli. *Journal of Accounting Research* (Spring 1975) *13*, pp. 38–72.

DUDYCHA, A. L., and NAYLOR, J. C. Characteristics of the Human Inference Process in Complex Choice Behavior Situations. *Organizational Behavior and Human Performance* (January 1966) *1*, pp. 110–128.

DYCKMAN, T. R. *Investment Analysis and General Price-Level Adjustments*. Studies in Accounting Research No. 1. Sarasota, Florida: American Accounting Association, 1969.

————. The Effects of Restating Financial Statements for Price Level Changes: A Comment. *Accounting Review* (October 1975) *50*, pp. 796–808.

————, DOWNES, D. H., and MAGEE, R. P. *Efficient Capital Markets and Accounting: A Critical Analysis*. Englewood Cliffs, N.J.: Prentice-Hall, 1975.

EBERT, R. J., and KRUSE, T. E. Bootstrapping the Security Analyst. *Journal of Applied Psychology* (February 1978) *63*, pp. 110–119.

EDWARDS, W. The Theory of Decision Making. *Psychological Bulletin* (July 1954) *51*, pp. 380–418.

————. Conservatism in Human Information Processing. *In* B. Kleinmuntz (ed.), *Formal Representation of Human Judgment*. New York: Wiley, 1968.

EHRENBERG, A. S. C. Some Rules of Data Presentation. *Statistical Reporter* (1977) *7*, pp. 305–310.

EINHORN, H. J. The Use of Nonlinear, Noncompensatory Models in Decision Making. *Psychological Bulletin* (February 1970) *73*, pp. 221–230.

————. Expert Measurement and Mechanical Combination. *Organizational Behavior and Human Performance* (February 1972) *7*, pp. 86–106.

————. Expert Judgment: Some Necessary Conditions and an Example. *Journal of Applied Psychology* (October 1974) *59*, pp. 562–571.

————. Synthesis: Accounting and Behavioral Science. *Studies on Human Information Processing in Accounting*, Supplement to *Journal of Accounting Research* (1976) *14*, pp. 196–206.

————. Overconfidence in Judgment. *In* R. Shweder and D. Fiske (eds.), *New Directions for Methodology of Social and Behavioral Science* (1980) *4*, pp. 1–16.

————, and HOGARTH, R. M. Unit Weighting Schemes for Decision Making. *Organizational Behavior and Human Performance* (April 1975), pp. 171–192.

————. Confidence in Judgment: Persistence of the Illusion of Validity. *Psychological Review* (1978) *85*, pp. 395–416.

————. Behavioral Decision Theory: Processes of Judgment and Choice. *Annual Review of Psychology* (1981) *32*, pp. 53–88.

————, KLEINMUNTZ, D. N., and KLEINMUNTZ, B. Linear Regression and Process Tracing Models of Judgment. *Psychological Review* (1979) *86*, pp. 465–485.

————, and McCOACH, W. P. A Simple Multiattribute Utility Procedure for Evaluation. *Behavioral Science* (July 1977) *22*, pp. 270–282.

————, and SCHACT, S. Decisions Based on Fallible Clinical Judgment. *In* M. F. Kaplan and S. Schwartz (eds.), *Human Judgment and Decision Processes in Applied Settings*. New York: Academic Press, 1977.

ELLIOTT, R. K., and WILLINGHAM, J. J. *Management Fraud: Detection and Deterrence*. New York: Petrocelli, 1980.

ELSTEIN, A. S. Clinical Judgment: Psychological Research and Medical Practice. *Science* (November 1976) *194*, pp. 696–700.

————, and BORDAGE, G. The Psychology of Clinical Reasoning: Current Research Approaches. *In* G. Stone, F. Cohen, and N. Adler (eds.), *Health Psychology*. E. Lansing, Mich.: Michigan State University, 1978.

————, SHULMAN, L. E., and SPRAFKA, S. A. *Medical Problem Solving: An Analysis of Clinical Reasoning*. Cambridge, Mass.: Harvard University Press, 1978.

ERICSSON, K. A., and SIMON, H. A. Verbal Reports as Data. *Psychological Review* (May 1980) *87*, pp. 215–251.

FELIX, W. L. Evidence on Alternative Means of Assessing Prior Probability Distributions for Audit Decision Making. *Accounting Review* (October 1976) *51*, pp. 800–807.

FISCHHOFF, B., SLOVIC, P., and LICHTENSTEIN, S. Knowing with Certainty: The Appropriateness of Extreme Confidence. *Journal of Experimental Psychology: Human Perception and Performance* (1977) *3*, pp. 552–564.

————, Fault Trees: Sensitivity of Estimated Failure Probabilities to Problem Representation. *Journal of Experimental Psychology: Human Perception and Performance* (1978) *4*, pp. 330–344.

FISHBURN, P. C. Mean-Risk Analysis with Risk Associated with Below-Target Returns. *American Economic Review* (1977) *67*, pp. 503–518.

FOSTER, G. *Financial Statement Analysis*. Englewood Cliffs, N.J.: Prentice-Hall, 1978.

FRYBACK, D. G., and THORNBURY, J. R. Informal Use of Decision Theory to Improve Radiological Patient Management. *Radiology* (1978) *129*, pp. 385–388.

GIBBINS, M. Human Inference, Heuristics and Auditors' Judgment Processes. Unpublished manuscript, presented at the C.I.C.A. Auditing Research Symposium, Laval University, Quebec, November 1977.

GIBBS, T. E., and SCHROEDER, R. G. Evaluating the Competence of Internal Audit Departments. In *Symposium on Auditing Research III*, Dept. of Accountancy, University of Illinois, Urbana, 1979.

GOLDBERG, L. R. Diagnosticians vs. Diagnostic Signs: The Diagnosis of Psychosis vs. Neurosis from the MMPI. *Psychological Monographs: General and Applied* (1965) *79*, No. 9, pp. 1–28.

————. Simple Methods or Simple Processes? Some Research on Clinical Judgments. *American Psychologist* (July 1968) *23*, pp. 483–496.

————. Man Versus Model of Man: A Rationale Plus Some Evidence for a Method of Improving on Clinical Inferences. *Psychological Bulletin* (June 1970) *73*, pp. 422–432.

GREEN, P. E., and RAO, V. R. *Applied Multidimensional Scaling: A Comparison of Approaches and Algorithms.* New York: Holt, Rinehart & Winston, 1972.

————, and WIND, Y. *Multiattribute Decisions in Marketing: A Measurement Approach.* New York: Holt, Rinehart & Winston, 1973.

GRETHER, D. M., and PLOTT, C. R. Economic Theory of Choice and the Preference Reversal Phenomenon. *American Economic Review* (September 1979) *69*, pp. 623–638.

HAMBURG, M. *Basic Statistics: A Modern Approach.* New York: Harcourt Brace Jovanovich, 1977.

HAMILTON, R. E., and WRIGHT, W. F. The Evaluation of Internal Controls over Payroll. Unpublished manuscript, University of Minnesota, Minneapolis, Minn., 1977.

HAMMOND, K. R. *Toward Increasing Competence of Thought in Public Policy Formation.* Washington, D.C.: American Association for the Advancement of Science, 1973.

————, and ADELMAN, L. Science, Values and Human Judgment. *Science* (1976) *194*, pp. 389–396.

————, Rohrbaugh, J., Mumpower, J. and Adelman, L. Social Judgment Theory: Applications in Policy Formation. *In* M. F. Kaplan and S. Schwartz (eds.), *Human Judgment and Decision Processes in Applied Settings.* New York: Academic Press, 1977.

————, and STEWART, T. R. The Interaction between Design and Discovery in the Study of Human Judgment. *Program of Research on Human Judgment and Social Interaction, Institute of Behavioral Science, University of Colorado, Paper 152,* 1974.

————, SUMMERS, D. A., and DEANE, D. H. Negative Effects of Outcome-Feedback on Multiple-Cue Probability Learning. *Organizational Behavior and Human Performance* (February 1973) *10*, pp. 30–34.

HARRELL, A. M. The Decision-Making Behavior of Air Force Officers and the Management Control Process. *Accounting Review* (October 1977) *52*, pp. 833–841.

HAYS, W. L. *Statistics for Psychologists.* New York: Holt, Rinehart & Winston, 1963.

HILTON, R. W. Integrating Normative and Descriptive Theories of Information Processing. *Journal of Accounting Research* (Autumn 1980) *18*, pp. 477–505.

————, SWIERINGA, R. J., and HOSKIN, R. E. Perception of Accuracy as a Determinant of Information Value. *Journal of Accounting Research* (Spring 1981) *19*.

HIRSCH, M. Disaggregated Probabilistic Accounting Information: The Effect of Sequential Events on Expected Value Maximization Decisions. *Journal of Accounting Research* (Autumn 1978) *16*, pp. 256–269.

HOFFMAN, P. J., SLOVIC, P., and RORER, L. G. An Analysis-of-Variance Model for the Assessment of Configural Cue Utilization in Clinical Judgment. *Psychological Bulletin* (May 1968) *69*, pp. 338–349.

HOFSTEDT, T., and Hughes, G. An Experimental Study of the Judgment Element in Disclosure Decisions. *Accounting Review* (April 1977) *52*, pp. 379–395.

HOGARTH, R. M. Cognitive Processes and the Assessment of Subjective Probability Distributions. *Journal of the American Statistical Association* (May 1975) *70*, pp. 271–289.

————. *Judgment and Choice: The Psychology of Decision.* New York: Wiley, 1980.

HOLSTRUM, G. L. Audit Judgment under Uncertainty: Empirical Evidence and Implications for Audit Practice. Unpublished manuscript, Deloitte, Haskins & Sells, New York, June 1980.

HORRIGAN, J. O. The Determination of Long Term Credit Standing with Financial Ratios. *Empirical Research in Accounting: Selected Studies 1966*, Supplement to *Journal of Accounting Research* (1966) *4*, pp. 44–62.

HURSCH, C., HAMMOND, K. R., and HURSCH, J. L. Some Methodological Considerations in Multiple Cue Probability Studies. *Psychological Review* (January 1964) *71*, pp. 42–60.

JOHNSON, E. J. Deciding How to Decide: the Effort of Making a Decision. Unpublished manuscript, Carnegie-Mellon University, Pittsburgh, December 1979.

JOYCE, E. J. Expert Judgment in Audit Program Planning. *Studies in Human Information Processing in Accounting,* Supplement to the *Journal of Accounting Research* (1976) *14*, pp. 29–60.

————, and BIDDLE, G. C. Anchoring and Adjustment in Probabilistic Inference in Auditing. *Journal of Accounting Research* (Spring 1981a).

————. Are Auditors' Judgments Sufficiently Regressive? *Journal of Accounting Research* (Autumn 1981b).

————, LIBBY, R. and SUNDER, S. Some Evidence on the Usefulness of SFAC No. 2: Qualitative Characteristics of Accounting Information. Unpublished manuscript, University of Michigan, February 1981.

KAHNEMAN, D., and TVERSKY, A. Subjective Probability: A Judgment of Representativeness. *Cognitive Psychology* (1972) *3*, pp. 430–454.

KAPLAN, R. S. *Advanced Cost Accounting.* Englewood Cliffs, N.J.: Prentice-Hall, forthcoming.

KEENEY, R. L., and RAIFFA, H. *Decisions with Multiple Objectives: Preferences and Value Tradeoffs.* New York: Wiley, 1976.

KENNEDY, H. A Behavioral Study of the Usefulness of Four Financial Ratios. *Journal of Accounting Research* (Spring 1975) *13*, pp. 97–116.

KEREN, G., and NEWMAN, J. R. Additional Considerations with Regard to Multiple Regression and Equal Weighting. *Organizational Behavior and Human Performance* (October 1978) *22*, pp. 143–164.

KERLINGER, F. N. *Foundations of Behavioral Research,* 2nd ed. New York: Holt, Rinehart & Winston, 1973.

KESSLER, L., and ASHTON, R. H. Feedback and Prediction Achievement in Financial Analysis. *Journal of Accounting Research* (Spring 1981) *19*.

KINNEY, W. R. A Decision Theory Approach to the Sampling Problem in Auditing. *Journal of Accounting Research* (Spring 1975), pp. 117–132.

————, and UECKER, W. C. Overcoming the Effects of the Anchoring and Adjustment Heuristic in Audit Judgments: An Experiment. Unpublished manuscript, University of Iowa, Iowa City, December 1979.

KORIAT, A., LICHTENSTEIN, S., and FISCHHOFF, B. Reasons for Confidence. Unpublished manuscript, Decision Research, A Division of Perceptronics, Inc., Eugene, Ore., 1979.

LEV, B. Industry Averages as Targets for Financial Ratios. *Journal of Accounting Research* (Autumn 1969) *7*, pp. 290–299.

LEWIS, B. L. Expert Judgment in Auditing: An Expected Utility Approach. *Journal of Accounting Research* (Autumn 1980) *18*, pp. 594–602.

LIBBY, R. The Use of Simulated Decision Makers in Information Evaluation. *Accounting Review* (July 1975a) *50*, pp. 475–489.

————. Accounting Ratios and the Prediction of Failure: Some Behavioral Evidence. *Journal of Accounting Research* (Spring 1975b) *13*, pp. 150–161.

————. Man versus Model of Man: Some Conflicting Evidence. *Organizational Behavior and Human Performance* (June 1976a) *15*, pp. 1–12.

————. Prediction Achievement as an Extension of the Predictive Ability Criterion: A Reply. *Accounting Review* (July 1976b) *51*, pp. 672–676.

————. Discussion of Cognitive Changes Induced by Accounting Changes: Experimental Evidence on the Functional Fixation Hypothesis. *Studies on Human Information Processing in Accounting,* supplement to *Journal of Accounting Research* (1976c) *14*, pp. 18–24.

————. Bankers' and Auditors' Perceptions of the Message Communicated by the Audit Report. *Journal of Accounting Research* (Spring 1979a) *17*, pp. 99–122.

————. The Impact of Uncertainty Reporting on the Loan Decision. *Studies on Auditing—Selections from the Research Opportunities in Auditing Program,* supplement to *Journal of Accounting Research,* (1979b) *17*, pp. 35–57.

————, and BLASHFIELD, R. K. Performance of a Composite as a Function of the Number of Judges. *Organizational Behavior and Human Performance* (April 1978) *21*, pp. 121–129.

―――, and FISHBURN, P. C. Behavioral Models of Risk Taking in Capital Budgeting. *Journal of Accounting Research* (Autumn 1977) *15*.

―――, and LEWIS, B. L. Human Information Processing Research in Accounting: The State of the Art. *Accounting, Organizations and Society* (1977) *2*, pp. 245–268.

―――. Human Information Processing in Accounting: The State of the Art in 1982. *Accounting, Organizations and Society* (1982).

LICHTENSTEIN, S., and FISCHHOFF, B. Training for Calibration. *Organizational Behavior and Human Performance* (October 1980) *26*, pp. 149–171.

―――, FISCHHOFF, B., and PHILLIPS, L. D. Calibration of Probabilities: The State of the Art. *In* H. Jungermann and G. de Zeeuw (eds.), *Decision Making and Change in Human Affairs*. Dordrecht-Holland: Riedel, 1977, pp. 275–324.

―――, Slovic, P., Fischhoff, B., Layman, M., and Combs, B. Perceived Frequency of Lethal Events. *Decision Research Report 78–2* (1978), Decision Research, a Branch of Perceptronics, Inc., Eugene, Ore.

LUSK, E. J. A Test of Differential Performance Peaking for a Disembedding Task. *Journal of Accounting Research* (Spring 1979) *17*, pp. 286–294.

McCLELLAND, G. Equal versus Differential Weighting for Multiattribute Decisions: There Are No Free Lunches. *Psychological Bulletin* (1979) *86*.

McNEIL, B. J., and PAUKER, S. G. The Patient's Role in Assessing the Value of Diagnostic Tests. *Radiology* (1979) *132*, pp. 605–610.

―――, WEICHSELBAUM, R., and PAUKER, S. G. Fallacy of the Five Year Survival in Lung Cancer. *New England Journal of Medicine* (1978) *299*, pp. 1397–1401.

MAGEE, R. P., and DICKHAUT, J. W. Effect of Compensation Plans on Heuristics in Cost Variance Investigations. *Journal of Accounting Research* (Autumn 1978) *16*, pp. 294–314.

MAIN, J. A New Way to Score with Lenders. *Money* (February 1977), pp. 73–74.

MARCHANT, G. A. Data Fixity: Some Further Empirical Evidence. Unpublished honors thesis, University of New South Wales, Kensington, 1979.

MEEHL, P. E. *Clinical versus Statistical Prediction*. Minneapolis: University of Minnesota Press, 1959.

MESSIER, W. F., and EMERY, D. R. Some Cautionary Notes on the Use of Conjoint Measurement for Human Judgment Modeling. *Decision Sciences*, forthcoming.

MOCK, T. J., and TURNER, J. L. The Effect of Changes in Internal Controls on Audit Programs. *In* T. J. Burns (ed.), *Behavioral Experiments in Accounting II*. Columbus, Ohio: College of Administrative Science, Ohio State University, 1979.

MONTGOMERY, R. H. *Auditing Theory and Practice*, 6th ed. New York: Wiley, 1940.

―――, LENHART, N. J., and JENNINGS, A. R. *Auditing*, 7th ed. New York: Wiley, 1949.

MORIARITY, S. Communicating Financial Information through Multi-Dimensional Graphics. *Journal of Accounting Research* (Spring 1979) *17*, pp. 205–223.

———, and BARRON, F. H. Modeling the Materiality Judgments of Audit Partners. *Journal of Accounting Research* (Autumn 1976) *14*, pp. 320–341.

———. A Judgment-Based Definition of Materiality. *Studies on Auditing—Selections from the Research Opportunities in Auditing Program,* supplement to *Journal of Accounting Research* (1979) *17*, pp. 114–135.

———, and ROACH, W. *Chernoff Faces as an Aid to Analytic Review.* Unpublished paper, presented to the Committee on Statistics in Accounting, American Statistical Association Annual Meeting, August 1977.

MUCHINSKY, P. M., and DUDYCHA, A. L. Human Inference Behavior in Abstract and Meaningful Environments. *Organizational Behavior and Human Performance* (June 1974) *13*, pp. 377–391.

VON NEUMANN, J., and MORGENSTERN, O. *Theory of Games and Economic Behavior,* 3rd. ed. Princeton, N.J.: Princeton University Press, 1947.

NEWELL, A. Judgment and Its Representation: An Introduction. *In* B. Kleinmuntz (ed.), *Formal Representation of Human Judgment.* New York: Wiley, 1968.

———, and SIMON, H. A. *Human Problem Solving.* Englewood Cliffs, N.J.: Prentice-Hall, 1972.

NEWMAN, J. R. Differential Weighting in Multiattribute Utility Measurement: When It Should Not and When It Does Make a Difference. *Organizational Behavior and Human Performance* (December 1977) *20*, pp. 312–324.

NEWTON, L. K. The Rick Factor in Materiality Decisions. *Accounting Review* (January 1977) *52*, pp. 97–108.

NISBETT, R. E., and ROSS, L. *Human Inference: Strategies and Shortcomings of Social Judgment.* Englewood Cliffs, N.J.: Prentice-Hall, 1980.

———, and WILSON, T. D. Telling More Than We Can Know: Verbal Reports on Mental Processes. *Psychological Review* (1977) *84*, pp. 231–259.

OLSON, C. L. Some Apparent Violations of the Representativeness Heuristic in Human Judgment. *Journal of Experimental Psychology: Human Perception and Performance* (1976) *2*, pp. 599–608.

PANKOFF, L. D., and VIRGIL, R. L. Some Preliminary Findings from a Laboratory Experiment on the Usefulness of Financial Accounting Information to Security Analysts. *Empirical Research in Accounting: Selected Studies, 1970.* Supplement to *Journal of Accounting Research* (1970) *8*, pp. 1–48.

PAUKER, S. G. Coronary Artery Surgery: The Use of Decision Analysis. *Annals of Internal Medicine* (1976) *85*, pp. 8–18.

———, Garry, G., Kassirer, J and Schwartz, W. Towards the Simulation of Clinical Cognition: Taking a Present Illness by Computer. *American Journal of Medicine* (1976) *60,* pp. 981–996.

PAYNE, J. W. Task Complexity and Contingent Processing in Decision

Making: An Information Search and Protocol Analysis. *Organizational Behavior and Human Performance* (December 1976) *16*, pp. 366–387.

――――, BRAUNSTEIN, M. L., and CARROLL, J. S. Exploring Pre-decisional Behavior: An Alternative Approach to Decision Research. *Organizational Behavior and Human Performance* (February 1978) *22*, pp. 17–44.

PEAT, MARWICK, MITCHELL, & Co. *Audit Sampling*, ASB 1980–6. New York: Author, 1980.

POSTMAN, L., and TOLMAN, E. C. Brunswik's Probabilistic Functionalism. *In* S. Kock (ed.), *Psychology: A Study of a Science, 1.* New York: McGraw-Hill, 1959.

RAIFFA, H. *Decision Analysis.* Reading, Mass.: Addison-Wesley, 1968.

ROCKNESS, H. O., and NIKOLAI, L. A. An Assessment of A.P.B. Voting Patterns. *Journal of Accounting Research* (Spring 1977) *15*, pp. 154–167.

ROMNEY, M. B., ALBRECHT, W. S., and CHERRINGTON, D. J. Auditors and the Detection of Fraud. *Journal of Accountancy* (May 1980) *149*, pp. 63–69.

RONEN, J. Some Effects of Sequential Aggregation in Accounting on Decision Making. *Journal of Accounting Research* (Autumn 1971) *9*, pp. 307–332.

ROOSE, J. E., and DOHERTY, M. E. A Social Judgment Theoretic Approach to Sex Discrimination in Faculty Salaries. *Organizational Behavior and Human Performance* (April 1978) *22*, pp. 193–215.

ROSE, J., Beaver, W., Becker, S., and Sorter, G. Toward an Empirical Measure of Materiality. *Empirical Research in Accounting: Selected Studies, 1970*, supplement to *Journal of Accounting Research* (1970) *8*, pp. 138–148.

RUSSO, J. E. Comments on Behavioral and Economic Approaches to Studying Market Behavior. *In* A. A. Mitchell (ed.), *The Effect of Information on Consumer and Market Behavior.* Chicago: American Marketing Association, 1978.

SAVAGE, L. J. *The Foundations of Statistics.* New York: Wiley, 1954.

SAWYER, J. Measurement and Prediction: Clinical and Statistical. *Psychological Bulletin* (September 1966) *66*, pp. 178–200.

SCHULTZ, J. J., and GUSTAVSON, S. G. Actuaries' Perceptions of Variables Affecting the Independent Auditor's Legal Liability. *Accounting Review* (July 1978) *53*, pp. 626–641.

SCHUM, D. A., and DuCHARME, W. M. Comments on the Relationship between the Impact and the Reliability of Evidence. *Organizational Behavior and Human Performance* (March 1971) *6*, pp. 111–131.

SHAKLEE, H., and FISCHHOFF, B. Limited Minds and Multiple Causes: Discounting in Multicausal Attributions. Unpublished manuscript, University of Iowa, Iowa City, 1979.

――――. Strategies of Information Search in Causal Analysis. Unpublished manuscript, University of Iowa, Iowa City, 1980.

SHIELDS, M.D. On the Use of an Accounting Information System: A

Behavioral Approach. Unpublished manuscript, University of North Carolina, Chapel Hill, October 1979.

————. Some Effects of Information Load on Search Patterns Used to Analyze Performance Reports. Unpublished manuscript, University of North Carolina, Chapel Hill, May 1980.

SIMON, H. A. A Behavioral Model of Rational Choice. *Quarterly Journal of Economics* (February 1955) *69*, pp. 174–184.

————. Information Processing Models of Cognition. *Annual Review of Psychology* (1979) *30*, pp. 363–396.

SLOVIC, P. Analyzing the Expert Judge: A Descriptive Study of a Stockbroker's Decision Process. *Journal of Applied Psychology* (August 1969), pp. 255–263.

————. Psychological Study of Human Judgment: Implications for Investment Decision Making. *Journal of Finance* (September 1972), pp. 779–799.

————, FISCHHOFF, B., and LICHTENSTEIN, S. Behavioral Decision Theory. *Annual Review of Psychology* (1977) *28*, pp. 1–39.

————, FLEISSNER, D., and BAUMAN, W. S. Analyzing the Use of Information in Investment Decision Making: A Methodological Proposal. *Journal of Business* (April 1972), pp. 283–301.

————, and LICHTENSTEIN, S. Comparison of Bayesian and Regression Approaches to the Study of Information Processing in Judgment. *Organizational Behavior and Human Performance* (November 1971) *6*, pp. 649–744.

SNOWBALL, D., and BROWN, C. Decision Making Involving Sequential Events: Some Effects of Disaggregated Data and Disposition Toward Risk. *Decision Sciences* (October 1979), pp. 527–546.

SORENSON, J. E., and SORENSON, T. L. Detecting Management Fraud: Some Organizational Strategies for the Independent Auditor. *In* R. K. Elliott and J. J. Willingham, (eds.). *Management Fraud: Detection and Deterrence.* New York: Petrocelli, 1980.

SPITZER, R. L., ENDICOTT, J., and ROBINS, E. Reliability of Clinical Criteria for Psychiatric Diagnosis. *American Journal of Psychiatry* (1975) *132*, pp. 1187–1192.

STEPHENS, R. G. Accounting Disclosures for User Decision Processes. *In* Y. Ijiri and A. B. Whinston, (eds.). *Quantitative Planning and Control.* New York: Academic Press, 1979, pp. 291–309.

SWIERINGA, R. J., DYCKMAN, T. R., and HOSKIN, R. E. Empirical Evidence about the Effects of an Accounting Change on Information Processing. *In* T. J. Burns (ed.). *Behavioral Experiments in Accounting II.* Columbus, Ohio: College of Administrative Science, Ohio State University, 1979.

————, Gibbins, M., Larsson, L., and Sweeney J.L. Experiments in the Heuristics of Human Information Processing. *Studies on Human Information Processing in Accounting,* supplement to *Journal of Accounting Research* (1976) *14*, p. 159–187.

TORGERSON, W. S. *Theory and Methods of Scaling.* New York: Wiley, 1958.

Touche Ross & Co. *Audit Manual: Field Test Draft—1977*. New York: Author, 1977.

Tucker, L. A Suggested Alternative Formulation in the Developments by Hursch, Hammond, and Hursch and by Hammond, Hursch and Todd. *Psychological Review* (November 1964), pp. 528–532.

Turner, J. L., and Mock, T. J. Economic Considerations in Designing Audit Programs. *Journal of Accountancy* (March 1980) *149*, pp. 65–74.

Tversky, A. Elimination by Aspects: A Theory of Choice. *Psychological Review* (1972) *79*, pp. 281–299.

————, and Kahneman, D. Availability: A Heuristic for Judging Frequency and Probability. *Cognitive Psychology* (1973) *5*, pp. 207–232.

————. Judgment under Uncertainty: Heuristics and Biases. *Science* (1974) *185*, pp. 1124–1131.

————. Causal Schemas in Judgments under Uncertainty. *In* M. Fishbein (ed.). *Progress in Social Psychology, Vol. 1*. Erlbaum: Hillsdale N.J., 1980.

————, and Sattath, S. Preference Trees. *Psychological Review* (1979) *86*, pp. 542–573.

Uecker, W. C. A Behavioral Study of Information System Choice. *Journal of Accounting Research* (Spring 1978) *16*, pp. 169–189.

————. The Effects of Knowledge of the User's Decision Model in Simplified Information Evaluation. *Journal of Accounting Research* (Spring 1980) *18*, pp. 191–213.

————, and Kinney, W. Judgmental Evaluation of Sample Results: A Study of the Type and Severity of Errors Made by Practicing CPA's. *Accounting, Organizations and Society* (1977) *2*, pp. 269–275.

Vasichek, O. A. A Note on Using Cross-Sectional Information in Bayesian Estimation. *Journal of Finance* (December 1973) *28*.

Wainer, H. Estimating Coefficients in Linear Models: It Don't Make No Nevermind. *Psychological Bulletin* (January 1976) *83*, pp. 213–217.

————. On the Sensitivity of Regression and Regressors. *Psychological Bulletin* (January 1978) *85*, pp. 267–273.

Wallsten, T. Bias in Evaluating Diagnostic Information. Unpublished manuscript, University of North Carolina, Chapel Hill, December 1978.

Ward, B. H. An Investigation of the Materiality Construct in Auditing. *Journal of Accounting Research* (Spring 1976) *14*, pp. 138–152.

Watts, R. L., and Zimmerman, J. L. The Markets for Independence and Independent Auditors. Unpublished manuscript, University of Rochester, July, 1979.

Whitbeck, V. S., and Kisor, M. A New Tool in Investment Decision-Making. *Financial Analysts Journal* (May–June 1963), pp. 55–62.

Wiener, L. Now Computer Will Take Human Factor out of Your Credit Rating. *Chicago Tribune,* Sunday May 22, 1977.

Winkler, R. L. *Introduction to Bayesian Inference and Decision*. New York: Holt, Rinehart & Winston, 1972.

_____, and MURPHY, A. H. Experiments in the Laboratory and the Real World. *Organizational Behavior and Human Performance* (April 1973) *10*, pp. 252–270.

WRIGHT, P. The Harassed Decision Maker: Time Pressures, Distractions and the Use of Evidence. *Journal of Applied Psychology* (October 1974) *59*, pp. 551–561.

WRIGHT, W. F. Cognitive Information Processing Models: An Empirical Study. *Accounting Review* (July 1977) *52*, pp. 676–689.

_____. Properties of Judgments in a Financial Setting. *Organizational Behavior and Human Performance* (February 1979a) *23*, pp. 73–85.

_____. Accuracy of Subjective Probabilities for a Financial Variable. *In* T. J. Burns (ed.). *Behavioral Experiments in Accounting II*. Columbus, Ohio: College of Administrative Science, Ohio State University, 1979b.

ZIMMER, I. A Lens Study of the Prediction of Corporate Failure by Bank Loan Officers. *Journal of Accounting Research* (Autumn 1980) *18*, pp. 629–636.

Index